HAL LEONARD

BASS LINES

AUDIO ACCESS INCLUDED

500 Grooves • All Styles • All Levels

BY MATT SCHARFGLASS

AF009441

	PAGE
Introduction	2
Rock and Pop	3
Blues and Jazz	69
Country	76
Electronic Dance Music (EDM)	79
Funk and R&B	87
Slap	112
Metal	122
World Music	133

PLAYBACK+
Speed • Pitch • Balance • Loop

To access audio visit:
www.halleonard.com/mylibrary

Enter Code
4236-0186-4829-0080

ISBN 978-1-4950-2874-8

7777 W. BLUEMOUND RD. P.O. BOX 13819 MILWAUKEE, WI 53213

In Australia Contact:
Hal Leonard Australia Pty. Ltd.
4 Lentara Court
Cheltenham, Victoria, 3192 Australia
Email: ausadmin@halleonard.au

Copyright © 2017 by HAL LEONARD LLC
International Copyright Secured   All Rights Reserved

No part of this publication may be reproduced in any form or by any means without
the prior written permission of the Publisher.

Visit Hal Leonard Online at www.halleonard.com

INTRODUCTION

When I was first approached to write a book of bass grooves, I was excited, then promptly overwhelmed. After all, there's so much that can be done with the electric bass guitar. Where do you even start? Then I remembered an occasion when I went to see a friend's band many years ago. I was younger, fresh out of college, and all about "chops" and speed at the time. As I watched them play—a typical four-piece ensemble with simple, catchy pop songs—I saw people dancing, smiling, and having a good time. None of the musicians were doing anything technically remarkable, particularly the bass player. But what they did, they did well, and the people responded. That's when it finally occurred to me that it's all about The Groove.

With that in mind, I humbly present to you a collection of bass lines that are accessible to players of all skill levels. Maybe you're an absolute beginner looking to jump in with both feet—many of these grooves will challenge you. Or, perhaps you're a seasoned player—maybe you'll find something in these pages that can help break you out of a rut. In either case, it's my hope that you'll take anything in this book that speaks to you and use it to inform your own approach to building bass lines.

These grooves span most styles and are deliberately written in various keys and feels. Some explore power in simplicity, others are more technical and contain a certain "wow" factor; all are effective, and grouped into sections each dedicated to a broad musical style while zoning in on several subgenres within that style. For example, the largest chapter, Rock and Pop, touches on hard rock, punk, ska, roots rock, soft rock, ballads, new wave, industrial, classic rock, and more.

Throughout these pages you'll be using techniques such as slides, pull-offs and hammer-ons, double- and triple-stops, rakes, bends, vibrato, slapping, and even a bit of two-handed tapping. We'll also explore the importance of silence (rests), note choice, note duration, grace notes and "dead" notes, staccato vs. legato articulation, and tempo. Care has been taken with every note, rest, and articulation to demonstrate interplay with the other instruments in the audio examples.

While following along with the audio examples, I encourage you to pay attention to each line's construction:

- Why are certain grooves in a lower octave rather than a higher one, or vice versa?
- How does octave choice affect the overall sound when the bass line is doubling the guitar?
- How do the rhythms interact with the drums and other instruments?
- Why are finger slides sometimes more effective than pull-offs or hammer-ons in certain licks?
- How does syncopation within a bass part serve to glue the drums to the chordal or melody instruments?
- Why is the bass playing notes other than roots in some examples, and how does this reharmonization affect the overall vibe or color of the music?
- Are you noticing common fretboard patterns and chord progressions, either within certain genres or even across genres?
- Are you noticing certain rhythmic properties with a particular style?

Regardless of your skill level, we can probably all agree that there's a special kind of magic in plugging into an amp, hitting a single note, and feeling those fat, low frequencies hit you in the chest, while silently confident in the knowledge that you are the foundation holding it all together. So, in that spirit—rejoice in The Groove! Let's play some bass.

Matt Scharfglass

New York City, 2017

ROCK AND POP

1. Garage Rock

2. Slinky Classic Rock

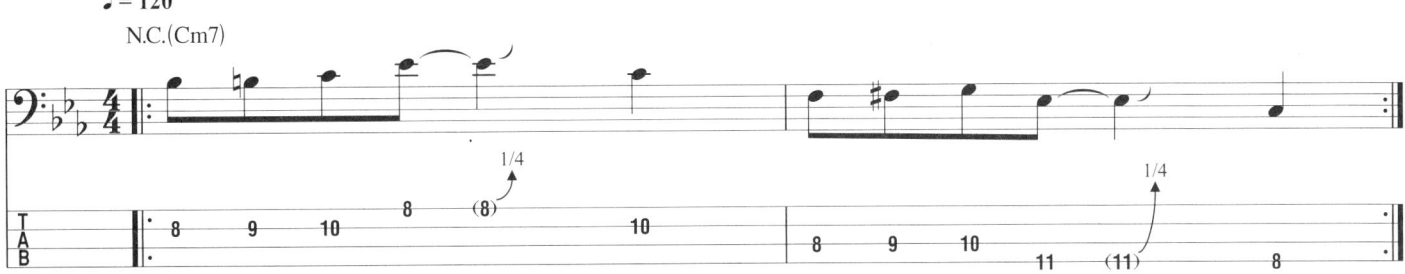

3. Moderate Classic Rock 16ths

4. Driving Eighth Notes

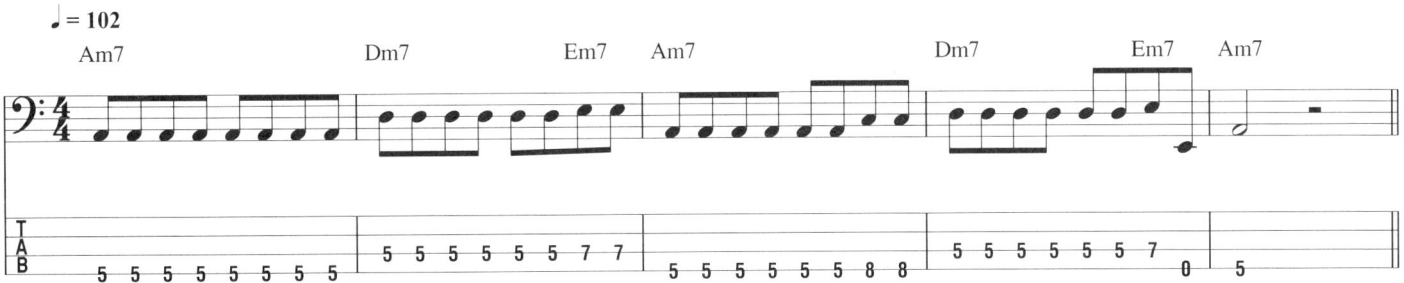

5. Open-String Groove

6. 7th/Octave Hammer Groove

7. Octave Pops 1

8. Octave Pops 2

9. Octave Backbeats

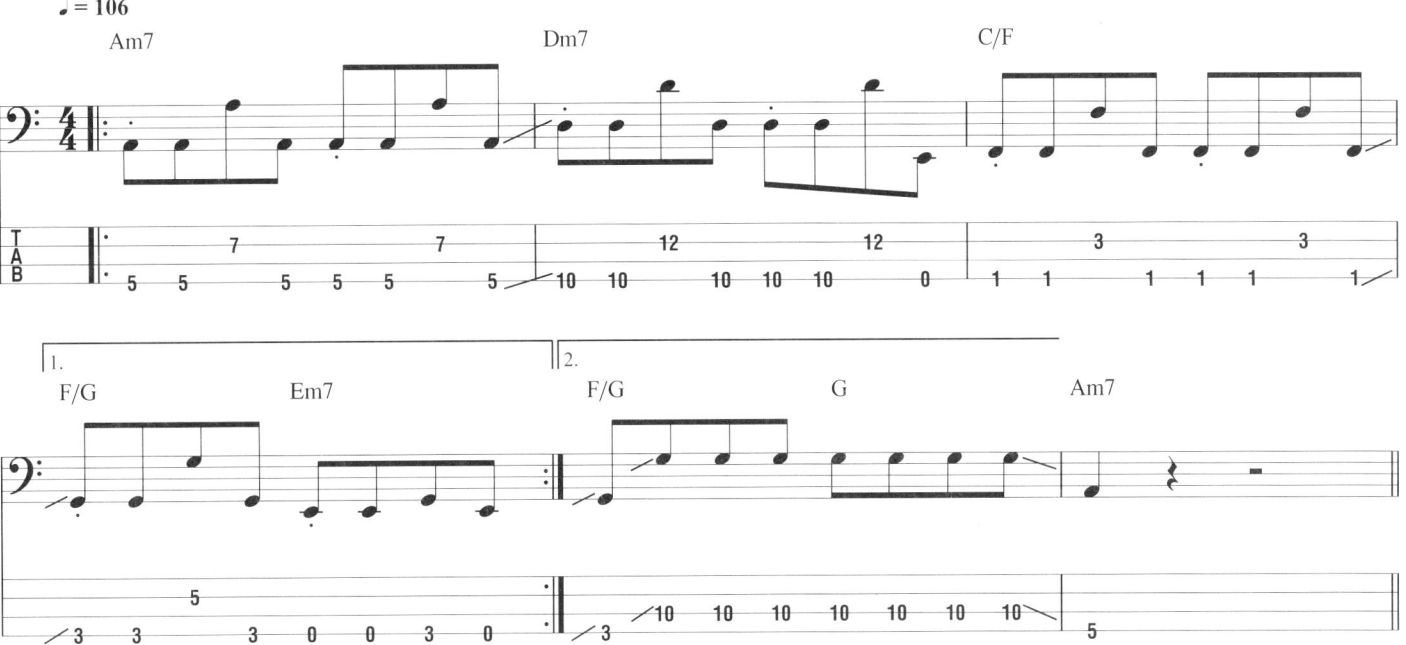

10. Moody Major Mellifluousness

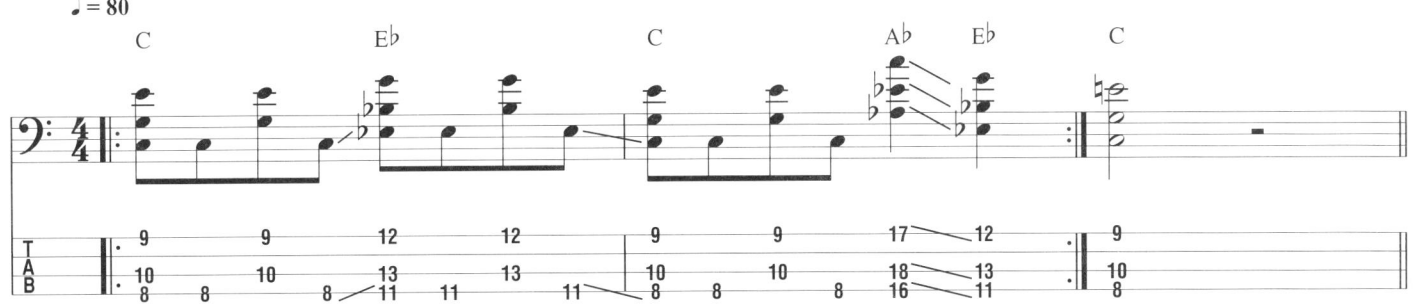

11. Bendy 1

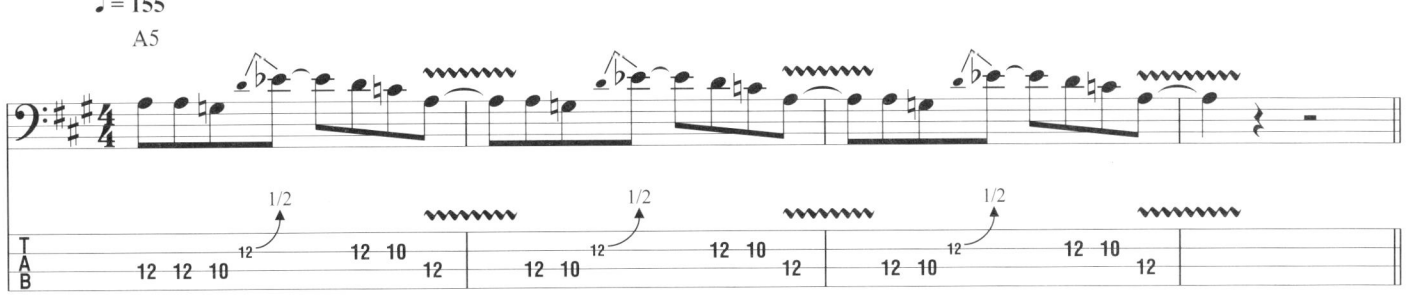

12. Bendy 2

13. Slightly Bendy 1

14. Slightly Bendy 2

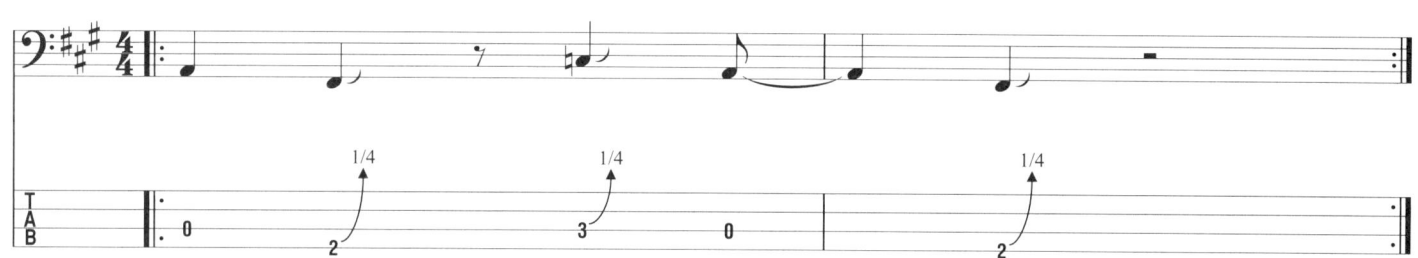

15. Chamber Pop 1

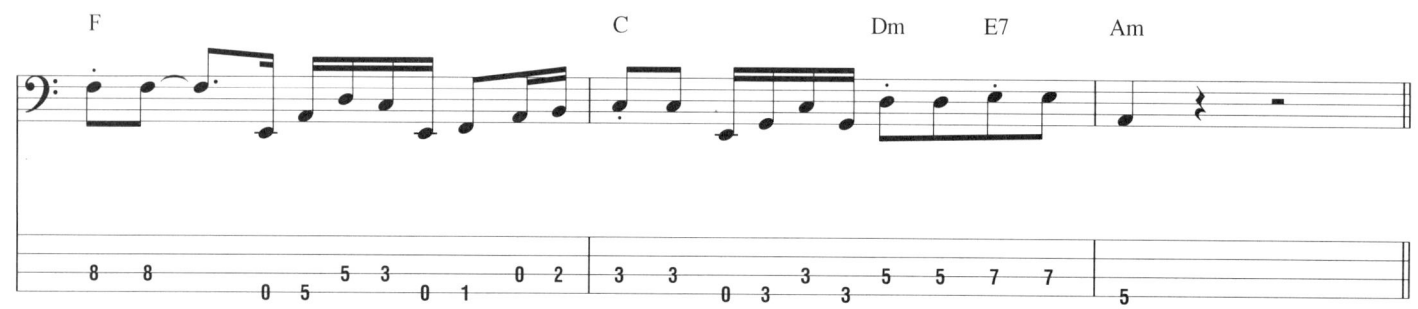

16. Chamber Pop 2

♩ = 126
Half-time feel

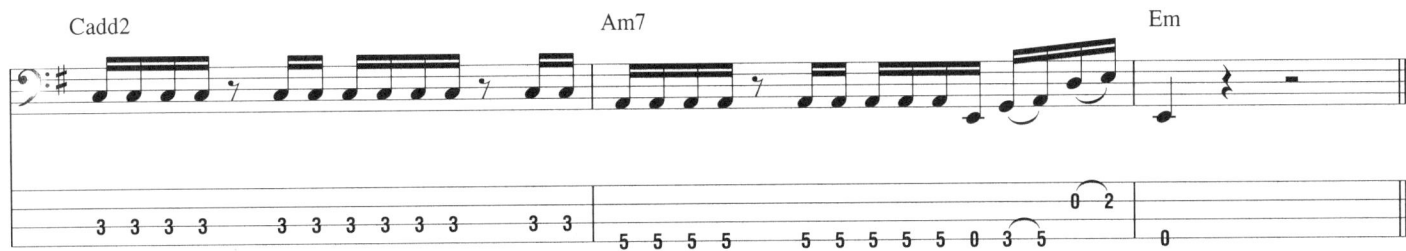

17. Stompin' 1

♩ = 126

18. Stompin' 2

Drop D tuning:
(low to high) D-A-D-G

♩ = 86

19. Stompin' 3

20. Stompin' 4

21. Stompin' 5

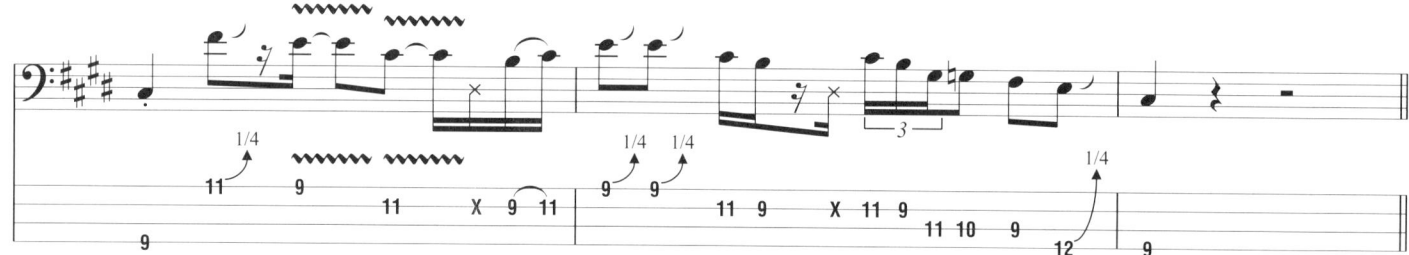

22. Stompin' 6

23. Stompin' 7

24. Stompin' 8

25. Stompin' 9

26. Power Chords

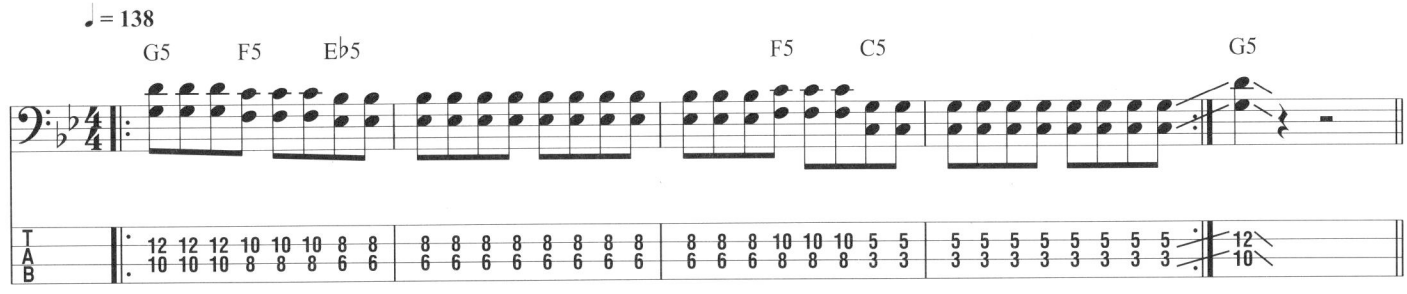

27. Backbeat 1
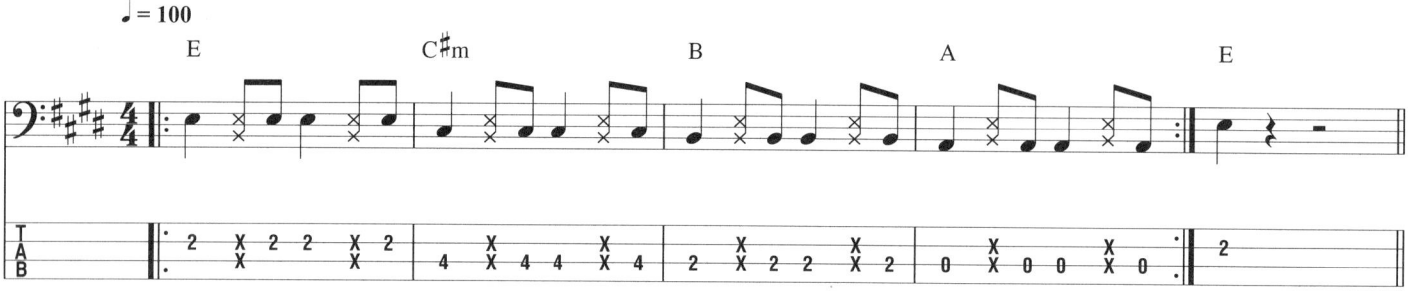

28. Backbeat 2

29. Backbeat 3
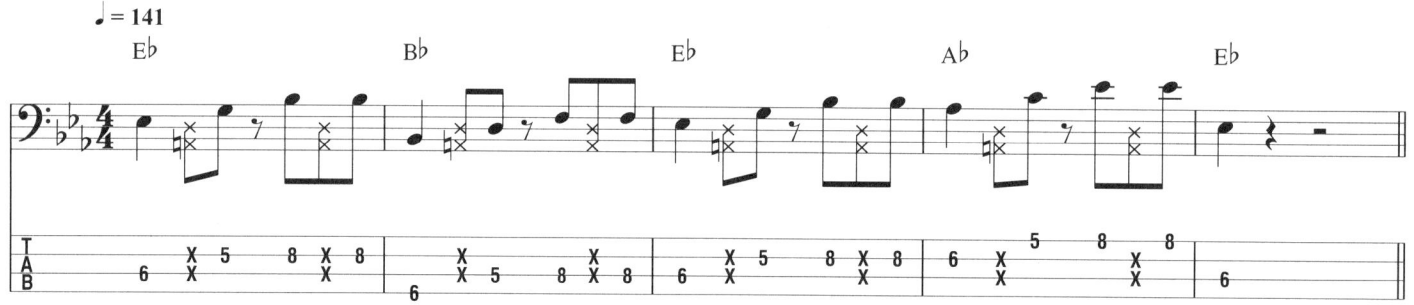

30. Backbeat 4

31. Lydian Line 1

32. Lydian Line 2

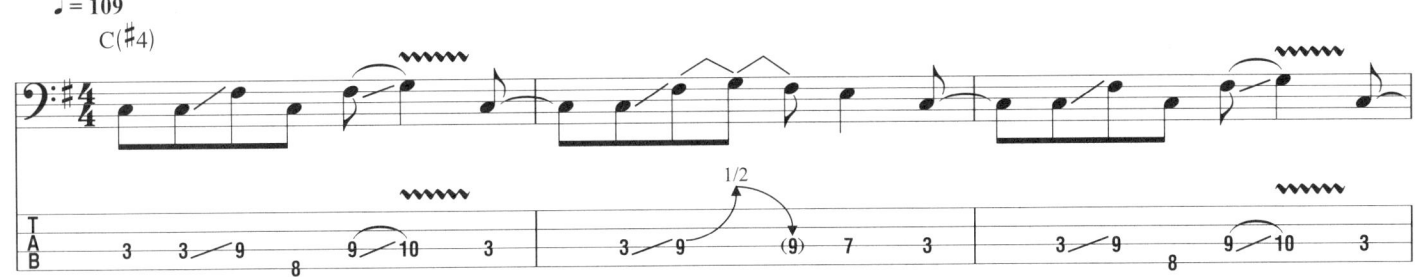

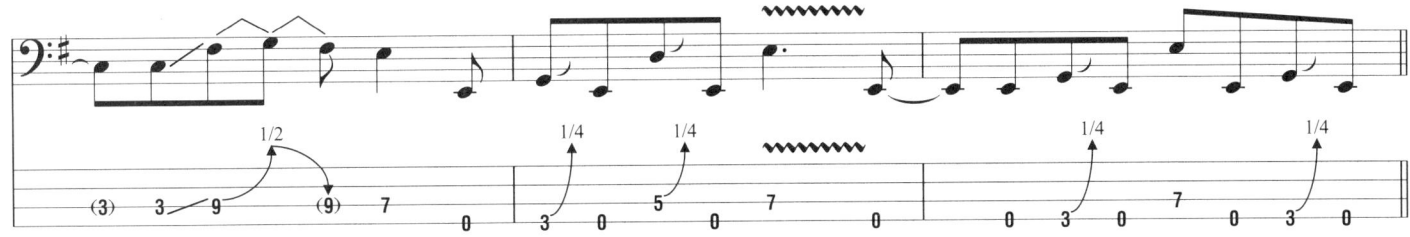

33. Angular Riff 1

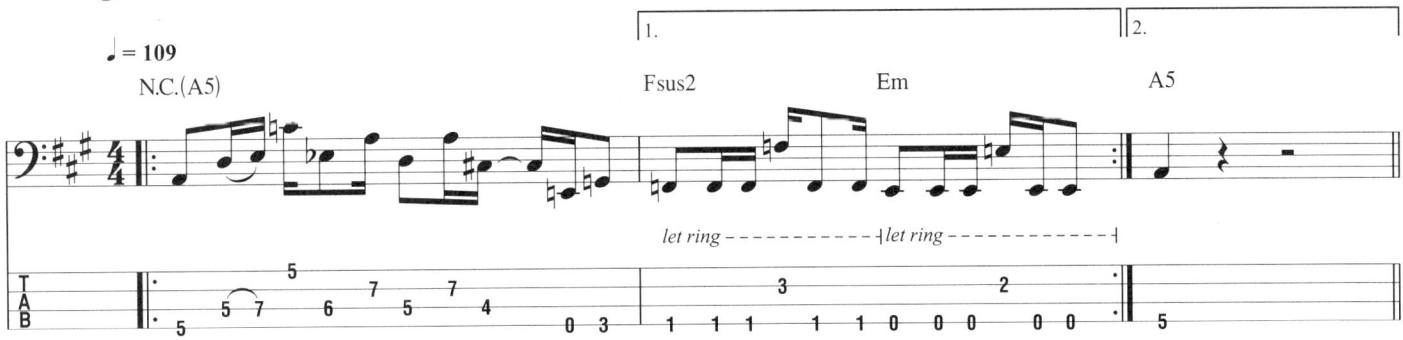

34. Angular Riff 2

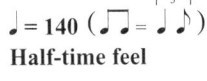

Half-time feel

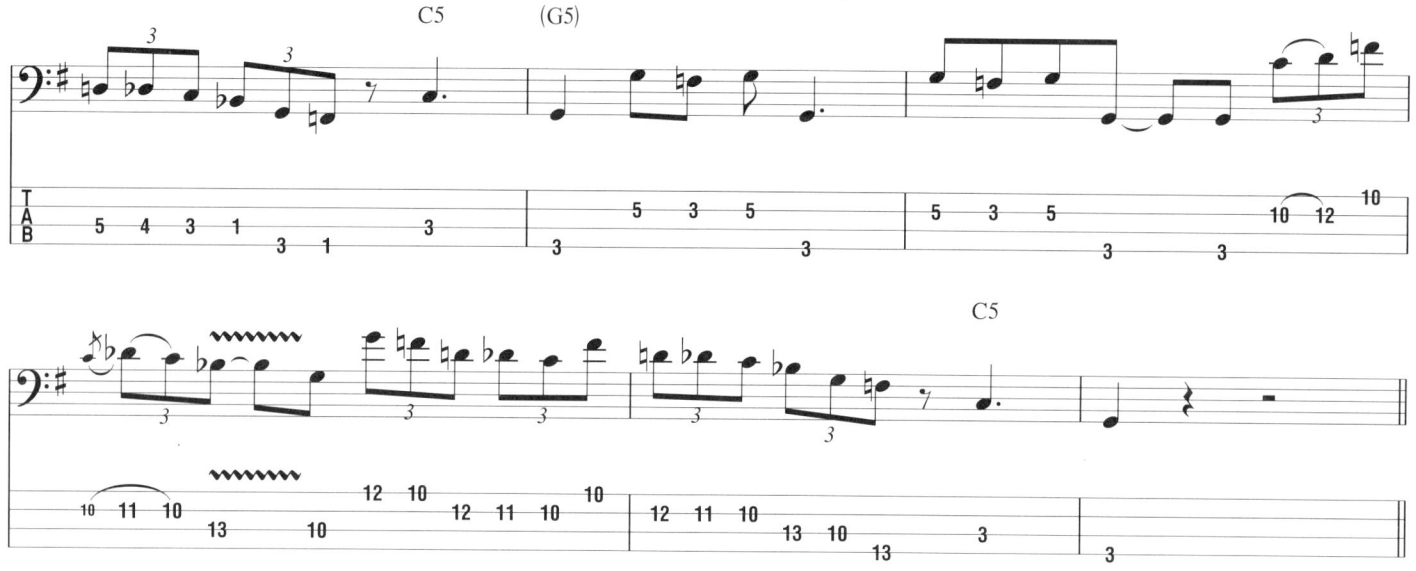

35. Reharmonization 1

36. Reharmonization 2

37. Reharmonization 3

38. Fast Blues Scale Riff

39. Doubled With Guitar

40. Cake and Eat It
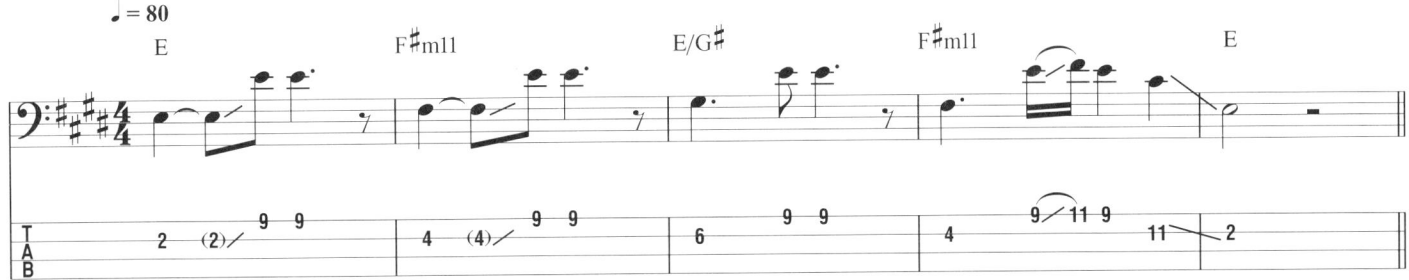

41. Inverted Pedal Tone Ballad

42. Ve Vill Pump You Up

43. Doo de Doot Doot

44. Melodic Major 7th Line

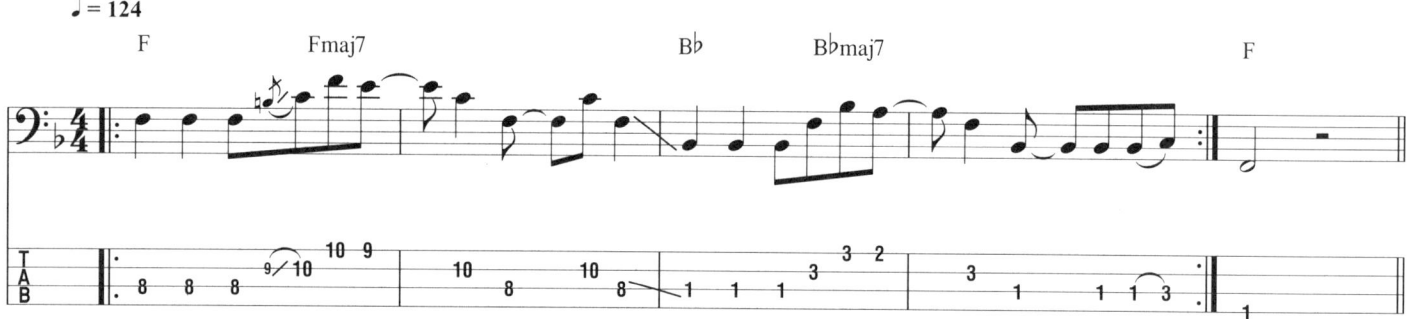

45. Ballad Major 7th Line

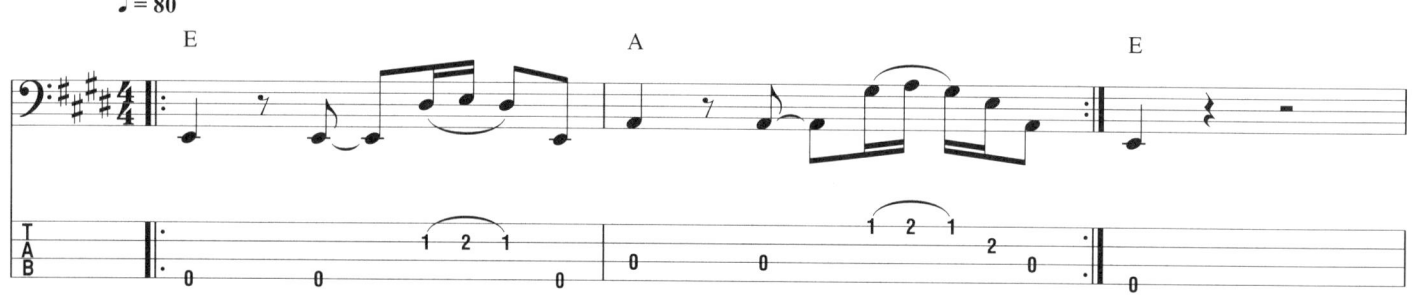

46. Southern Train

47. Single-String Symphony 1

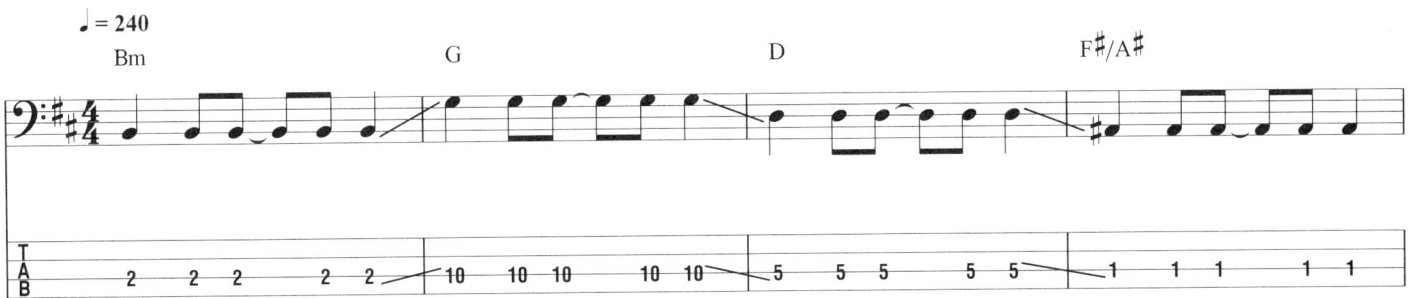

48. Single-String Symphony 2

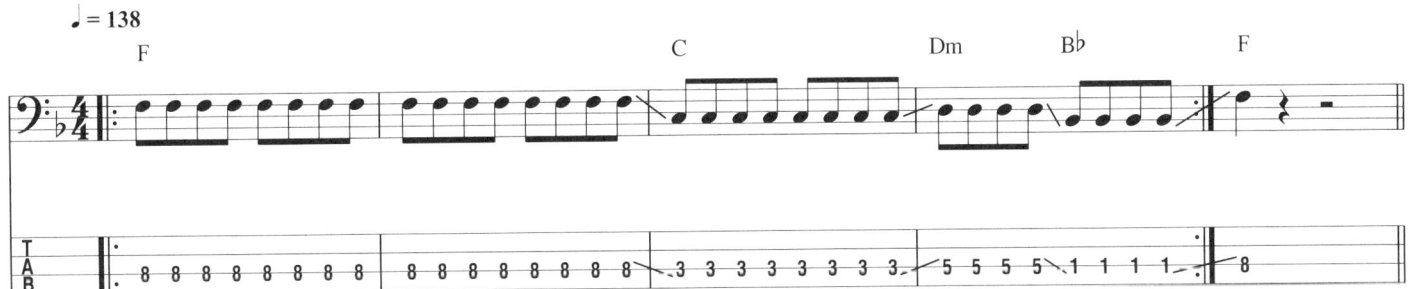

49. Single-String Symphony 3

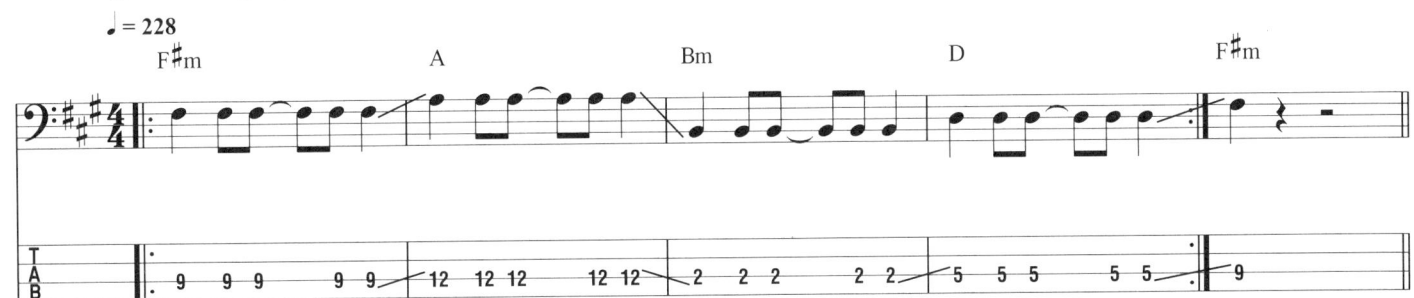

50. Single-String Symphony 4

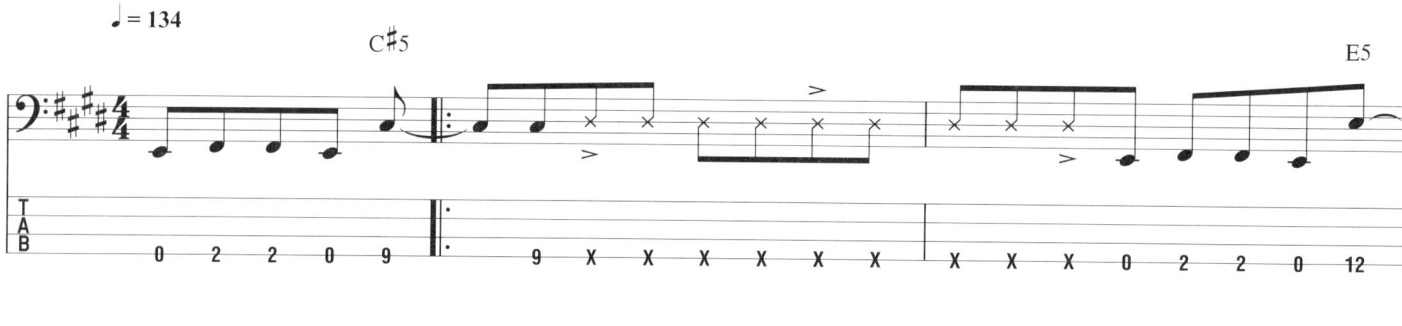

51. Single-String Symphony 5

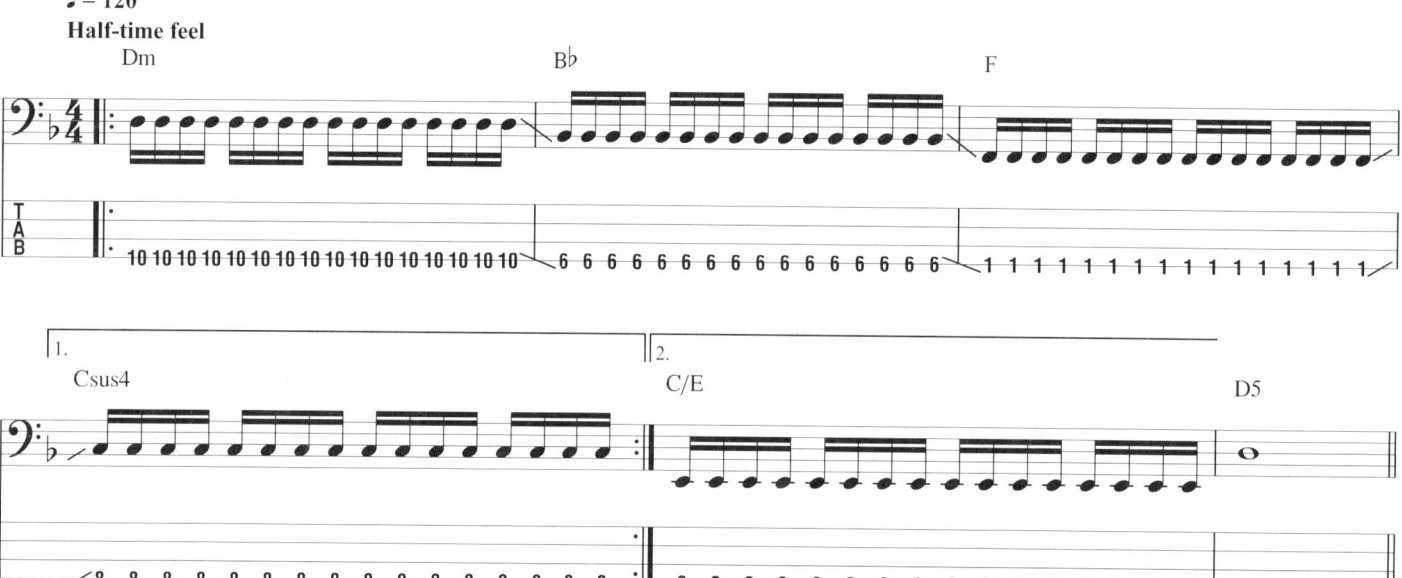

52. Single-String Symphony 6

53. Single-String Symphony 7

54. Single-String Symphony 8

55. Single-String Symphony 9 (8th notes)

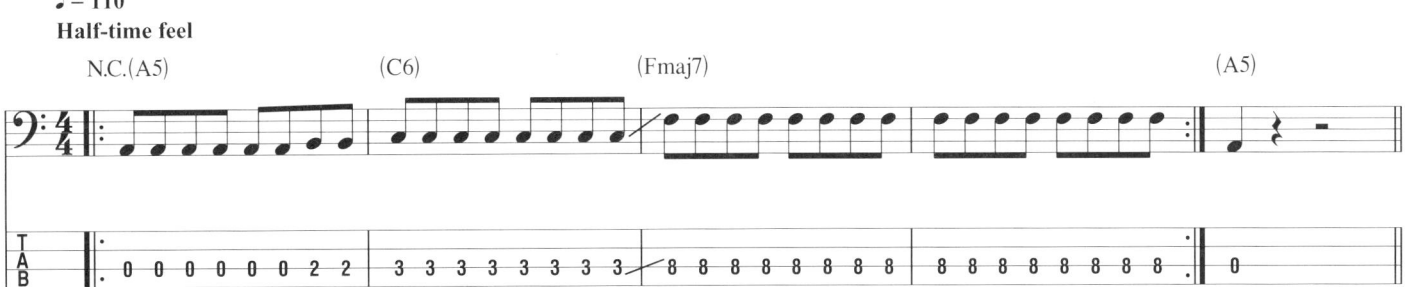

56. Single-String Symphony 9 (16th notes)

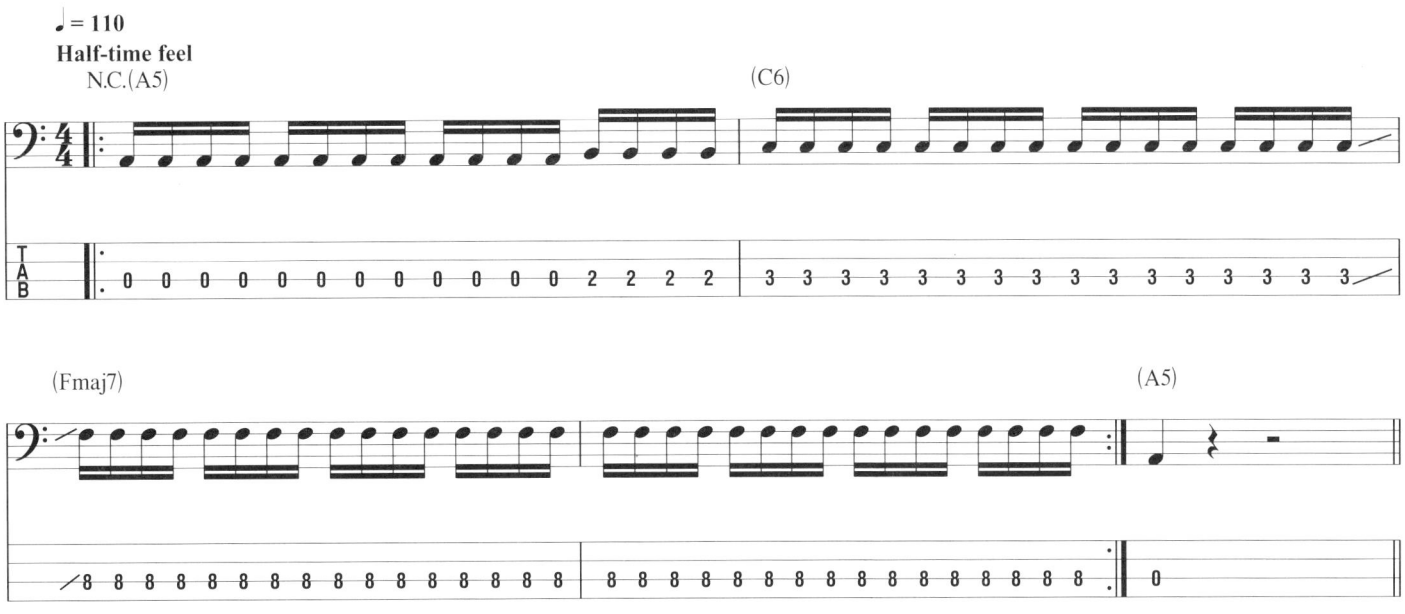

57. Single-String Symphony 10

58. Single-String Symphony 11

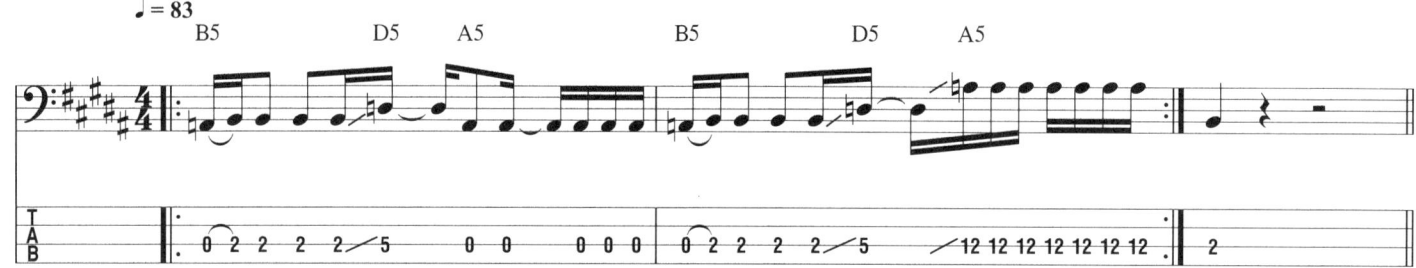

59. Rock 'n' Roll Blues Ending

60. Dancehall

61. Ska 1

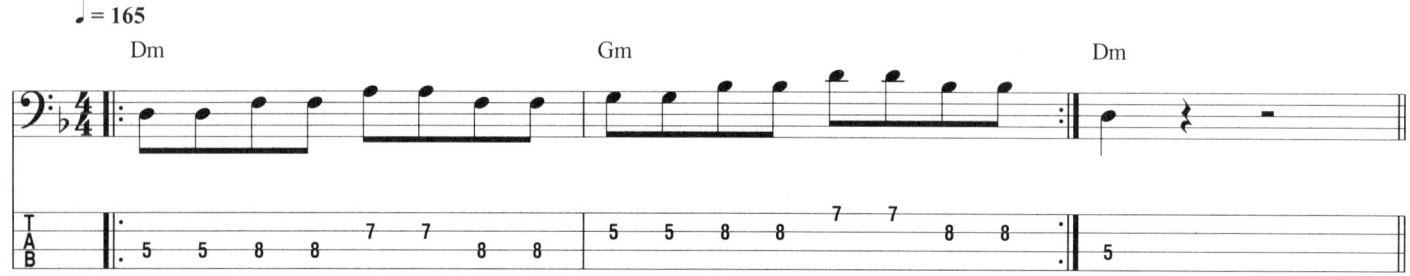

62. Ska 2

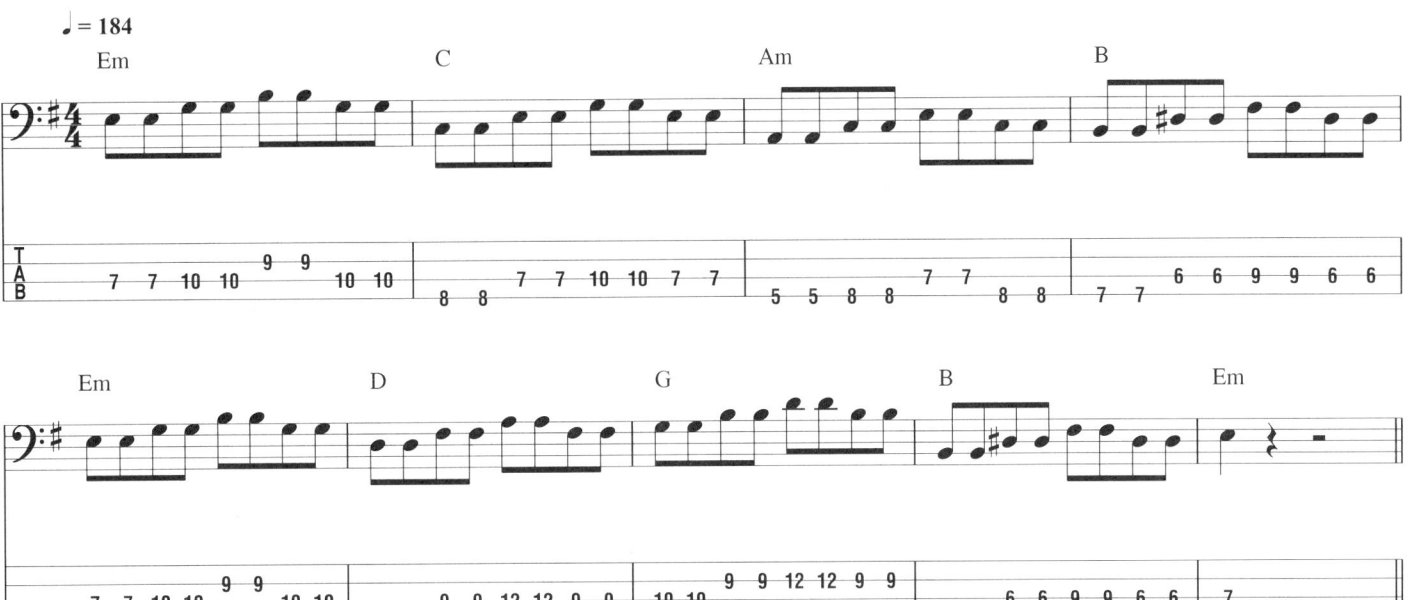

63. Ska 3

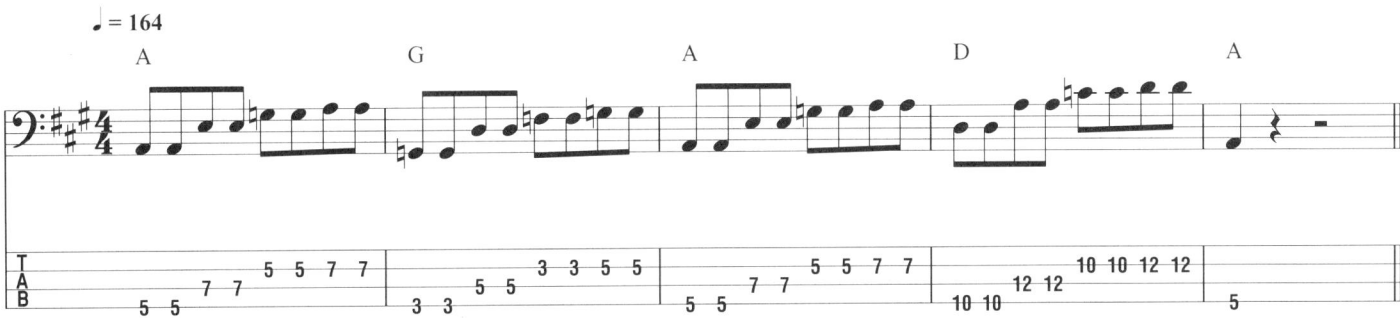

64. Drama-Building Octave Jump

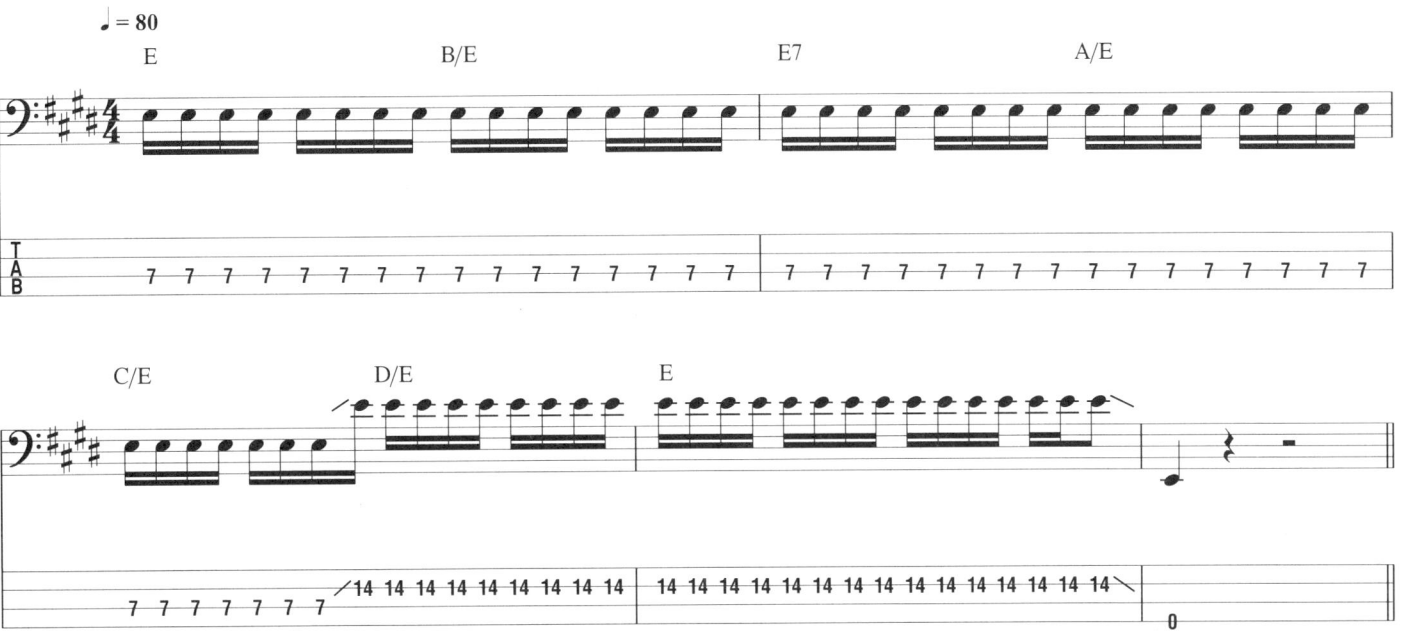

65. Up-Jump the Octave 1

66. Up-Jump the Octave 2

67. Groove with a Side of Open Strings 1

68. Groove with a Side of Open Strings 2

69. Groove with a Side of Open Strings 3

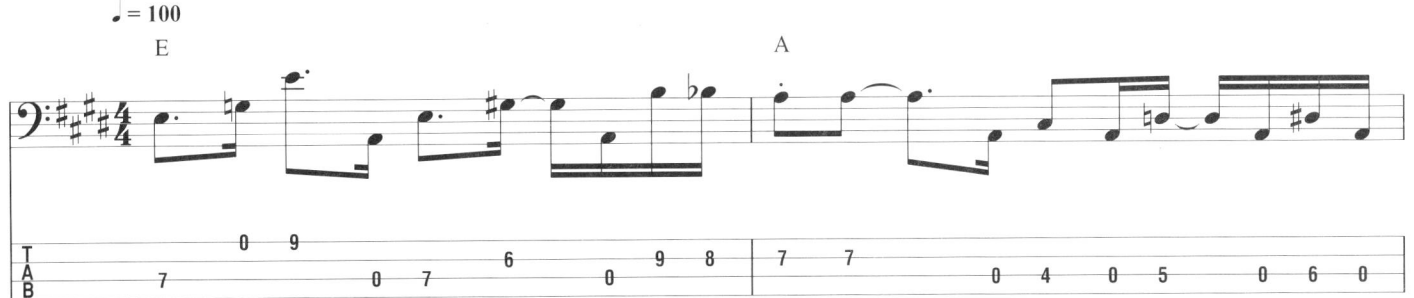
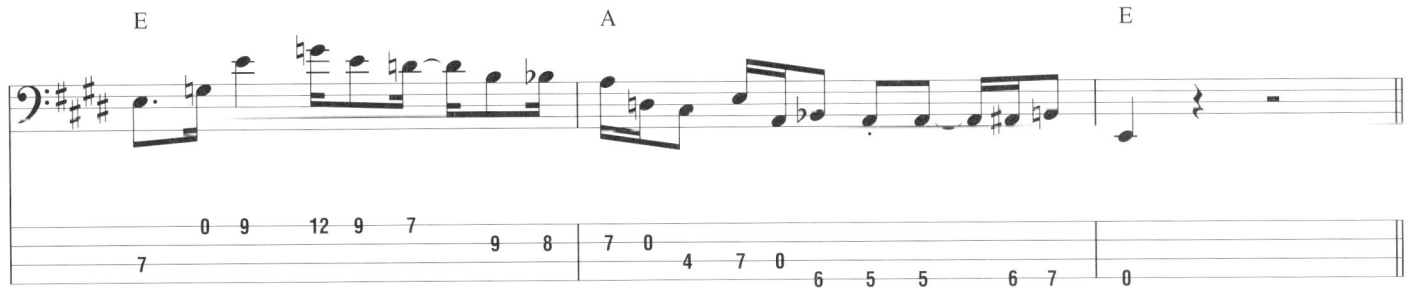

70. Droney 1

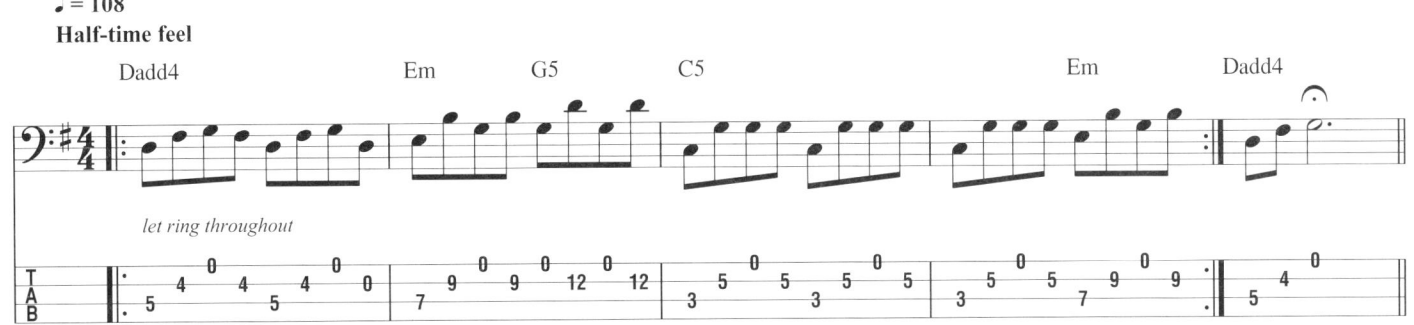

71. Droney 2

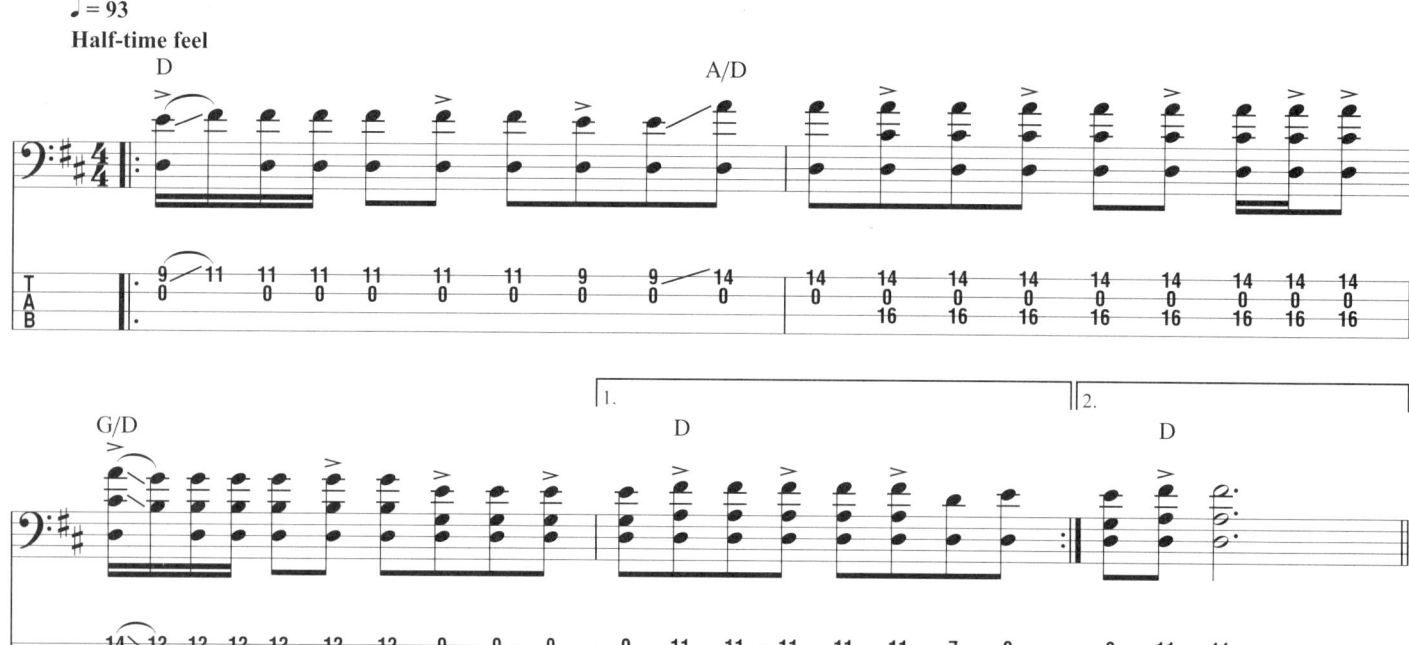

72. Droney 3

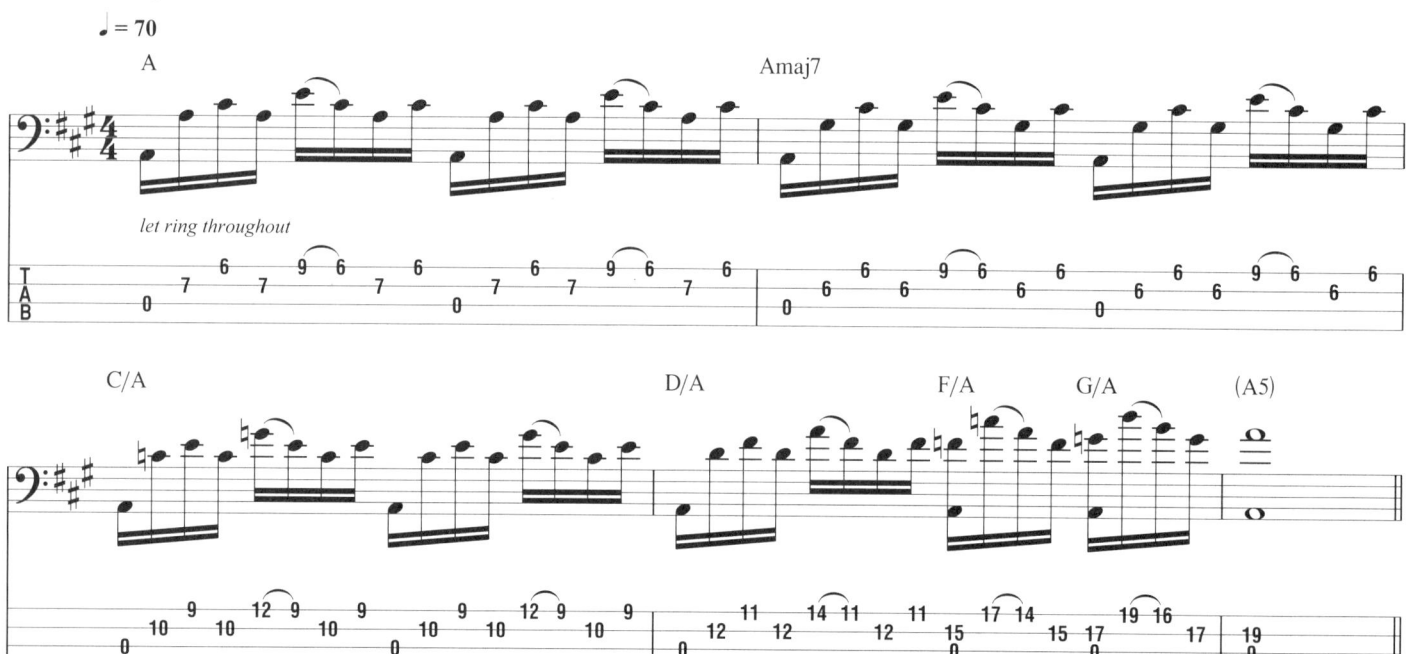

73. Power Pop Pedal

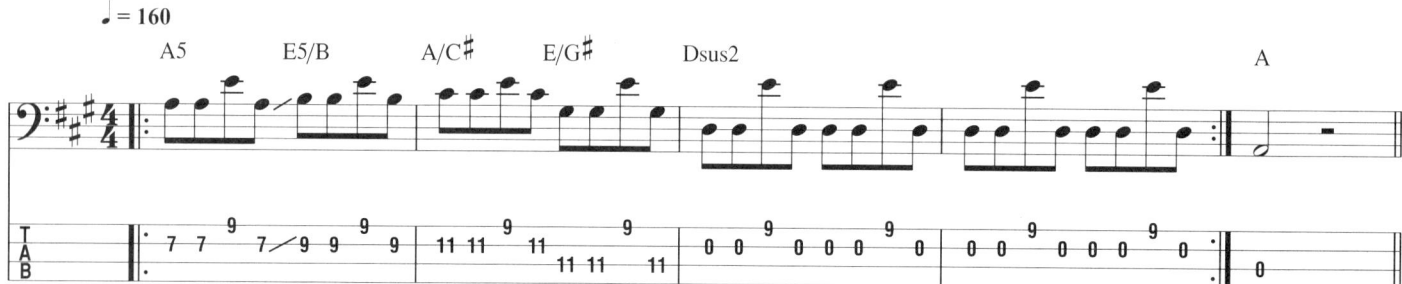

74. Pedal Pop 1

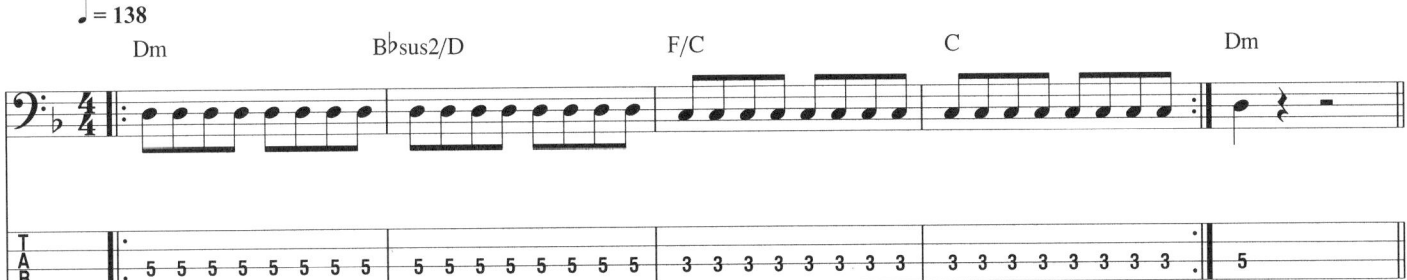

75. Pedal Pop 2

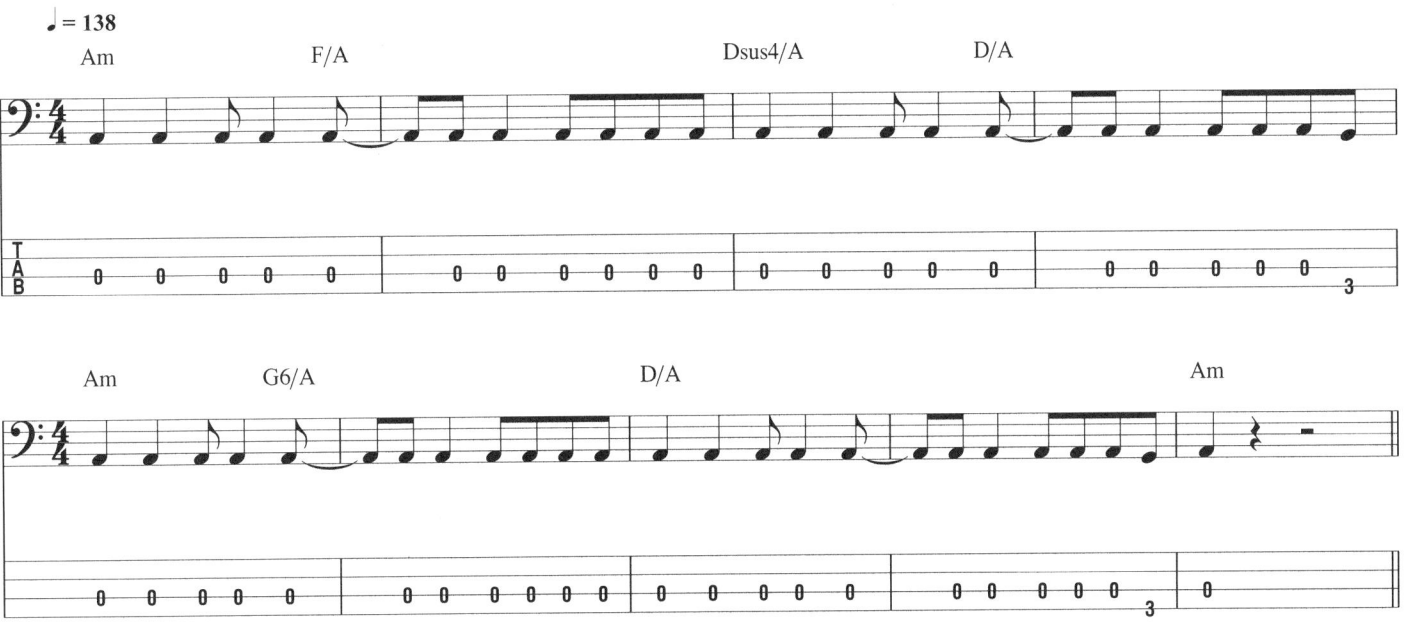

76. Pedal Pop 3

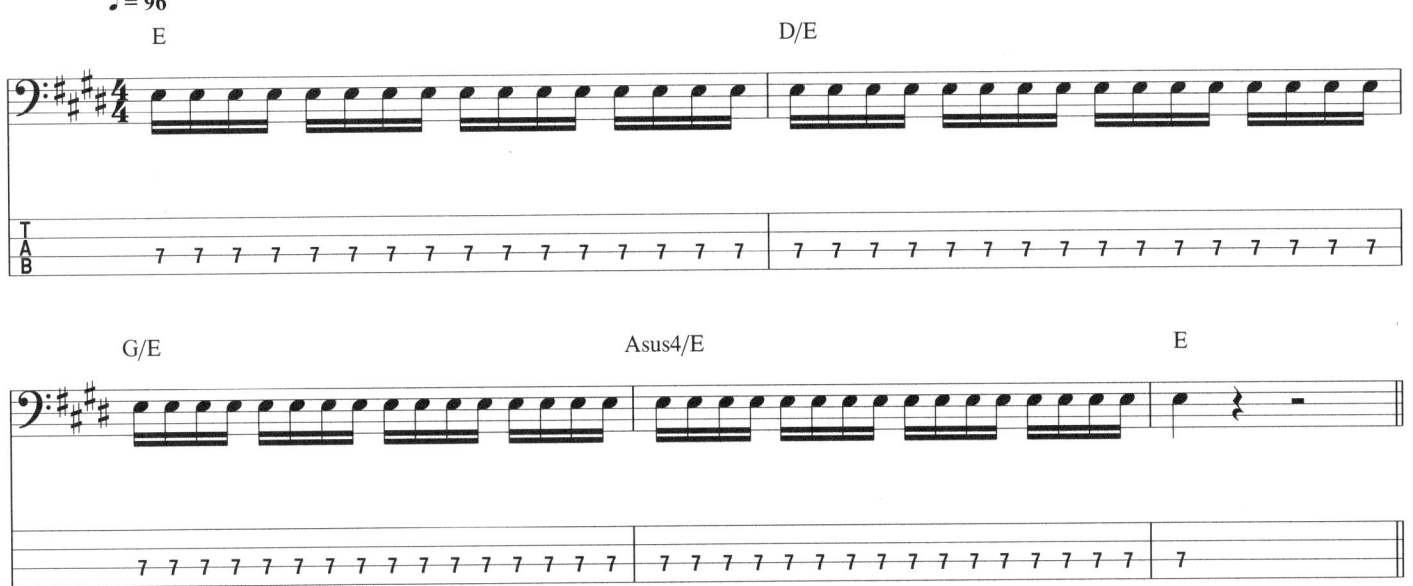

77. Pedal-Tone Line with Scale-Tone Hits

78. Heavy Pedal-Tone Groove with Riff

79. Mid-Tempo Natural Minor Groove 1

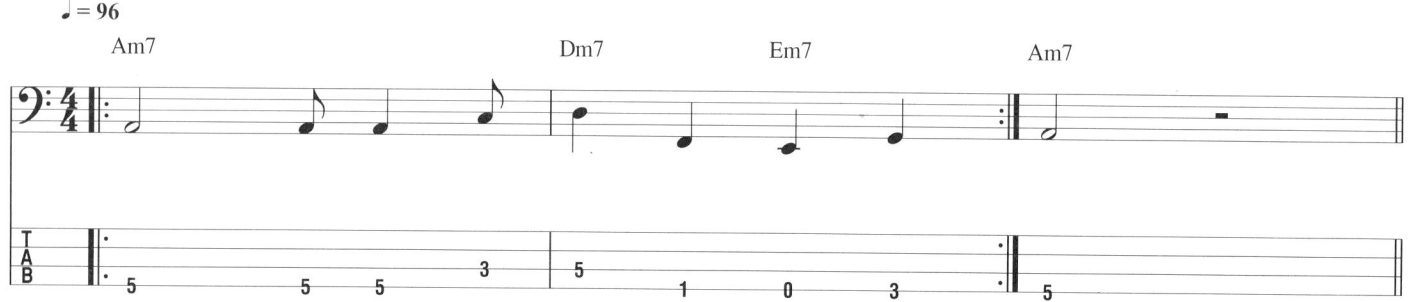

80. Mid-Tempo Natural Minor Groove 2

81. Fast Natural-Minor Rock Groove

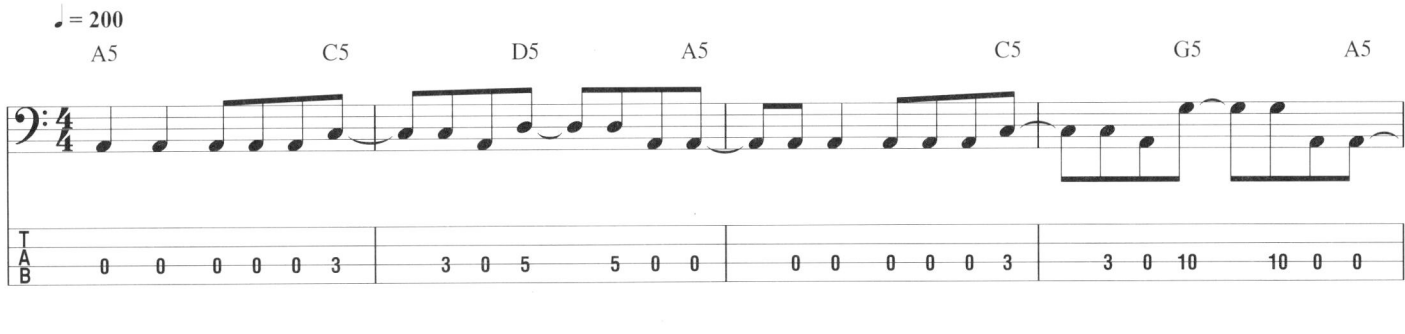

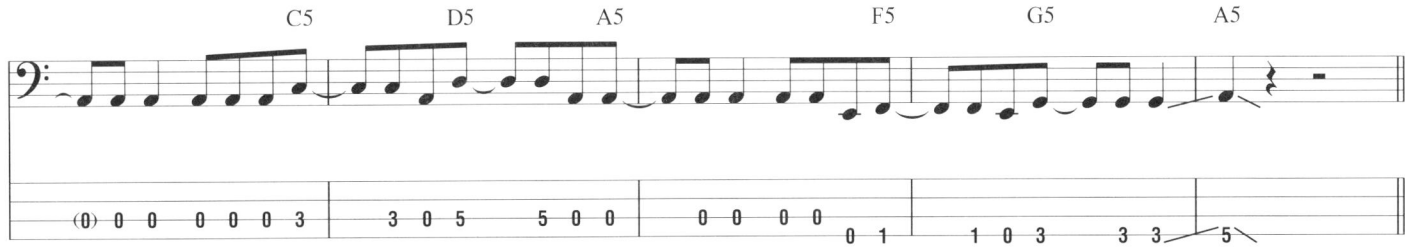

82. Latin Rock

83. Simple Latin-Rock Groove

84. Geezerish

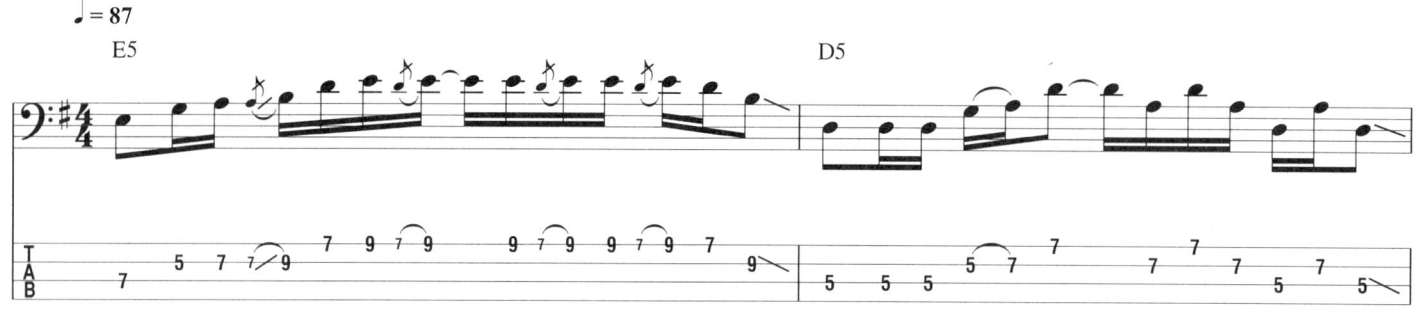

85. Ethereal Mid-Tempo Ballad

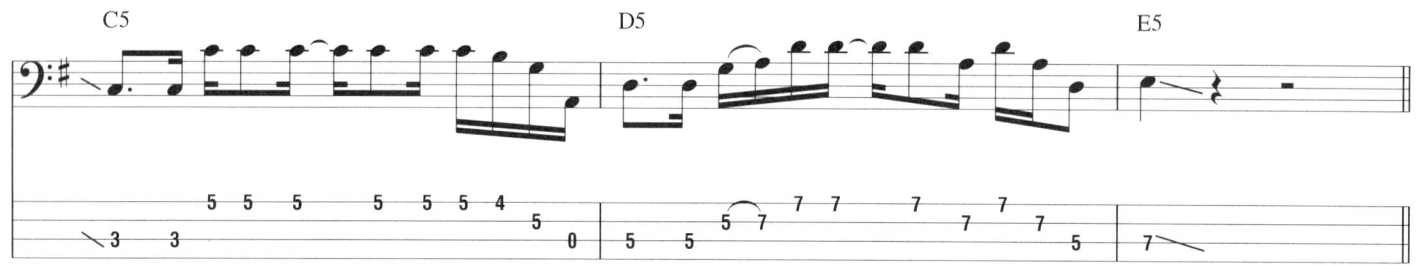

86. Bring in the Octave Reinforcements

87. Sustained Octave Climb

88. Ballad Groove with Sustained Octave Slides

89. Wall of Sound 1

90. Wall of Sound 2

27

91. Moody Modal
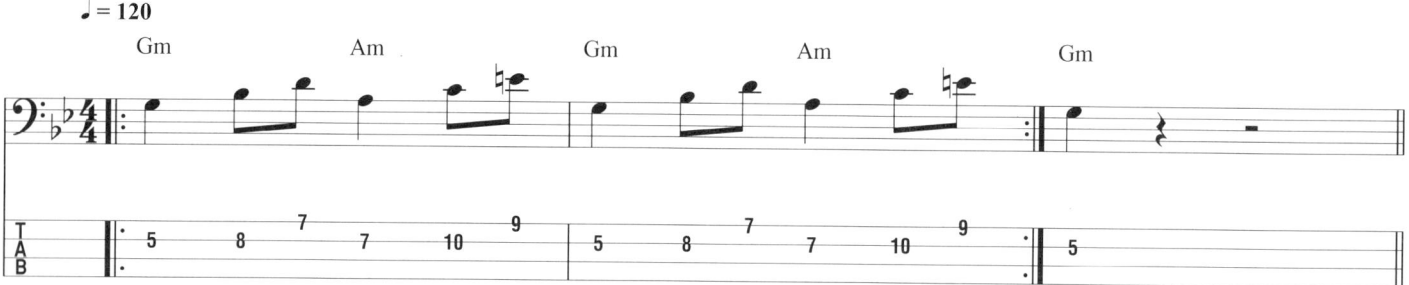

92. Jazzy Turnaround
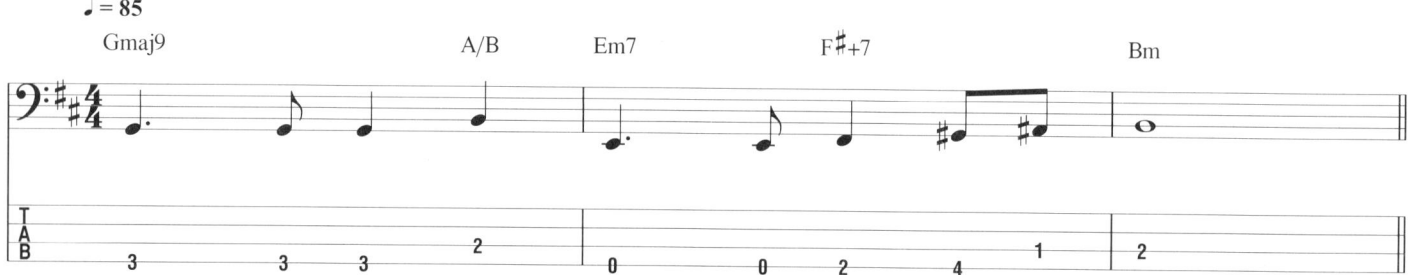

93. Melodic Minor Pop
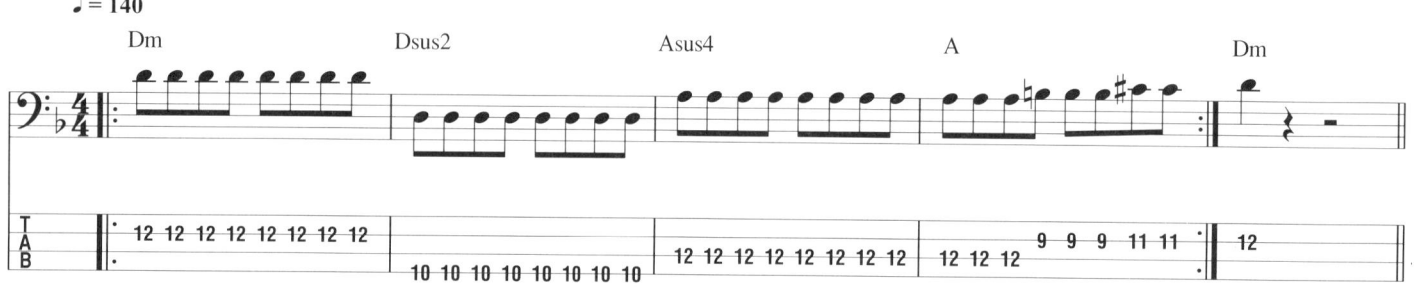

94. Pop

95. Quarter-Tone Rub
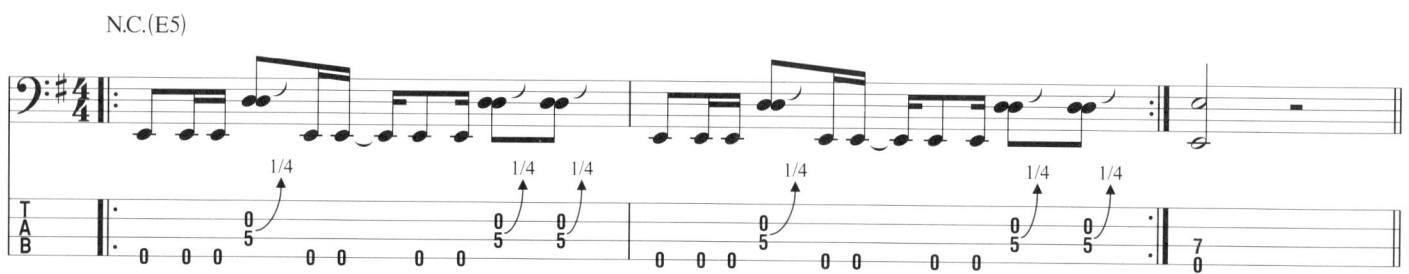

96. Moody Sus2 Line 1
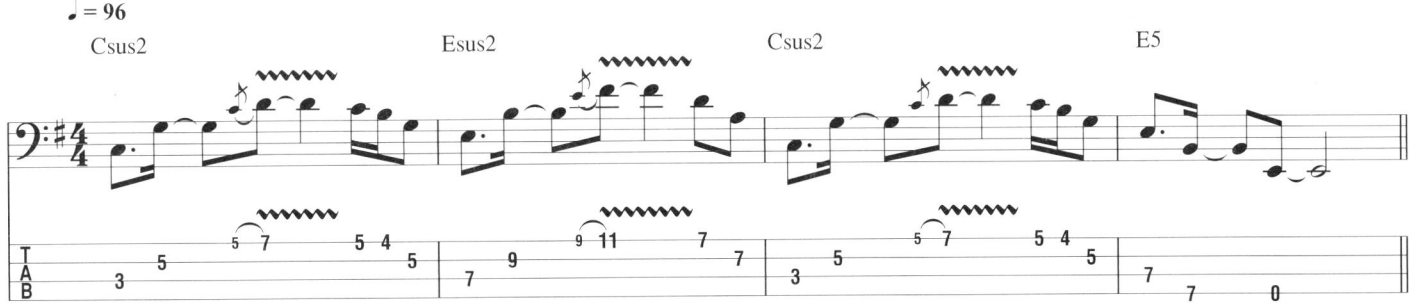

97. Moody Sus2 Line 2

98. Line Cliché 1

99. Line Cliché 2
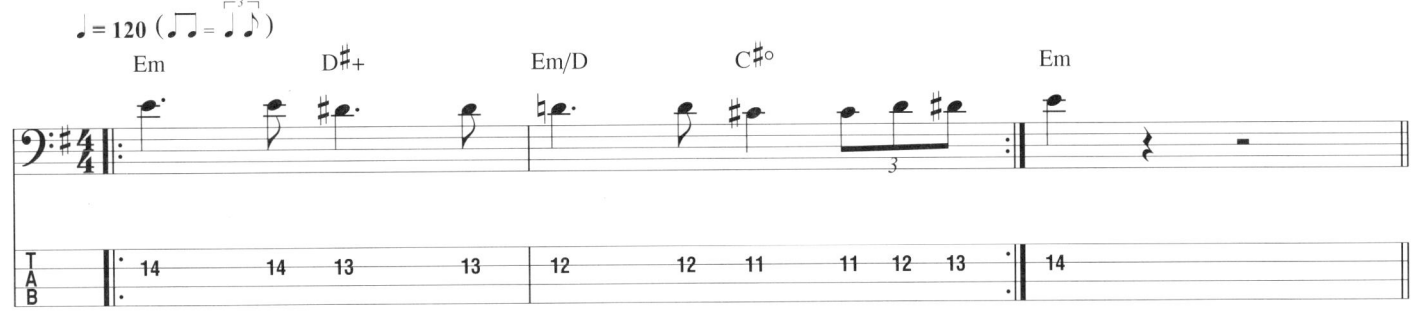

100. Line Cliché 3
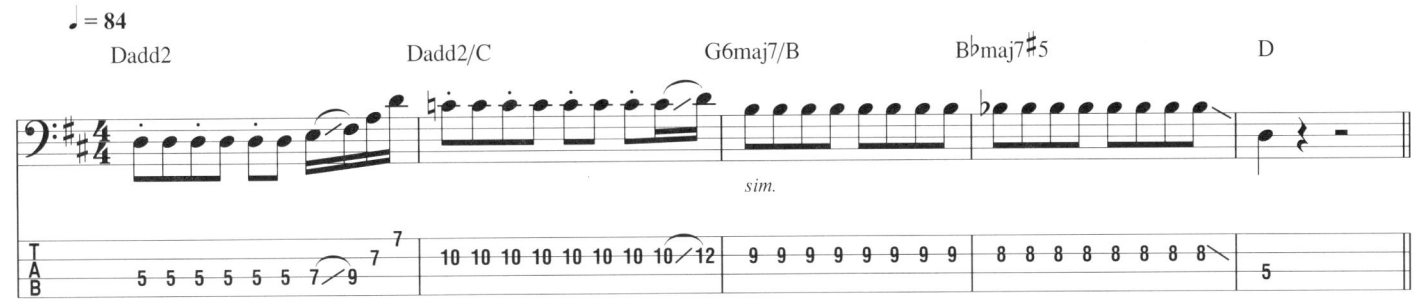

101. Half-Time Shuffle with the Fatness

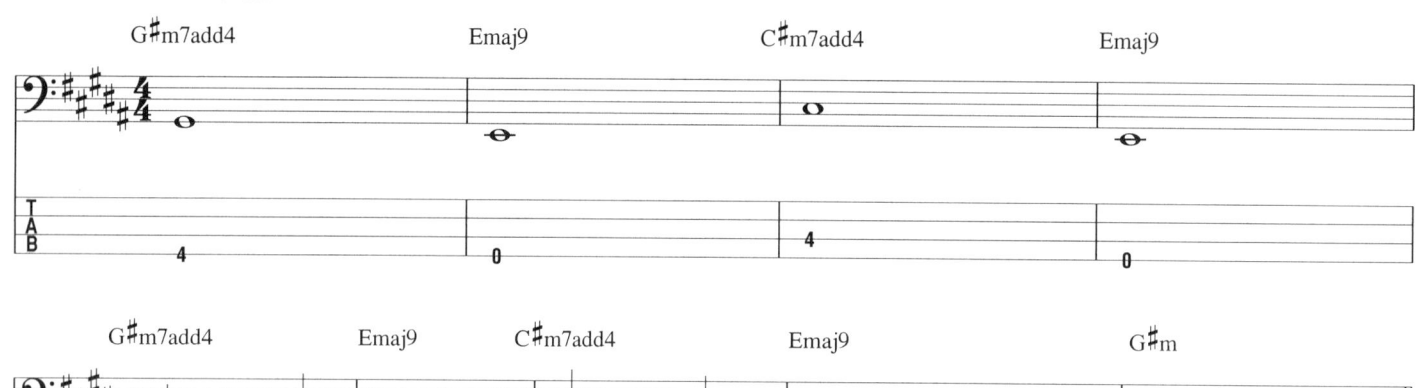

102. Half-Time Shuffle with Funky Spaces

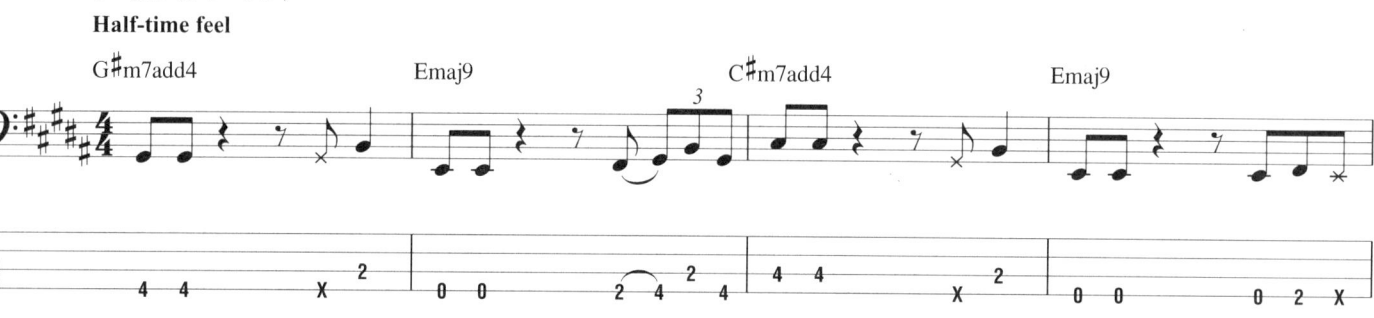

103. One-Man Band 1

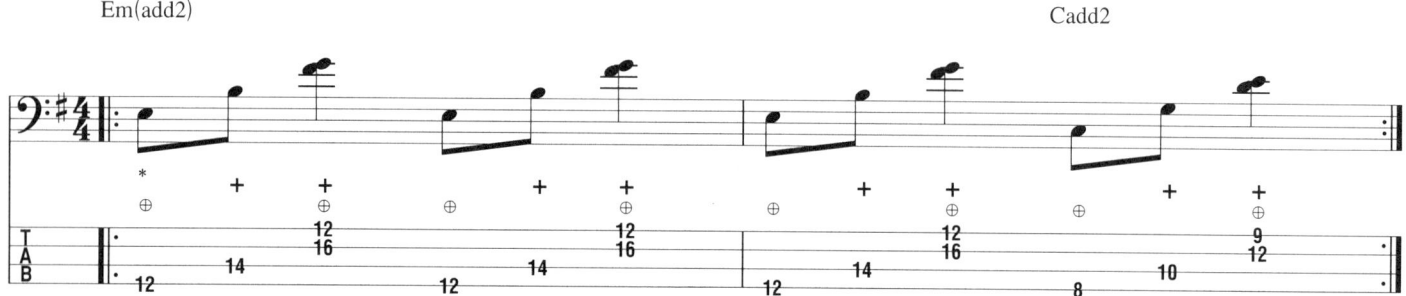

*Fingering: E string: fret-hand index; A string: pick-hand index; D-string: pick-hand ring; G-string: fret-hand pinky

104. One-Man Band 2

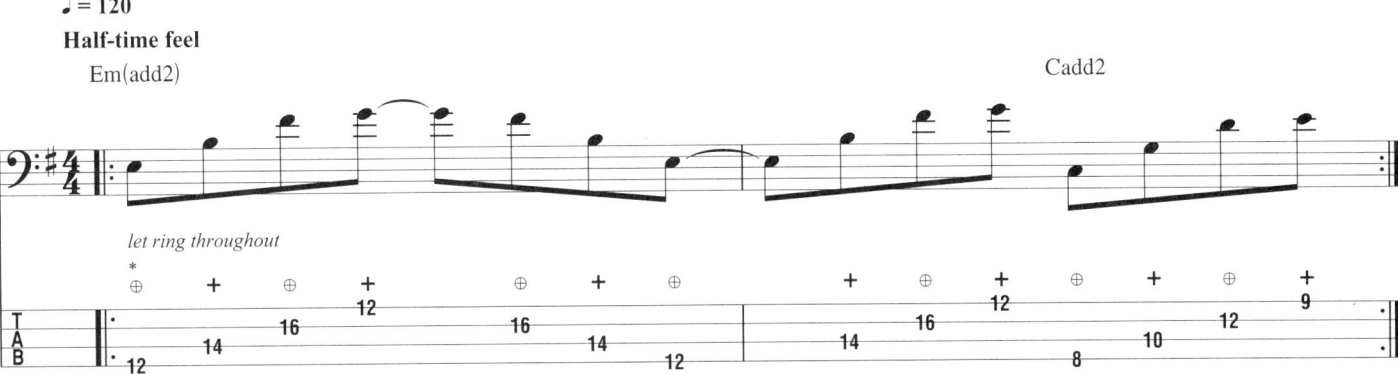

*Fingering: E string: fret-hand index; A string: pick-hand index; D-string: pick-hand ring; G-string: fret-hand pinky

105. Every Pop-Rock Bass Line You've Ever Heard 1

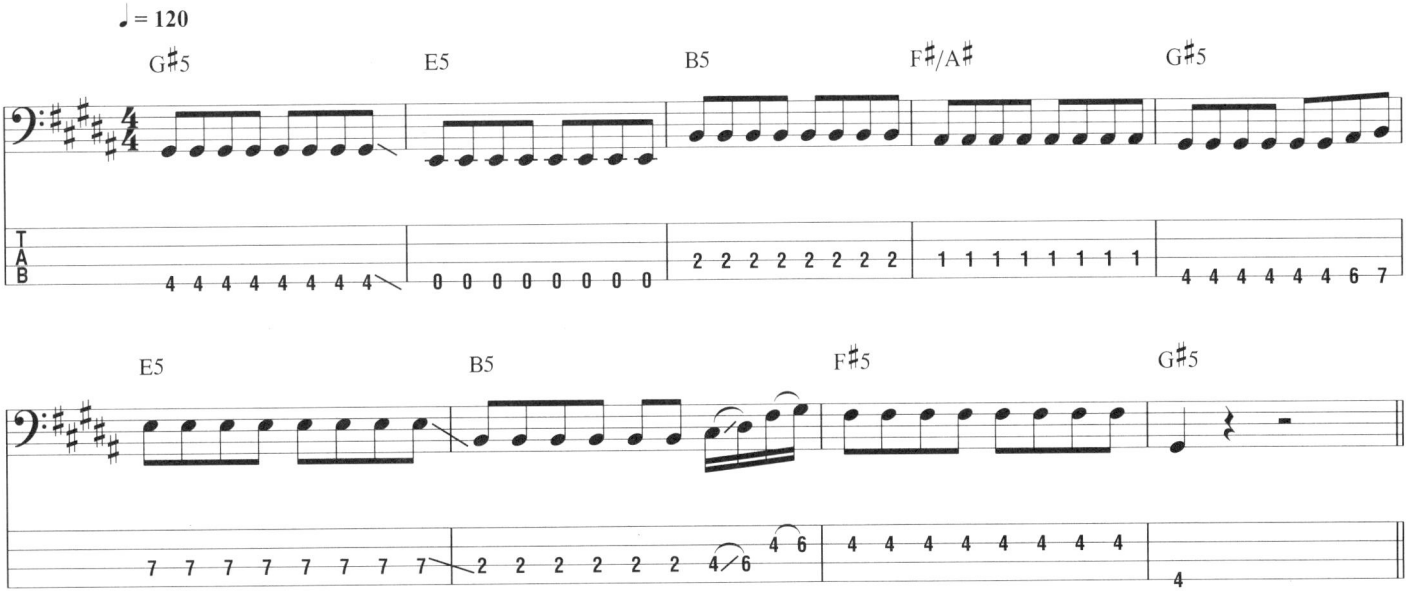

106. Every Pop-Rock Bass Line You've Ever Heard 2

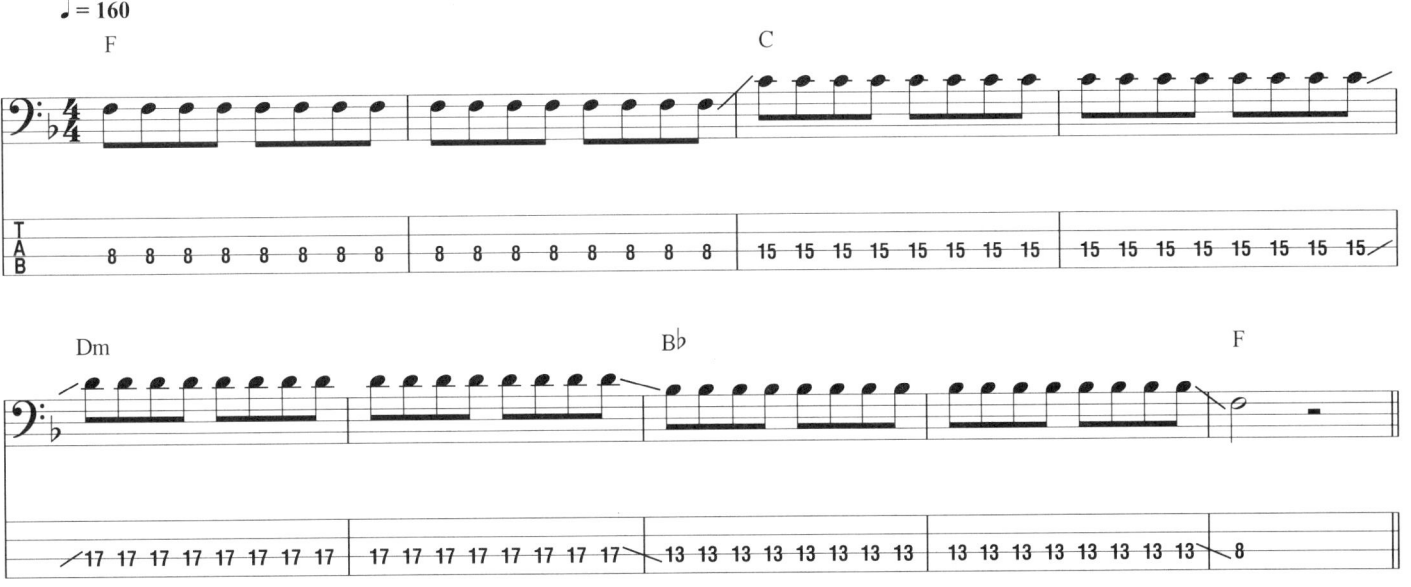

107. Every Pop-Rock Bass Line You've Ever Heard 3

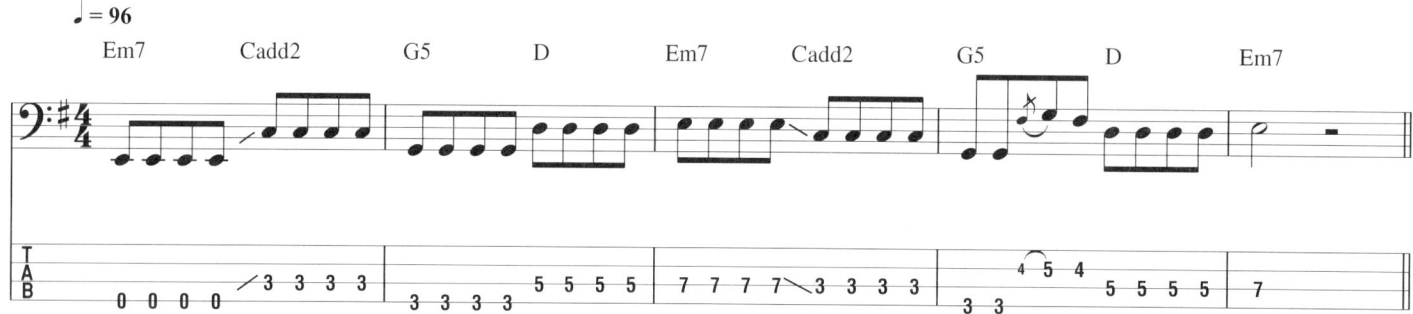

108. The Notes You *Don't* Play Are Just as Important 1

109. The Notes You *Don't* Play Are Just as Important 2

110. The Notes You *Don't* Play Are Just as Important 3

111. Slinky 1

112. Slinky 2

113. Simple Ballad

114. Delicate Melodic Ballad 1

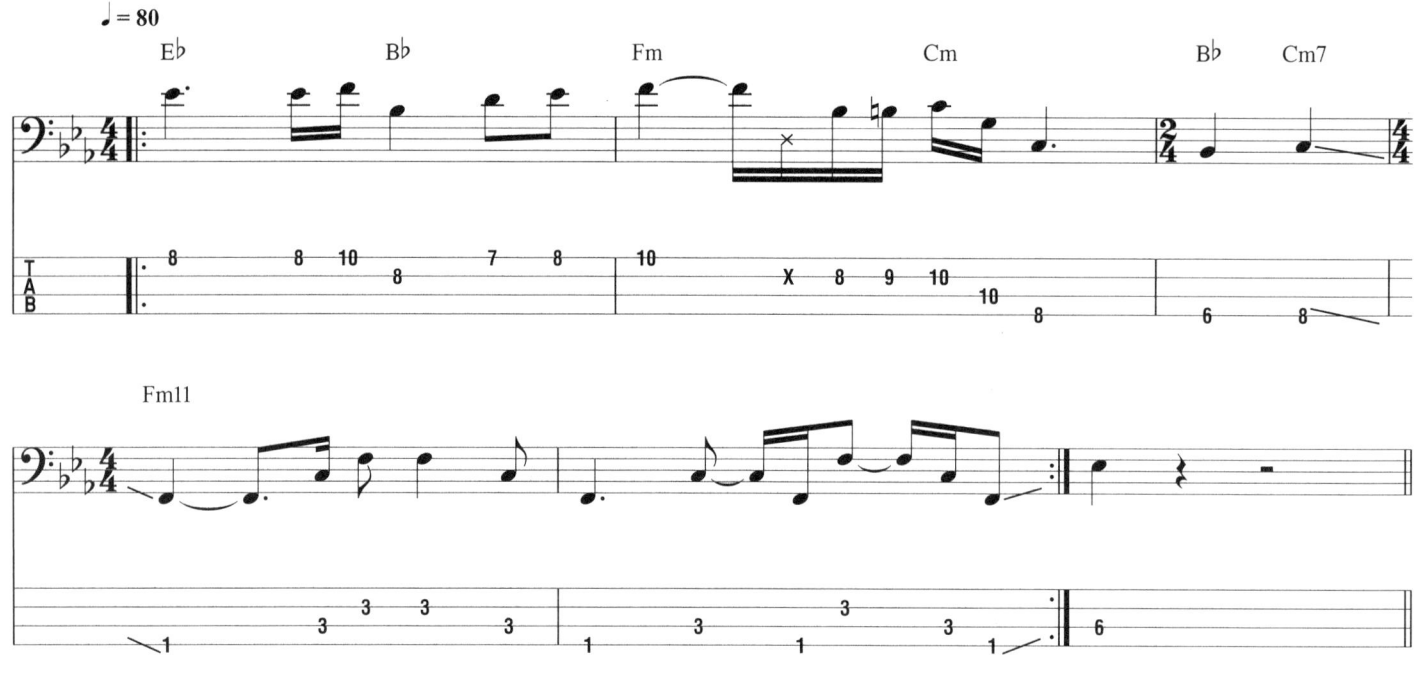

115. Delicate Melodic Ballad 2

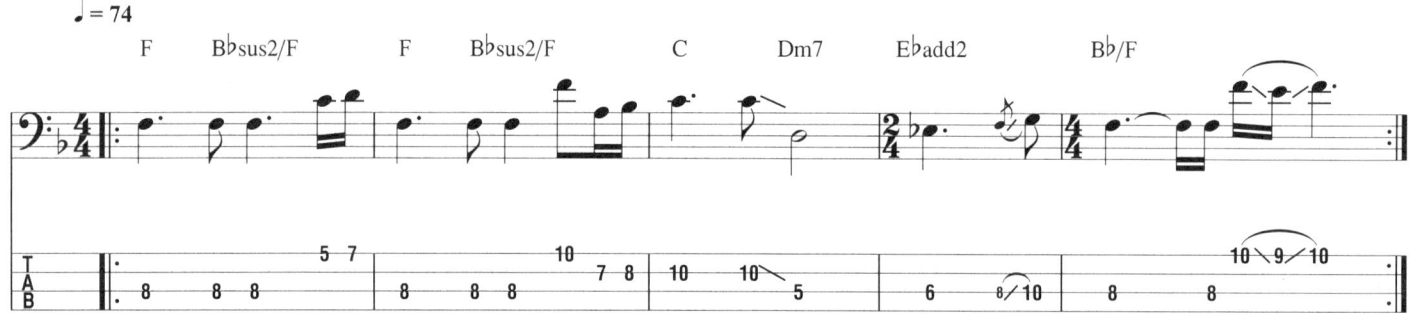

116. '70s Ballad

117. Dramatic Gallop Climb

118. Soft Vibrato Ballad Groove

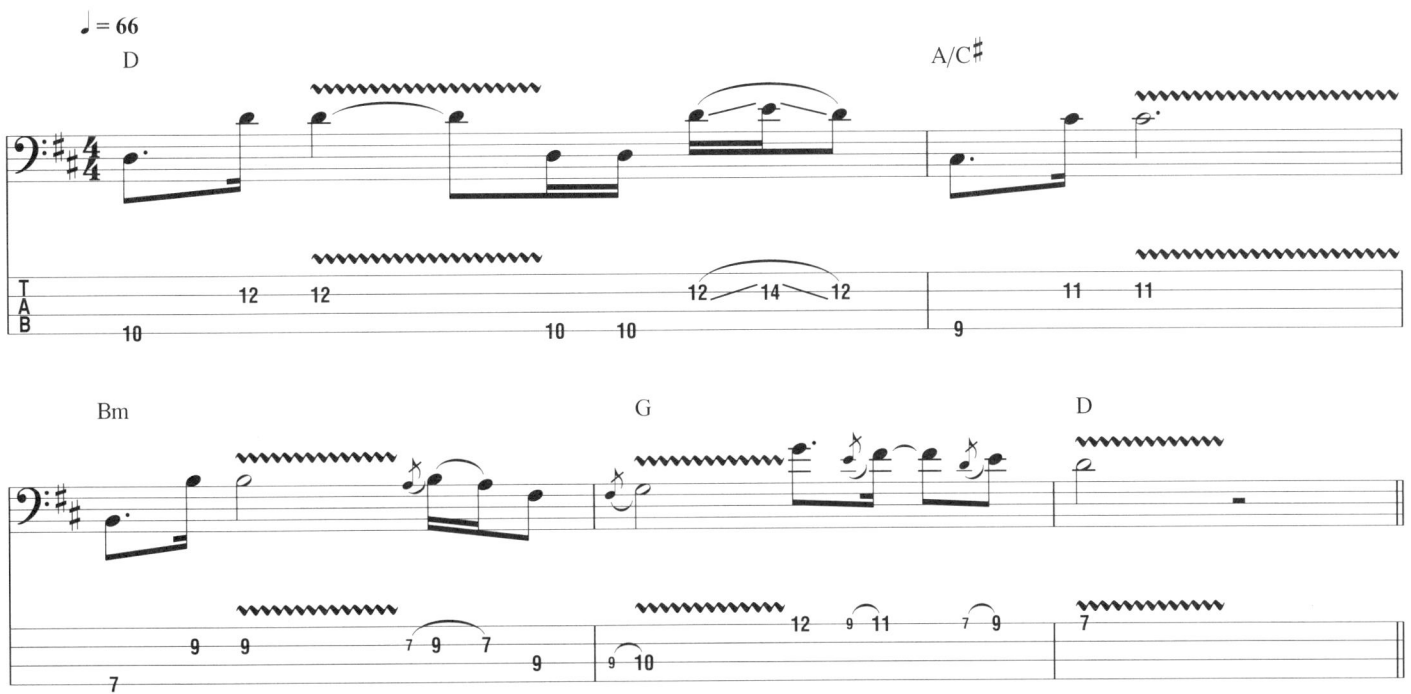

119. Odd-Time Pop

120. Fast '50s Rock

121. Basic I-IV-V Variation 1

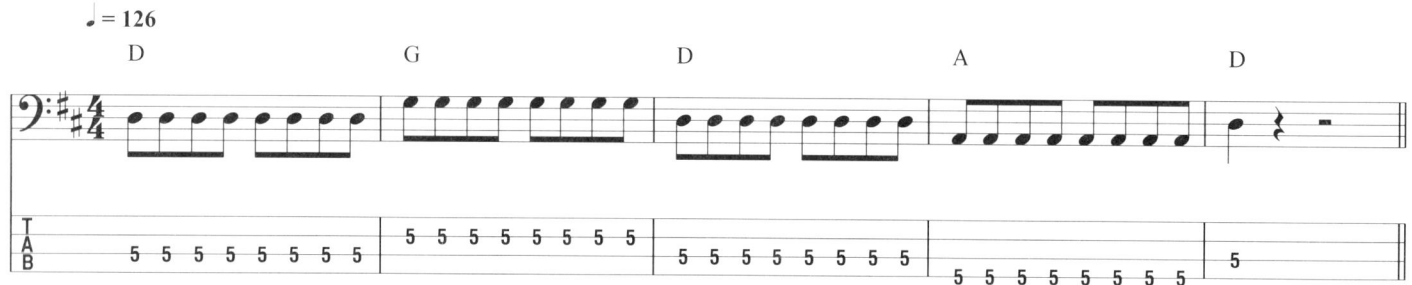

122. Basic I-IV-V Variation 2

123. Basic I-IV-V Variation 3

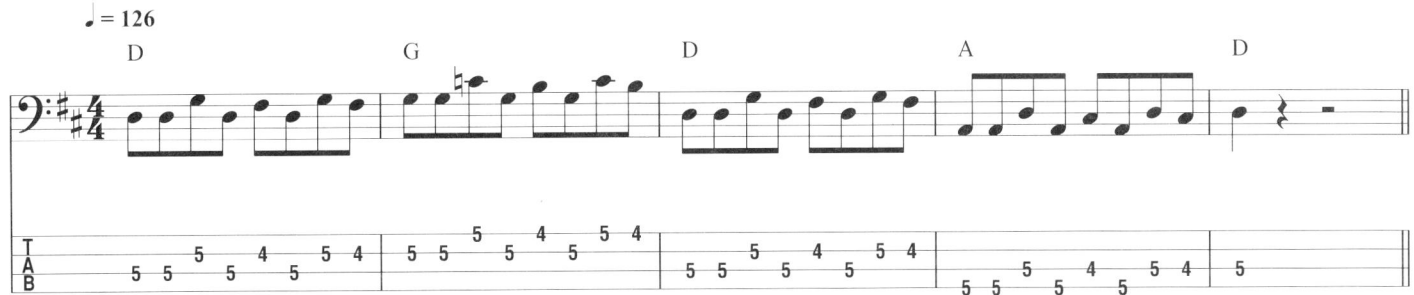

124. Half-Time Pop Variation 1

125. Half-Time Pop Variation 2

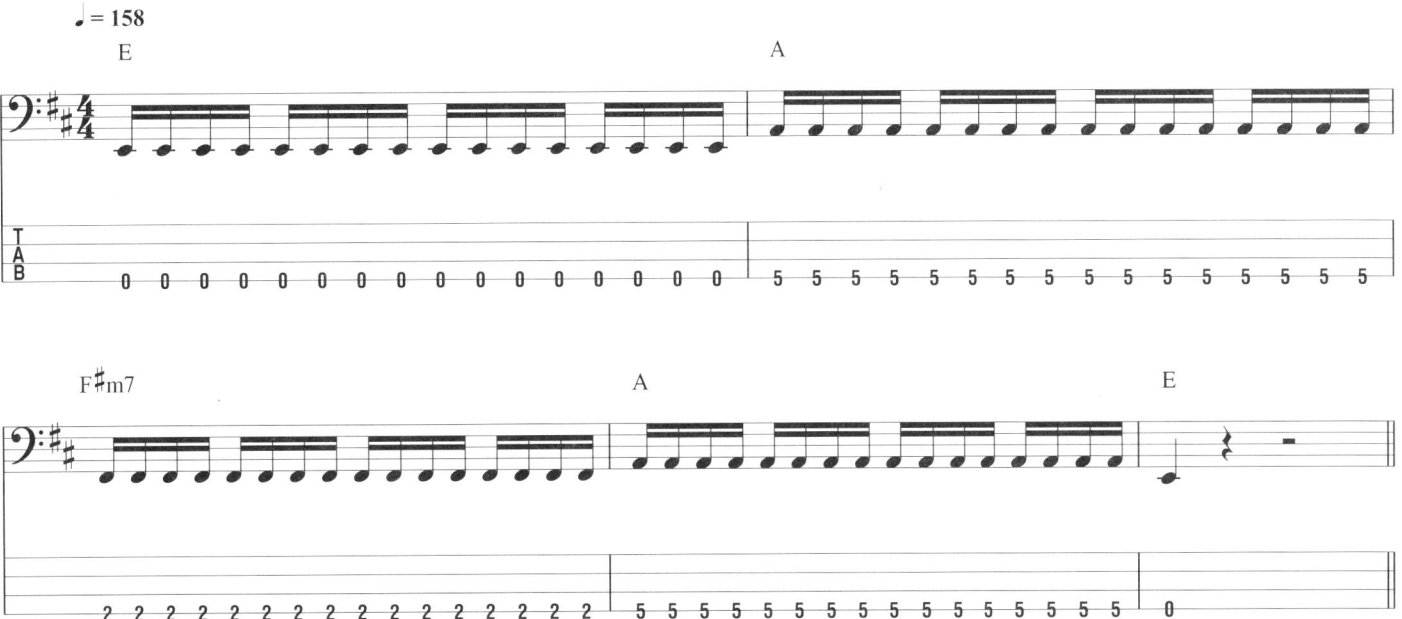

126. Lite Melodic Pop

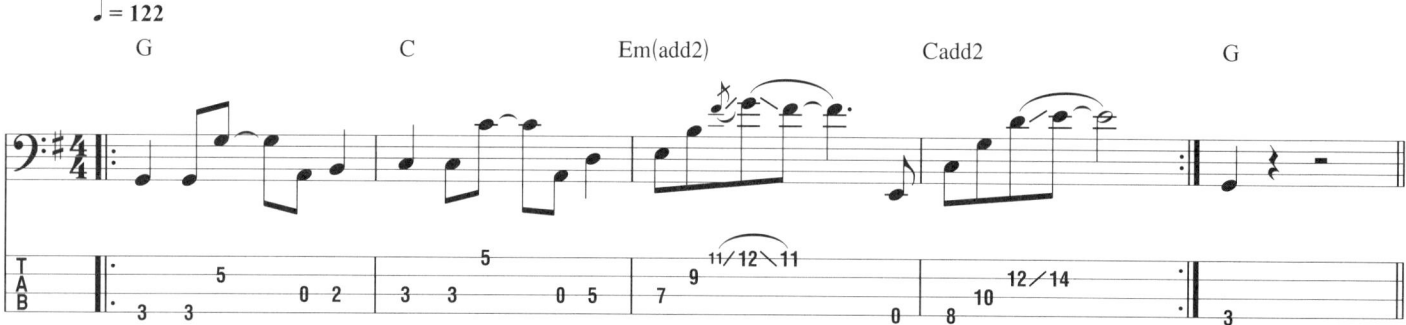

127. Groove from That Music They Play in European-Based Clothing Retail Chains

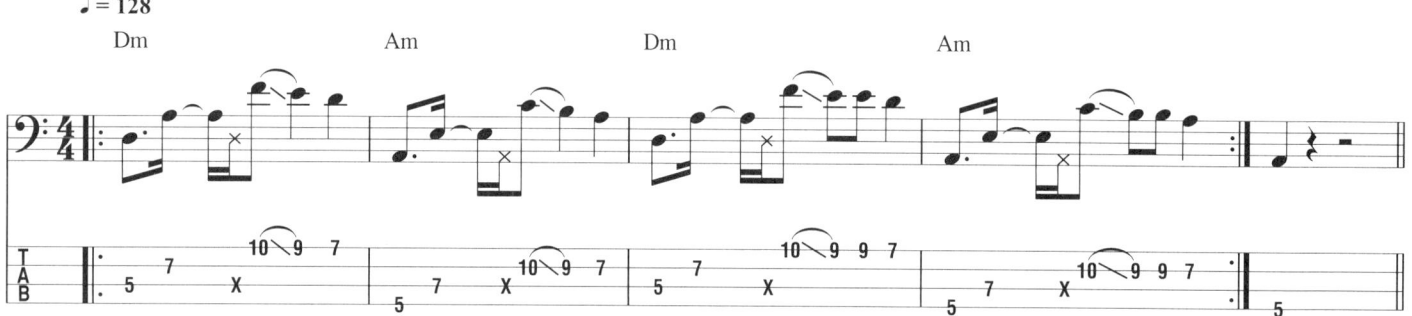

128. Power Pop

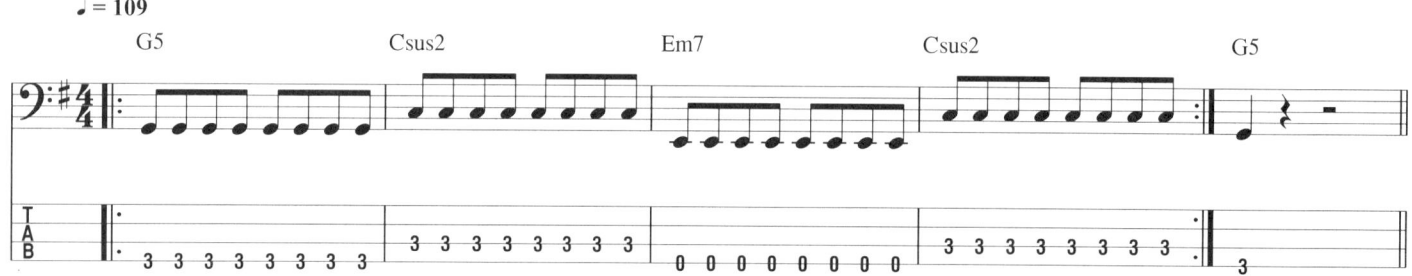

129. Dance-y Pop

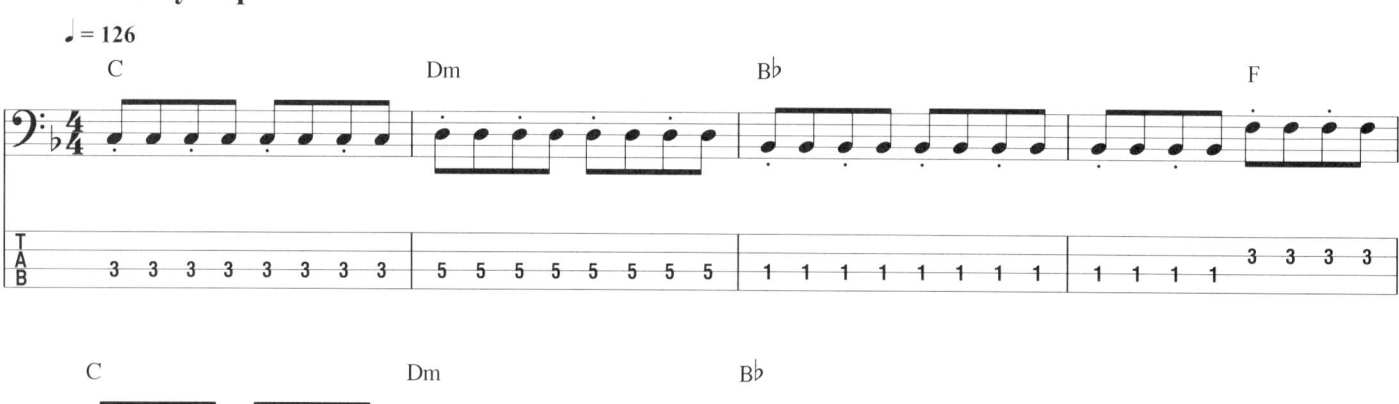

130. Slow Ballad

131. Funky Rock Offbeats

132. Open-String-Based Pop Line

133. Busy Mid-Tempo Groove

134. Up the Fretboard

135. Grungy Quarter-Tone Bends

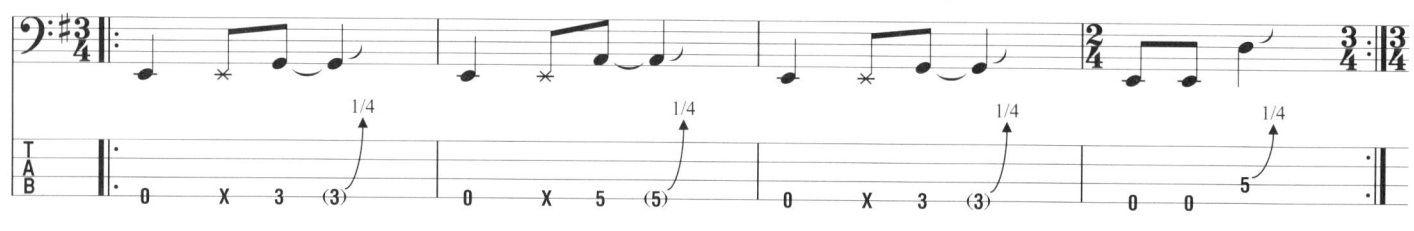

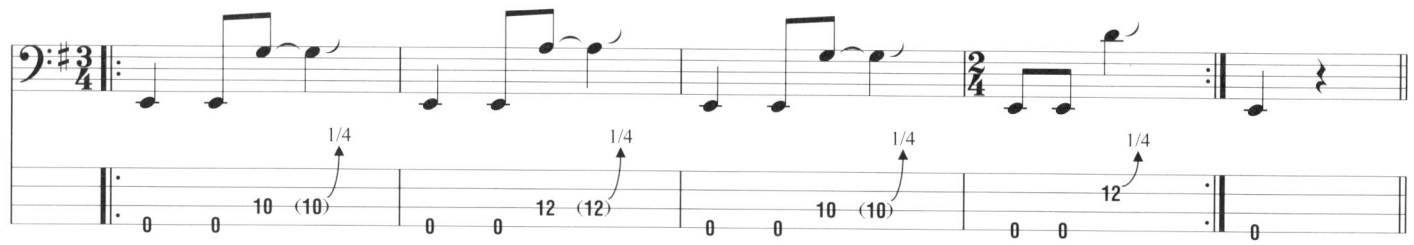

136. Stoner Jam

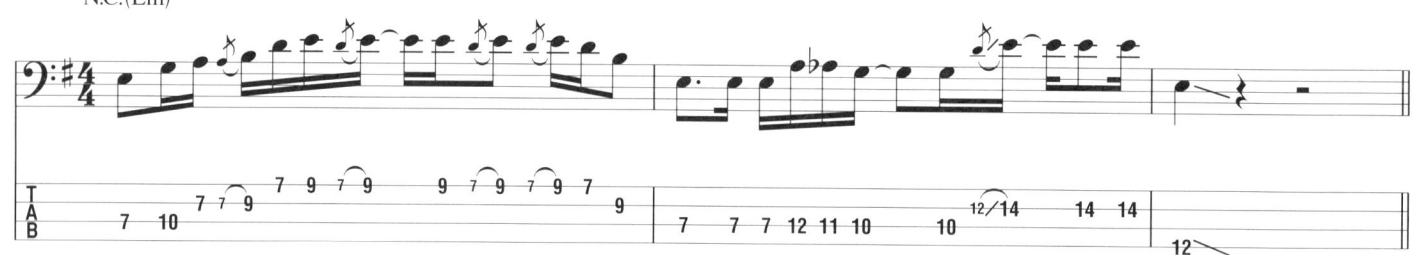

137. Dig In

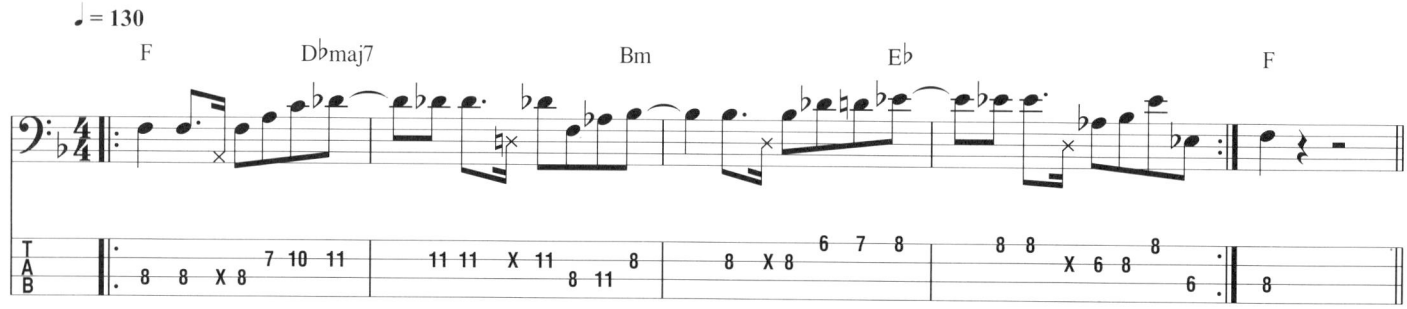

138. Baroque 1

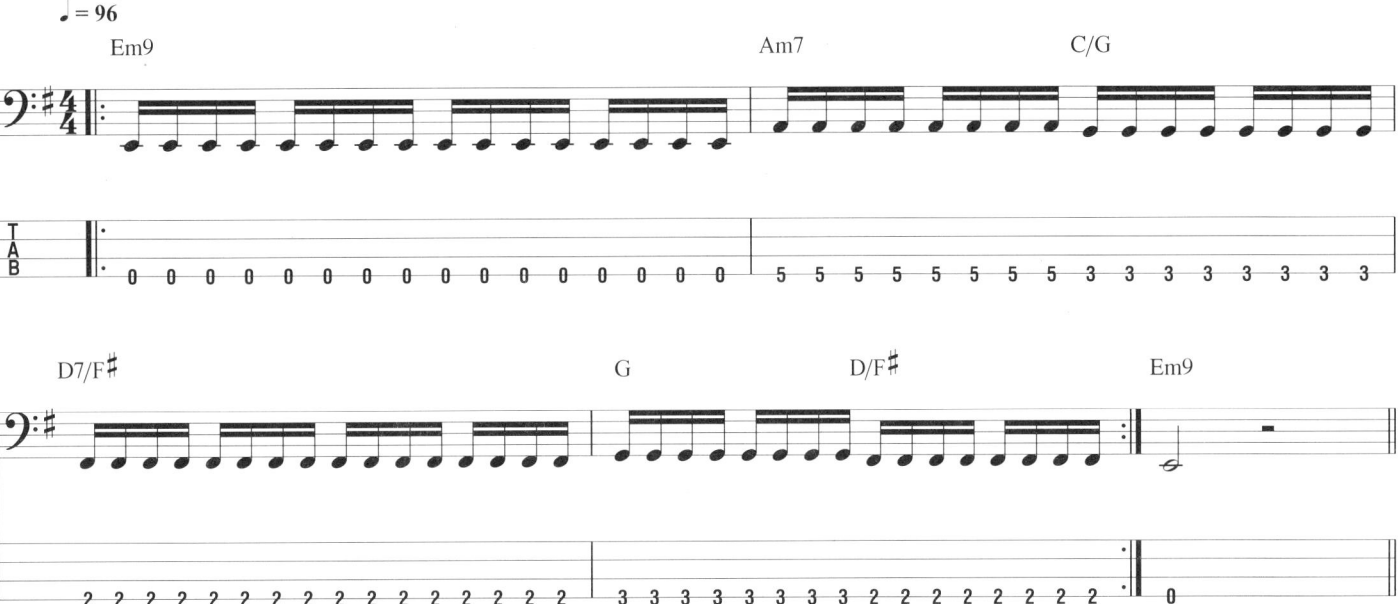

139. Deep Rock Groove

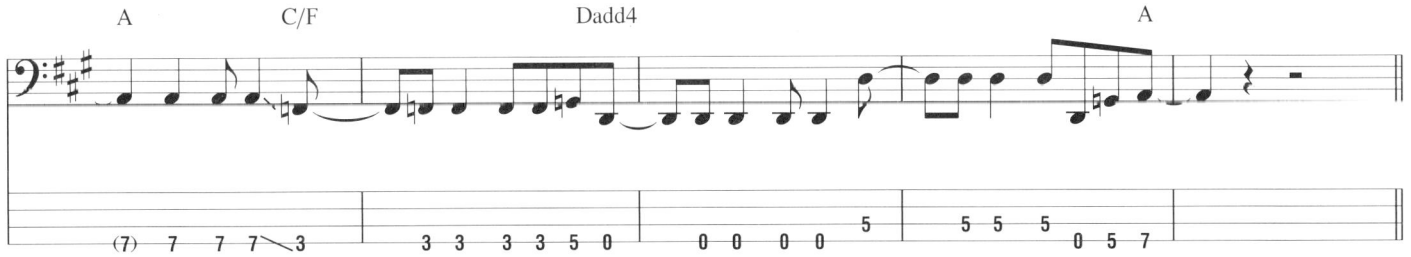

140. Pop Go the Off-Beats

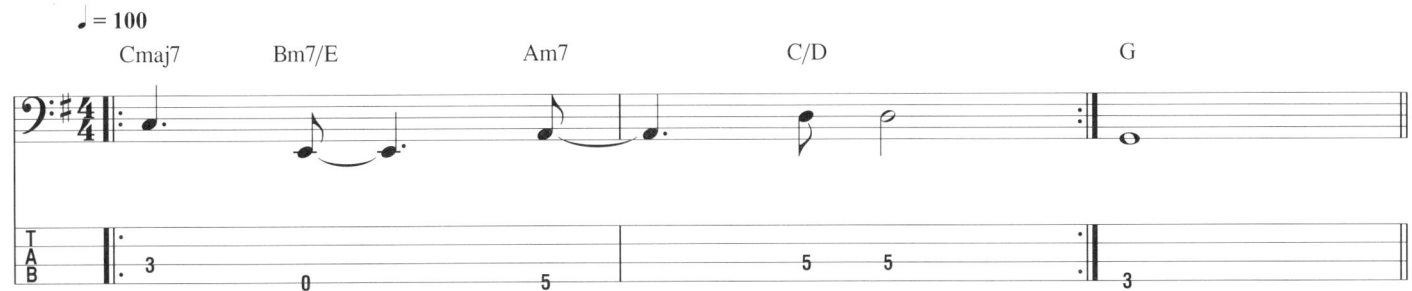

141. Rock Octaves

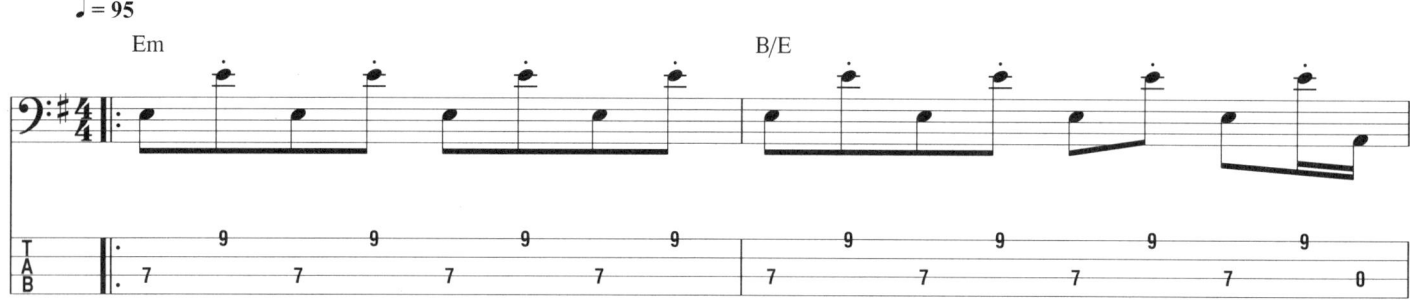

142. Stax-ish 1

143. Bass Riff Lead-In 1

Drop D tuning:
(low to high) D-A-D-G

144. Bass Riff Lead-In 2

145. Bass Riff Lead-In 3

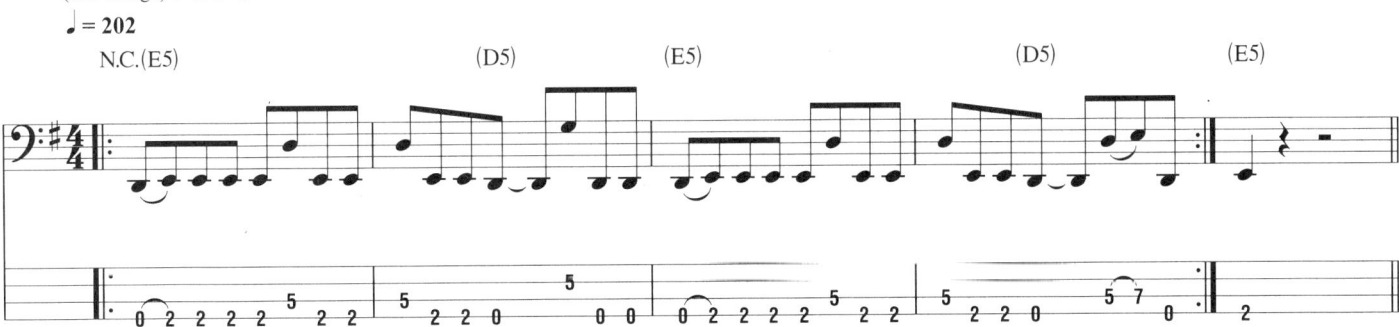

146. Tight Staccato Shuffle

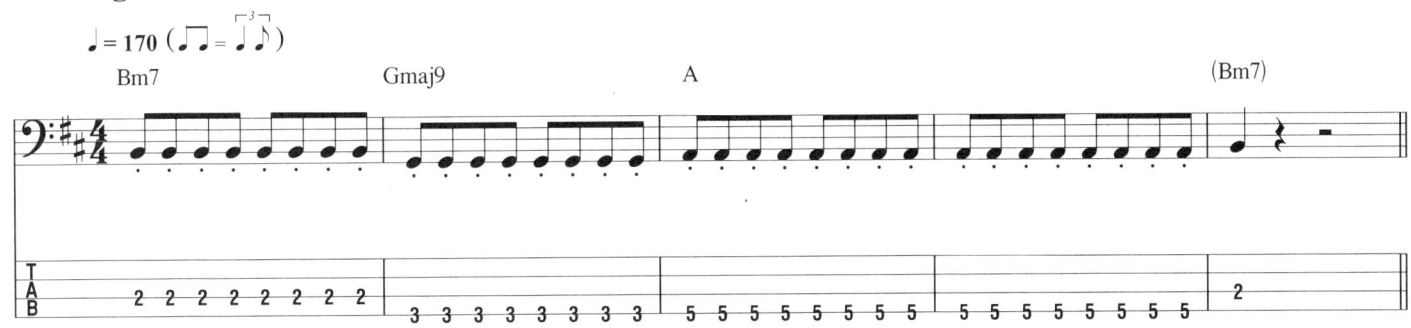

147. Smooth Pop-Soul Groove

148. Simple and Soulful

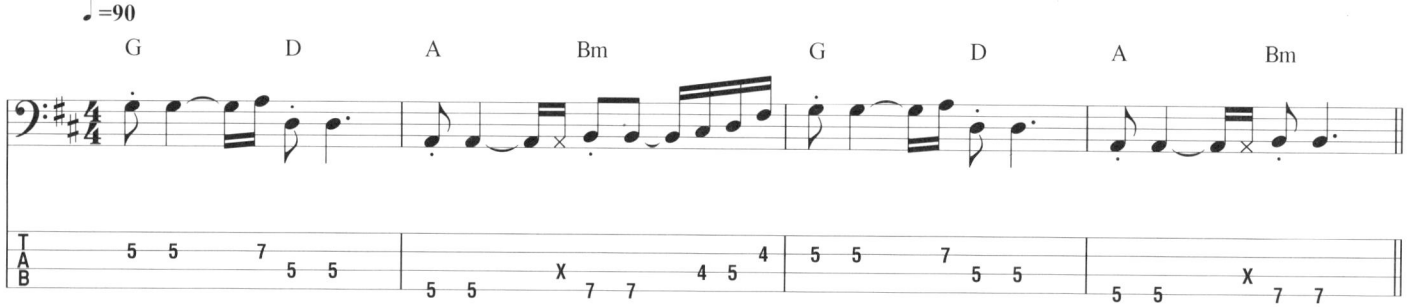

149. '90s 1

150. '90s 2

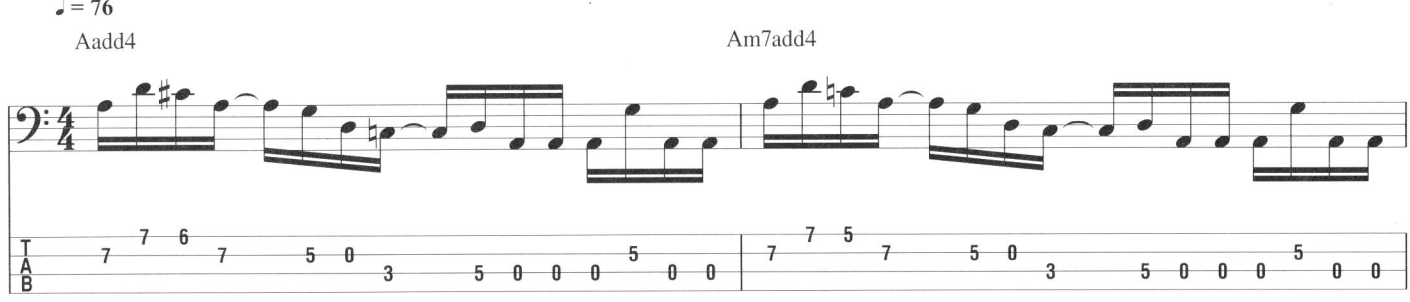

151. A Bass Guitar Is Still a Guitar 1

152. A Bass Guitar Is Still a Guitar 2

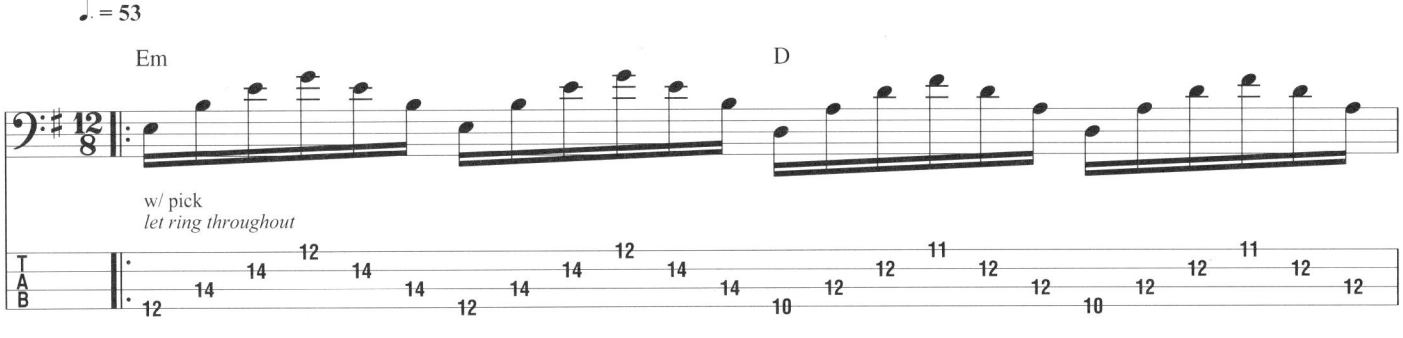
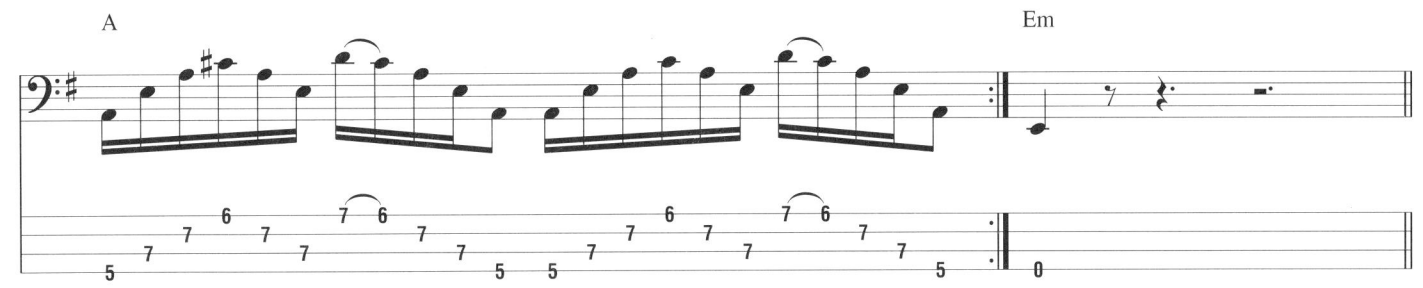

153. Funky Staccato Octaves
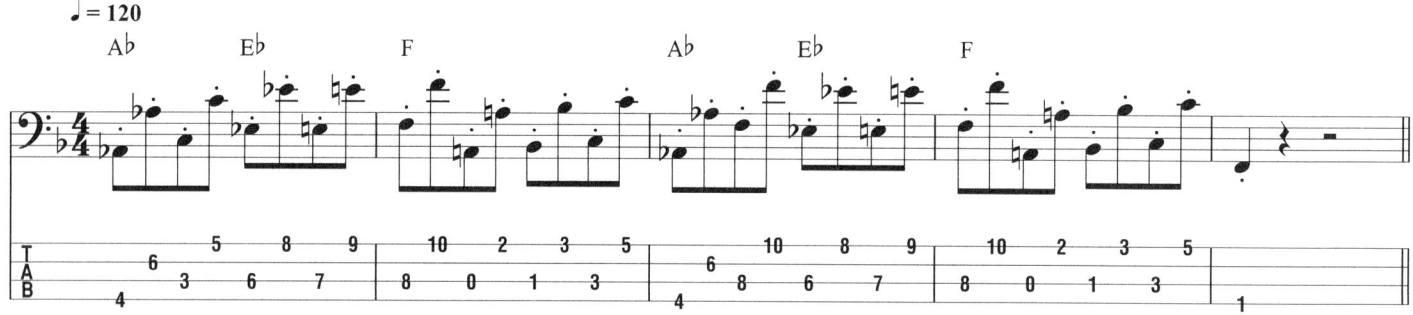

154. Reggae-Pop

155. I Could Tell She Was Trouble

156. Heavy Blues-Rock Syncopation

157. Uptempo Boogie

158. Island Rock

159. Harmonics

160. Rock & Soul 1

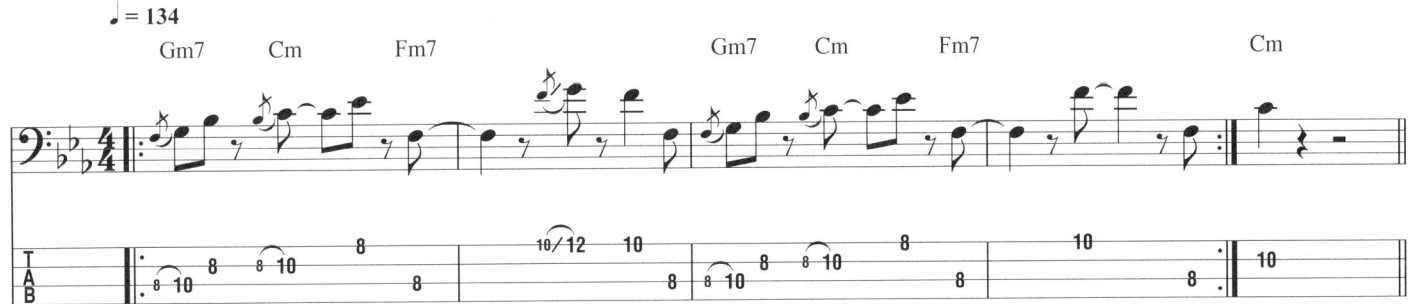

161. Rock & Soul 2

162. Rock & Soul 3

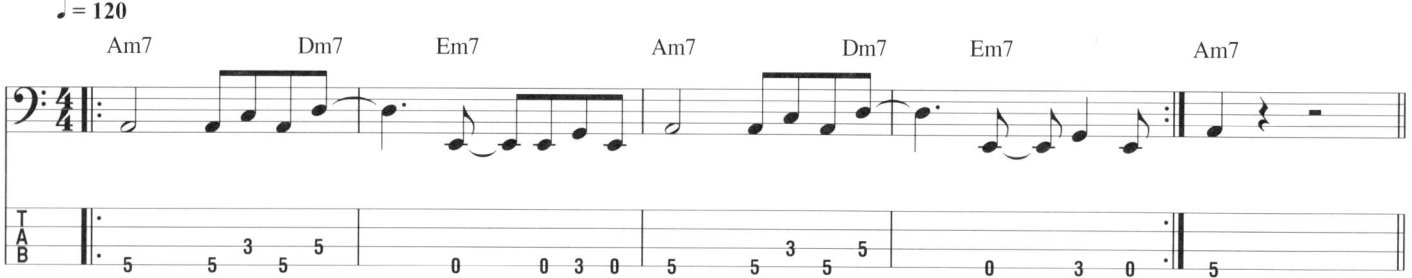

163. Hammermania 1

164. Hammermania 2

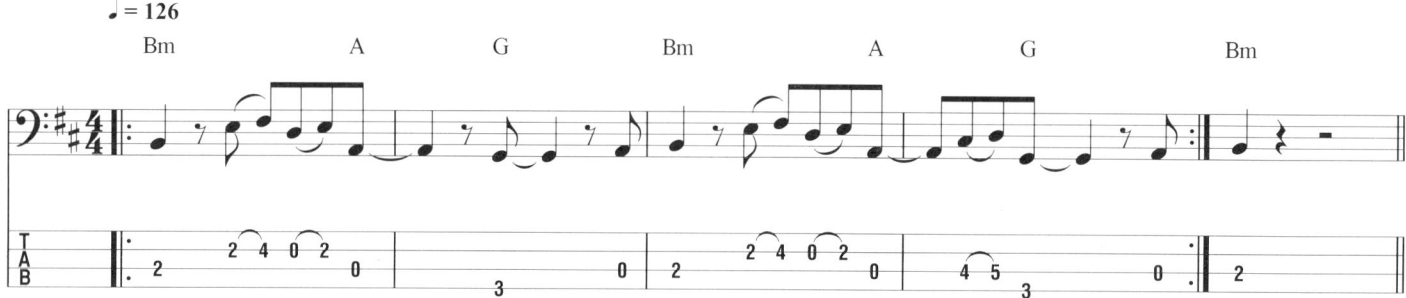

165. Calipunk

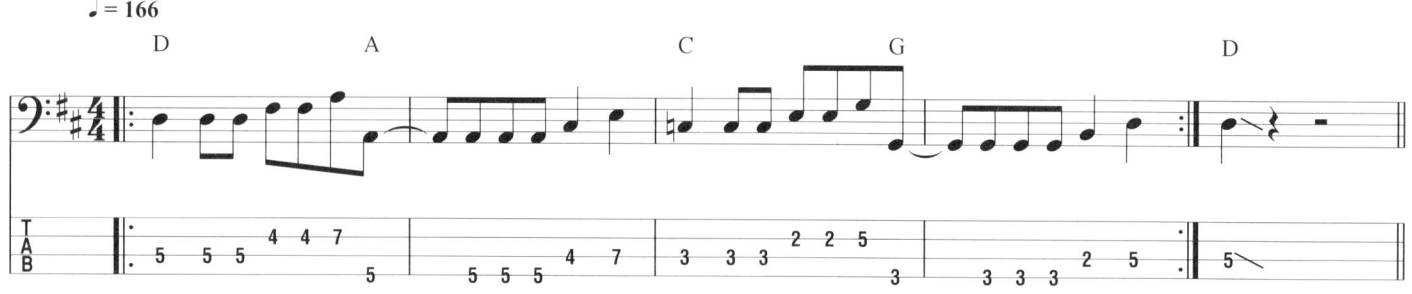

166. Fast Punk 1

167. Fast Punk 2

168. Pop Punk 1

169. Pop Punk 2

170. Grunge 1

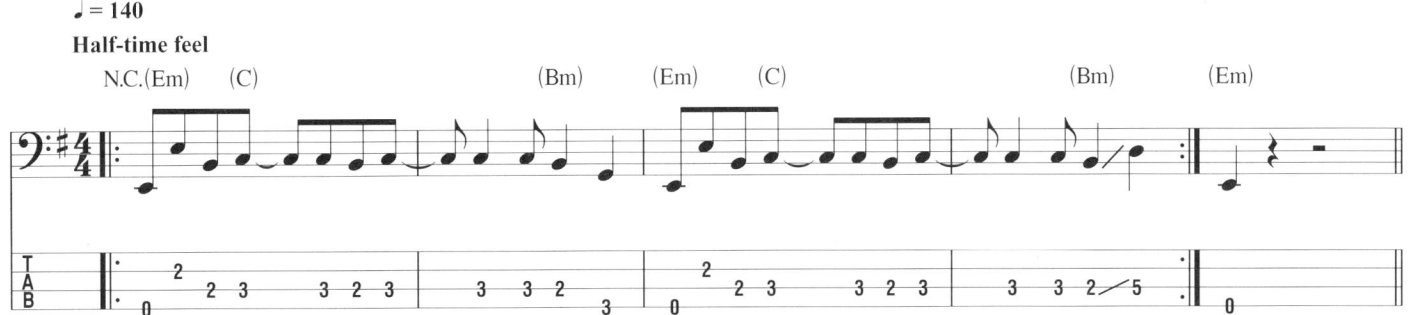

171. Grunge 2

172. Grunge 3

173. Grunge 4

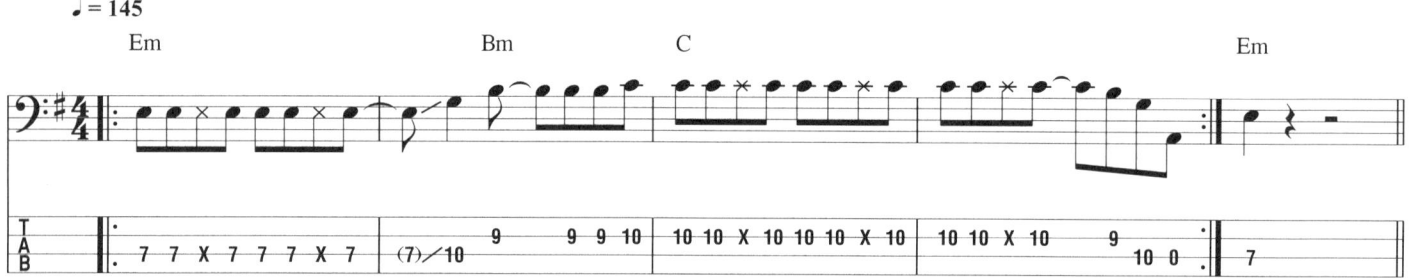

174. Slide

175. Jangle Pop 1

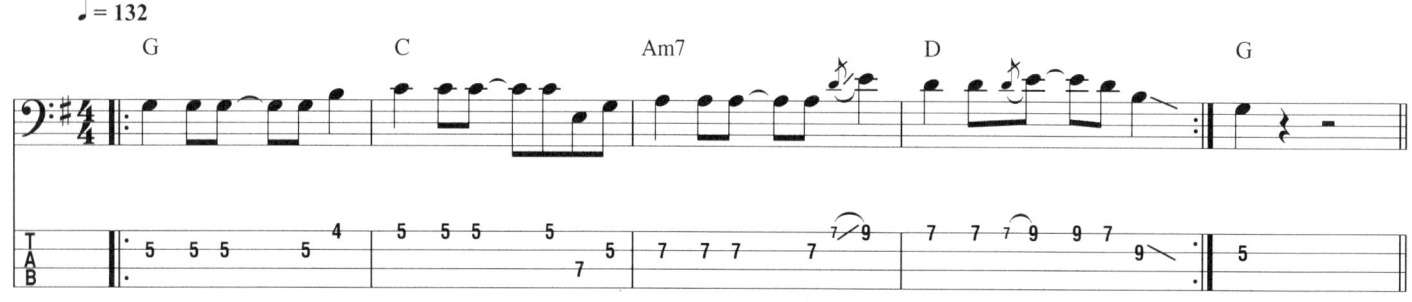

176. Jangle Pop 2

177. Chicago Shuffle 1

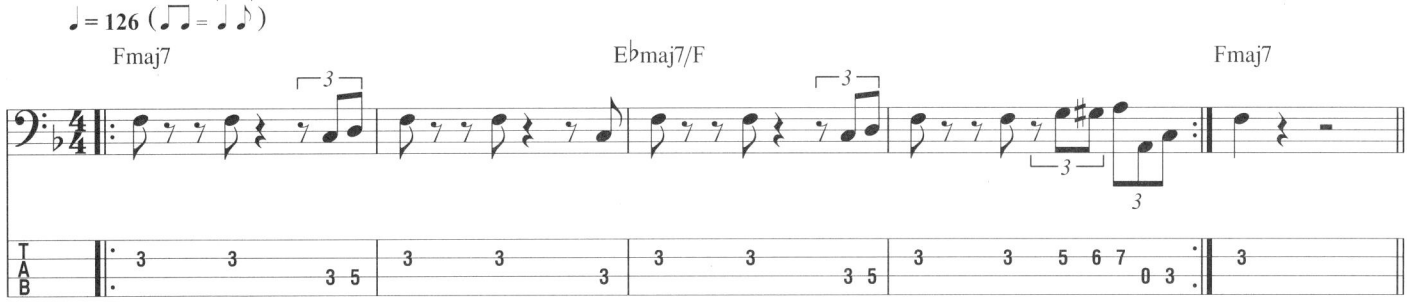

178. Chicago Shuffle 2

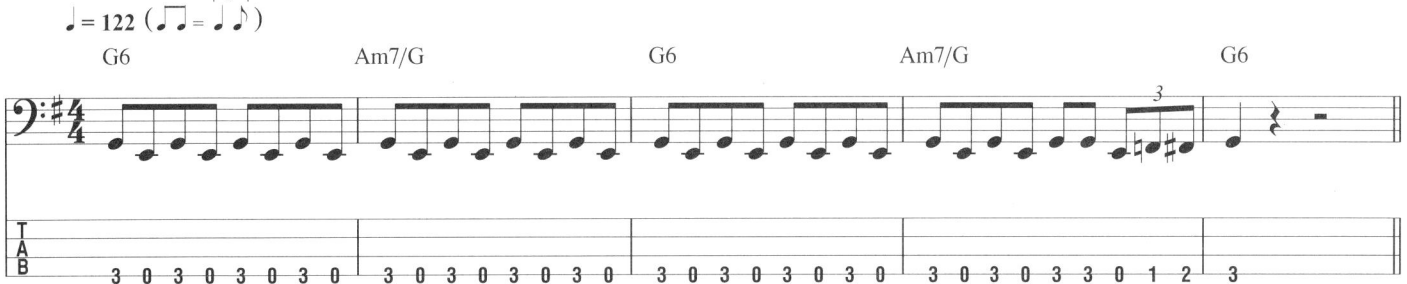

179. Swagger

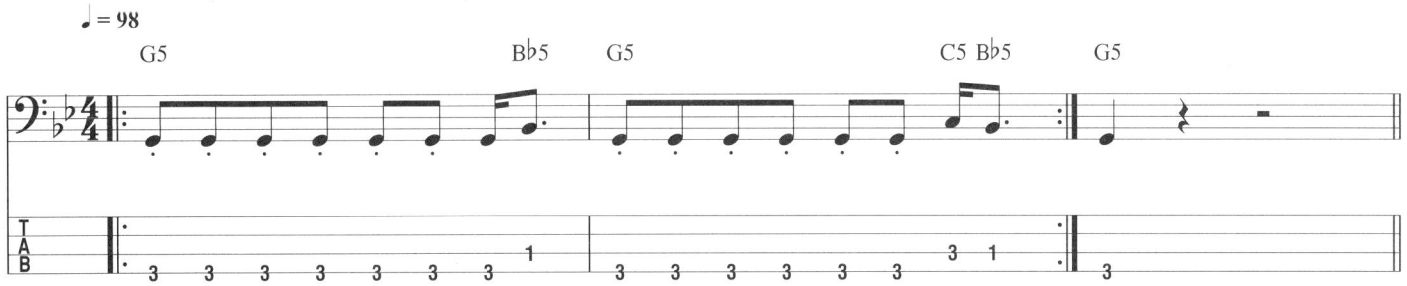

180. Melodic Rock

181. Roots Rock 1

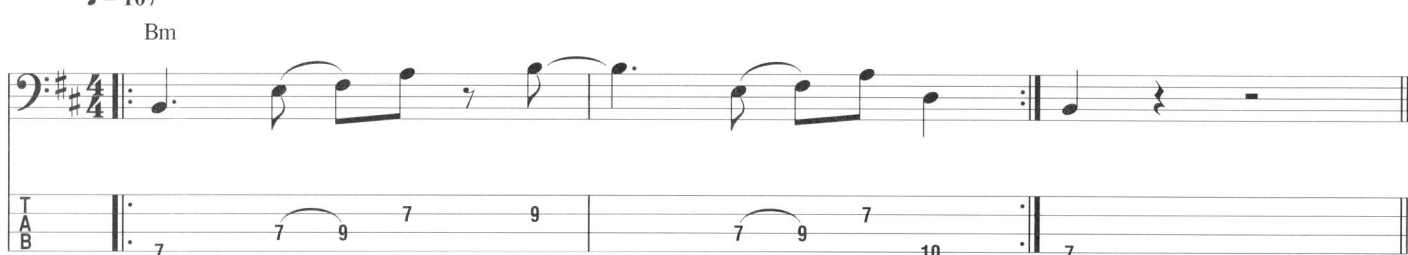

182. Roots Rock 2

183. Roots Rock 3

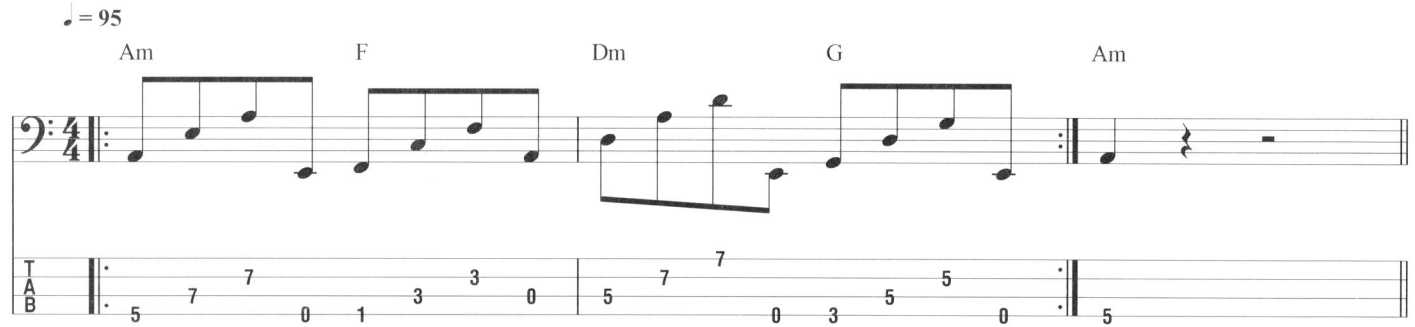

184. Roots Rock 4

185. Roots Rock 5

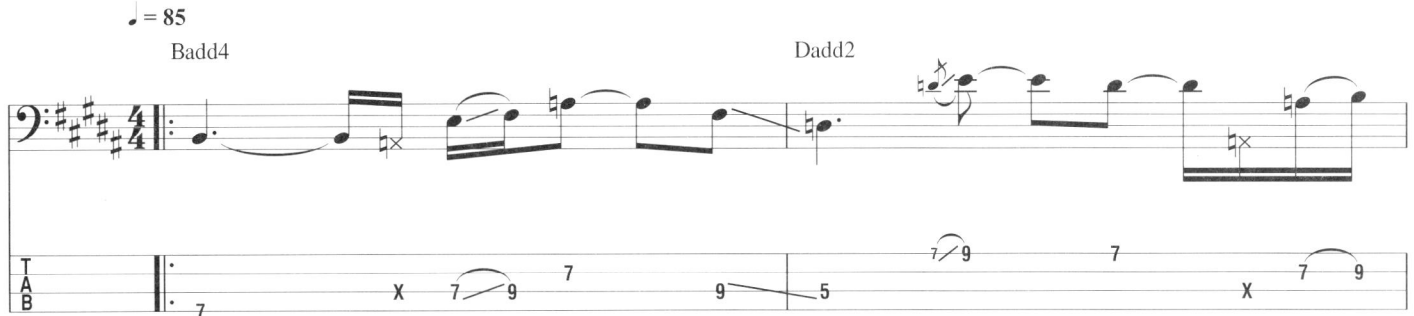

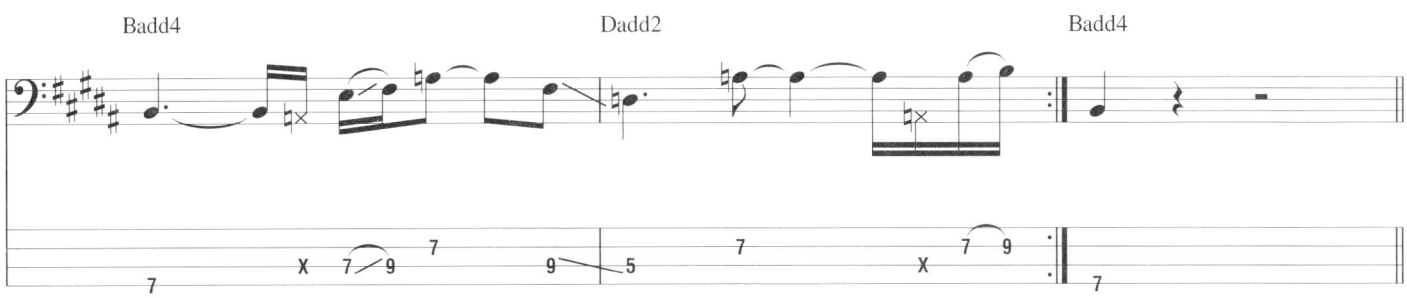

186. Roots Rock 6

187. Slinky Chromatics

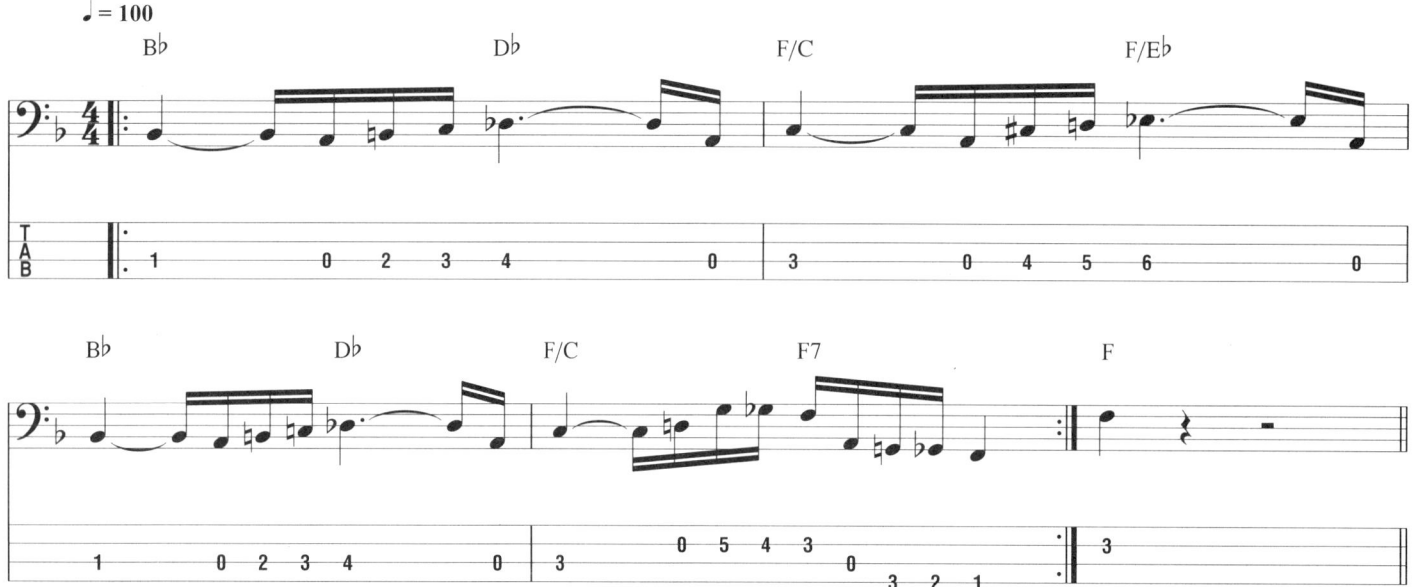

188. Holding It Down Hipster Style

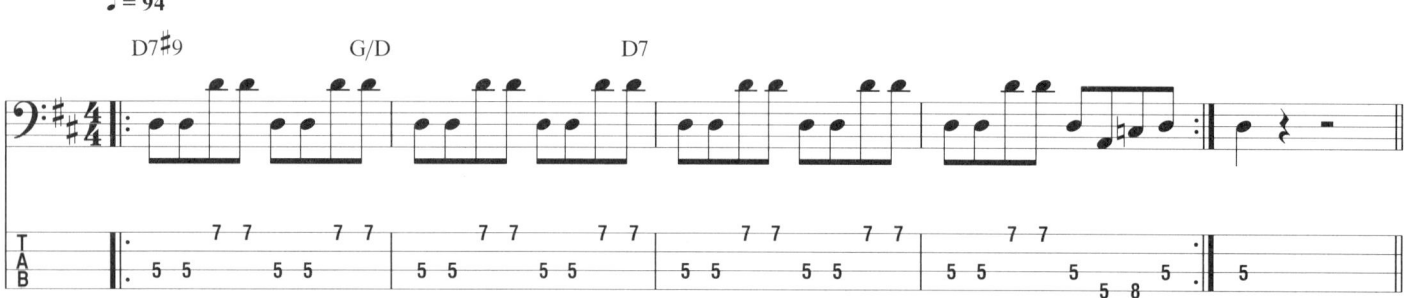

189. Spaces

190. Note Substitutions

191. Sequencer Bass 1

192. Arpeggio Pop

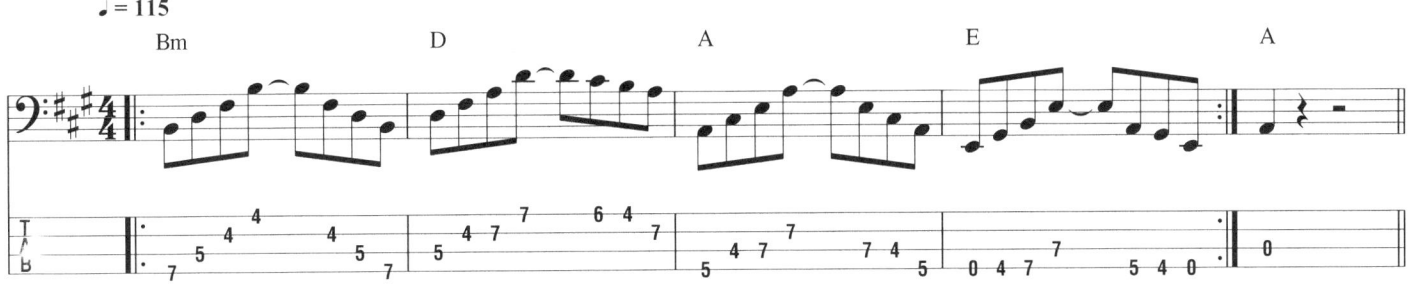

193. Trippy Alt-Rock 1

194. Trippy Alt-Rock 2

195. Fast Alt-Rock 1

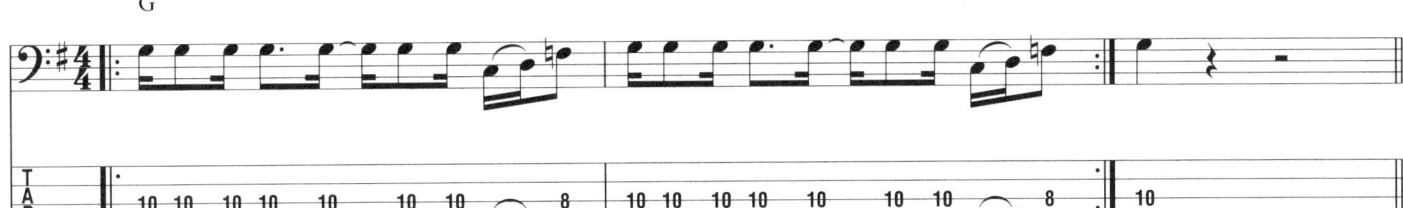

196. Fast Alt-Rock 2

197. Vaguely Industrial 1

198. Vaguely Industrial 2

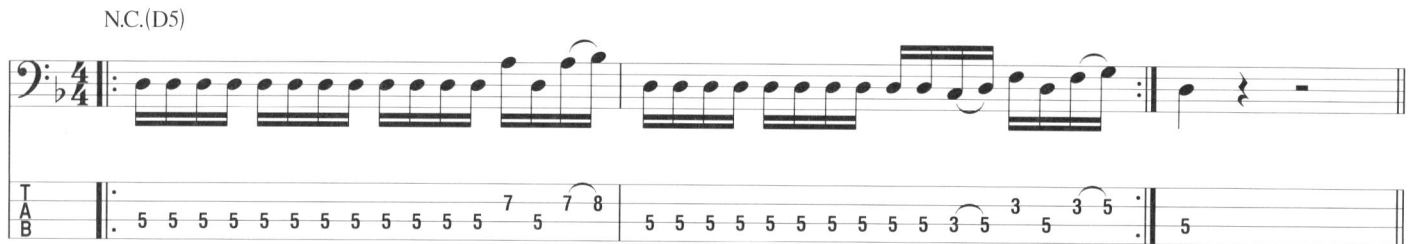

199. Vaguely Industrial 3

200. Vaguely Industrial 4

201. Vaguely Industrial 5

202. Vaguely Industrial 6

203. Vaguely Industrial 7

204. Vaguely Industrial 8

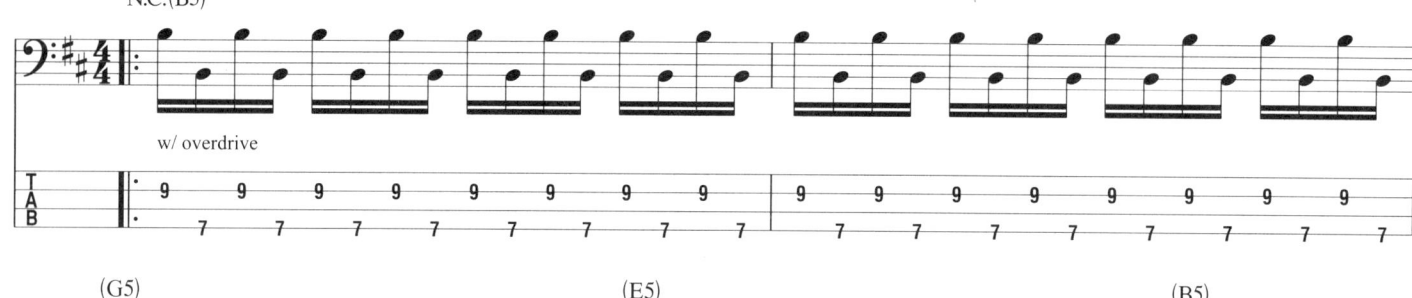

205. Vaguely Industrial 9

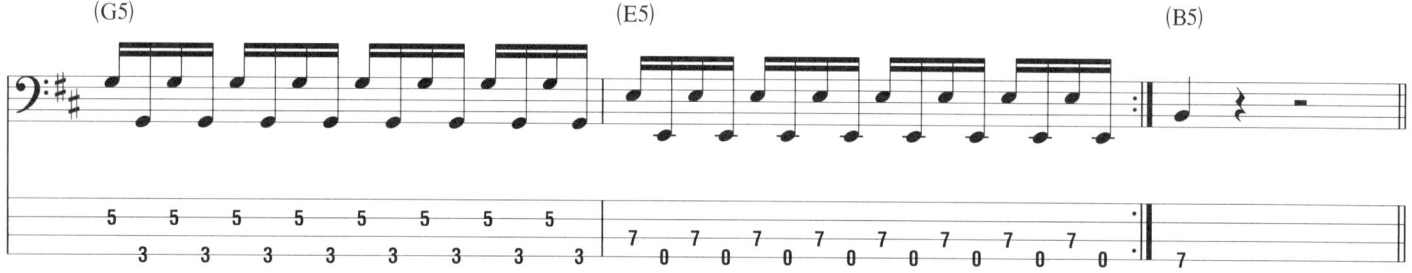

206. Vaguely Industrial 10

207. New Wave 1

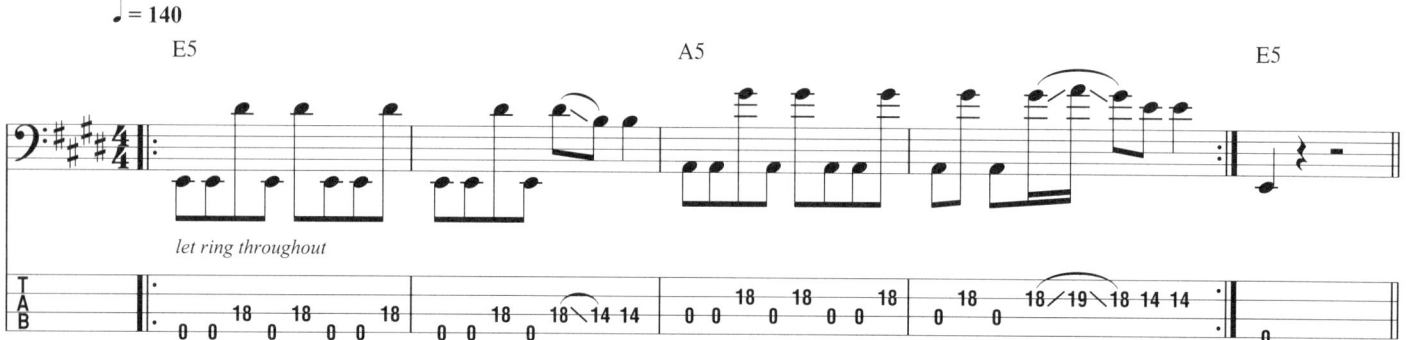

208. New Wave 2

209. New Wave 3

210. New Wave 4

211. New Wave 5

212. New Wave 6

213. New Wave 7

214. New Wave 8

215. New Wave 9

216. New Wave 10

217. New Wave 11

218. New Wave 12

219. New Wave 13

220. New Wave 14

221. New Wave 15

222. New Wave 16

223. New Wave 17

224. New Wave 18

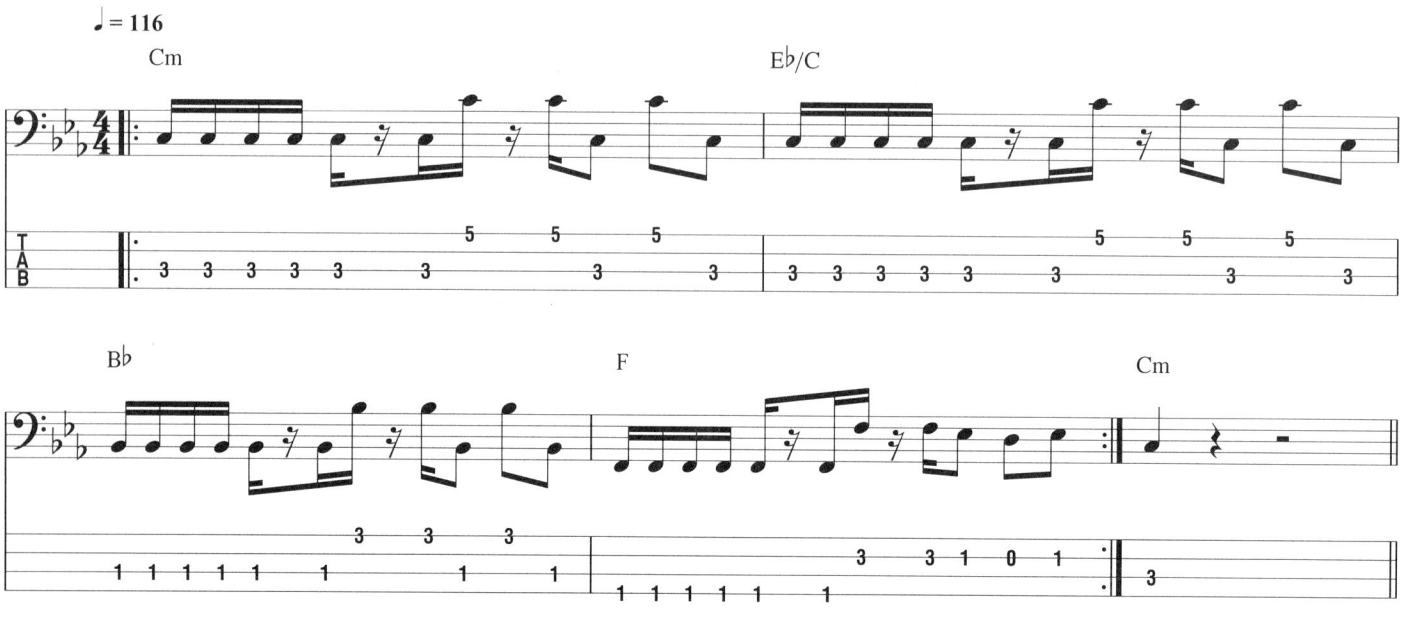

225. New Wave 19

226. New Wave 20

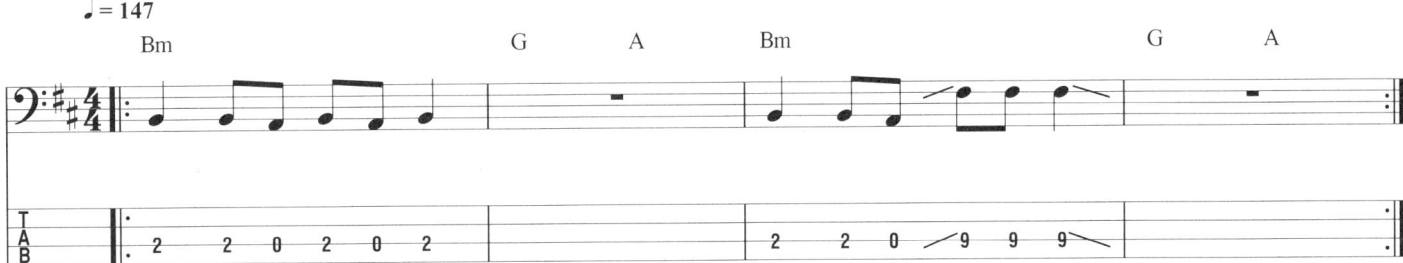

227. New Wave 21

228. New Wave 22

229. Hooked 1

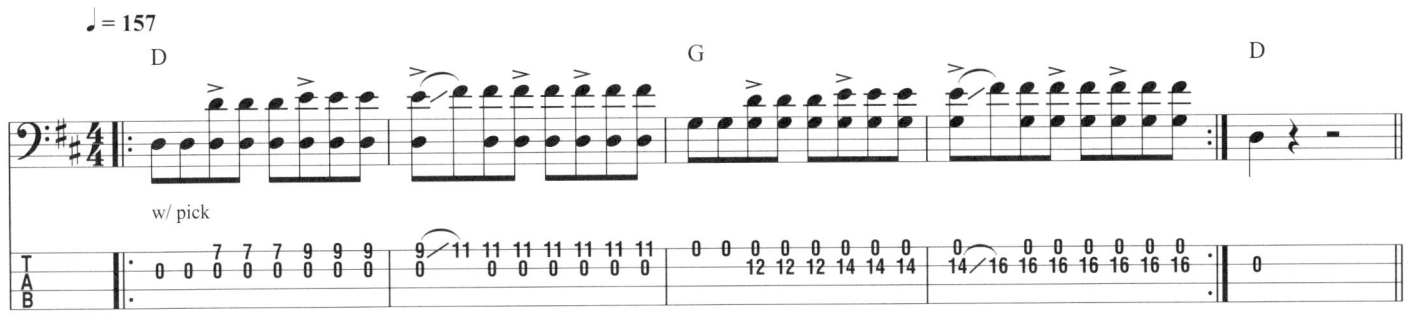

230. Hooked 2
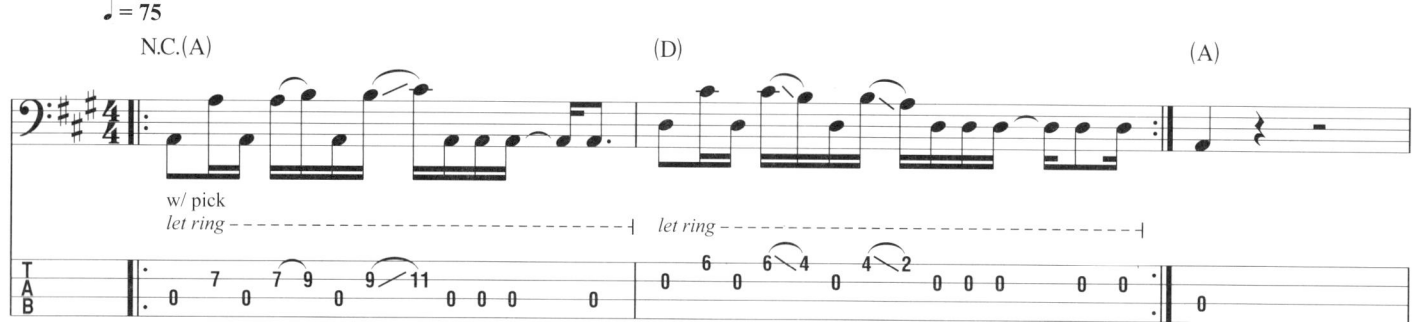

231. Hooked 3
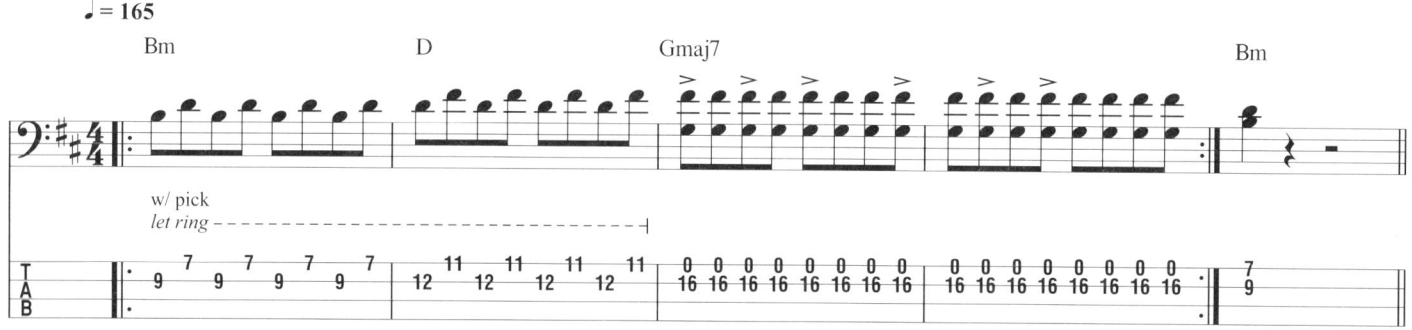

232. Hooked 4
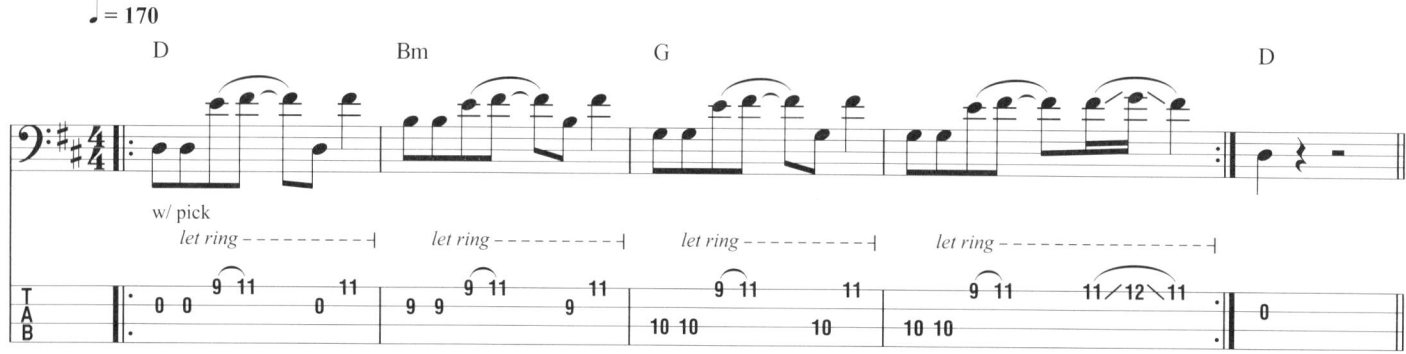

233. 3rd in the Bass
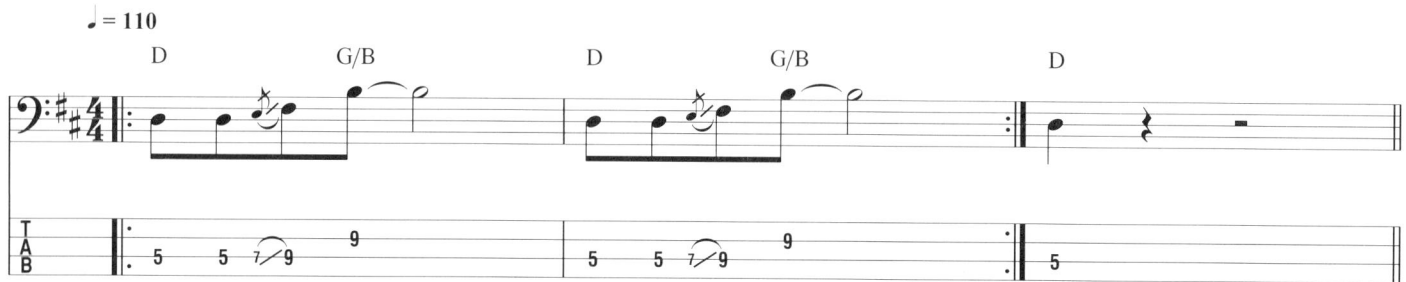

234. Freedom Rock

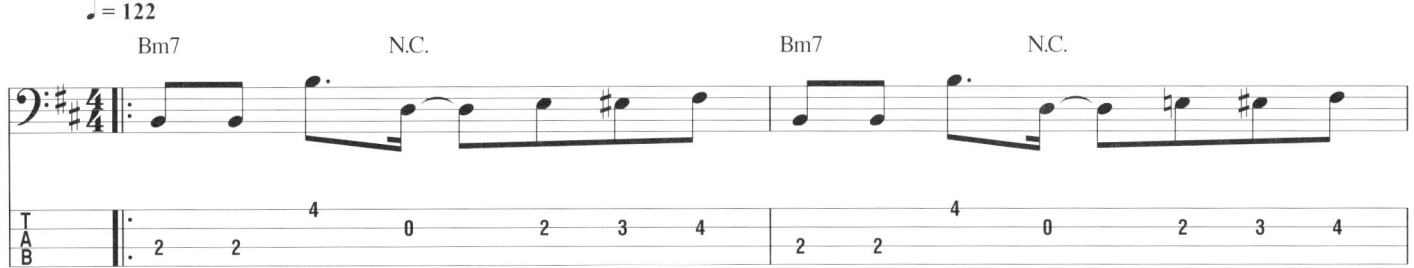

235. Nu 1

236. Nu 2

237. Nu 3

238. Chromatic Sludge 1

239. Chromatic Sludge 2

240. Soft Alt-Rock

241. Soft Rock 1

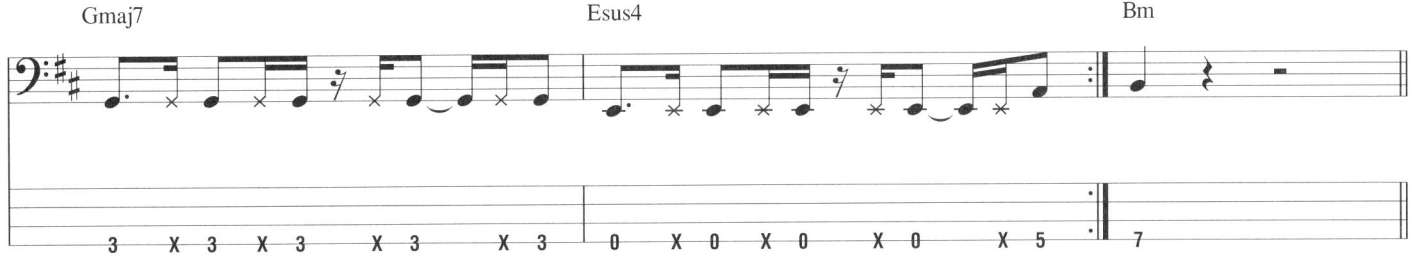

242. Soft Rock 2

243. Soft Rock 3

244. Soft Rock 4

245. Funky Pop-Rock 1
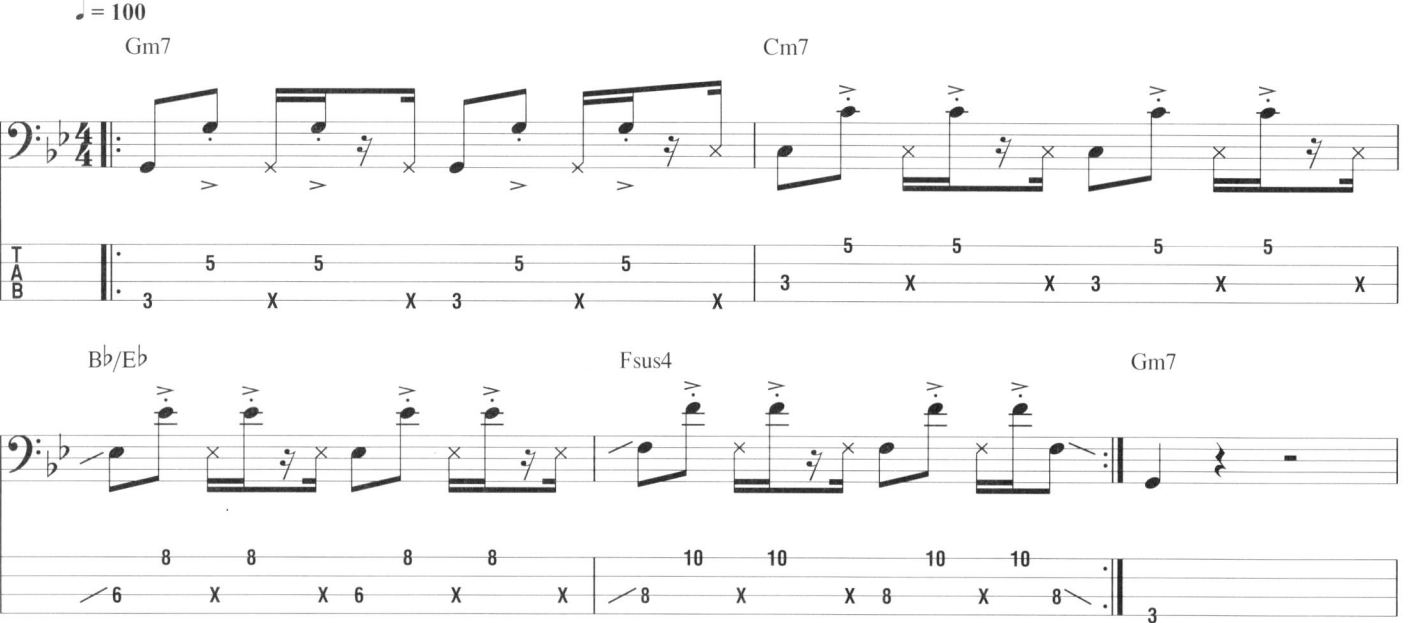

246. Funky Pop-Rock 2

247. Funky Pop-Rock 3
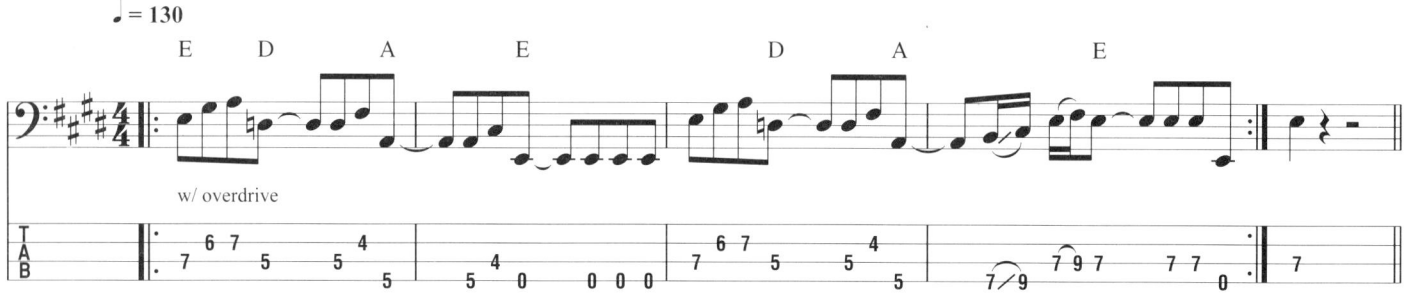

BLUES AND JAZZ

248. Dirty Walk

249. Basic Walk

250. Walk of Funk

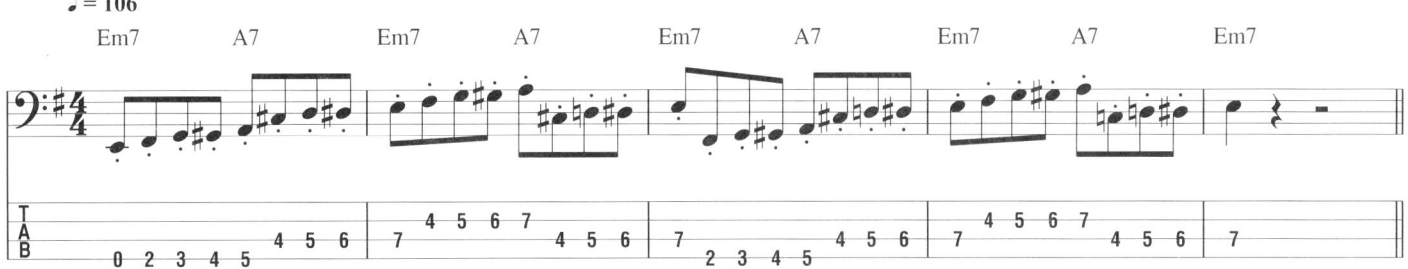

251. Rock 'n' Roll Walk 1

252. Rock 'n' Roll Walk 2

253. Rock 'n' Roll Walk 3

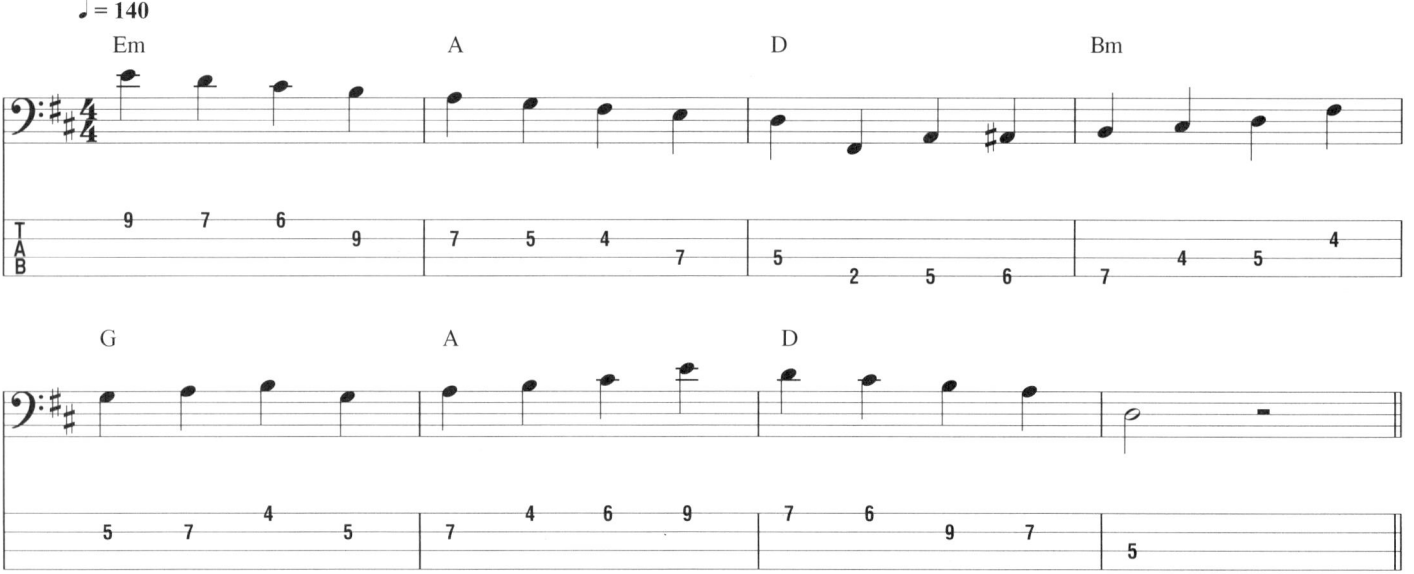

254. Walking Rave-Up

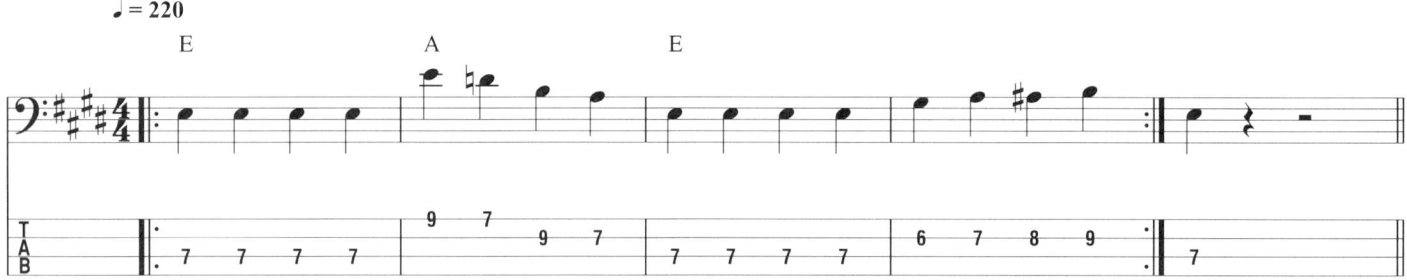

255. Walking Rave-Up

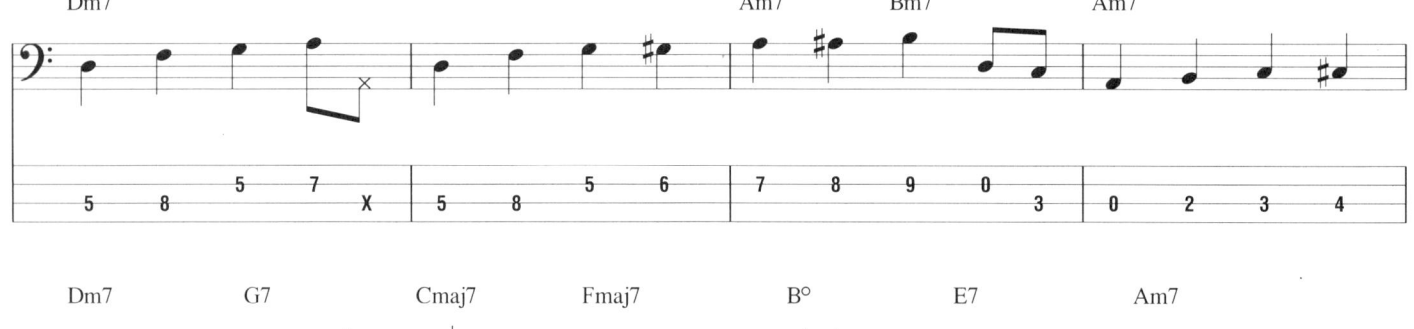
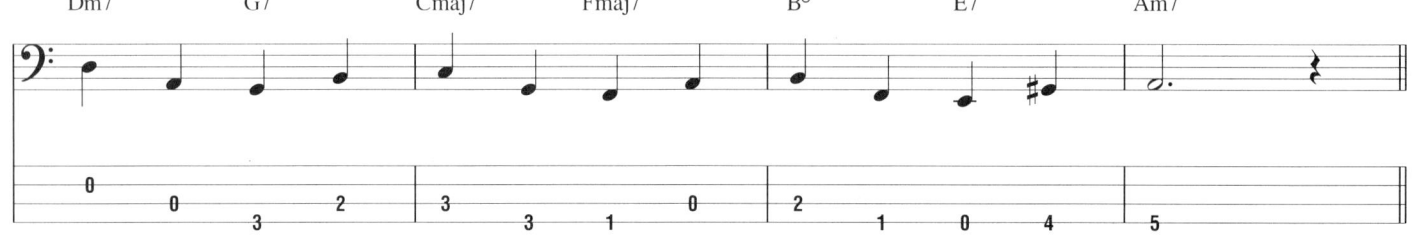

256. 12-Bar Jazz

257. 12-Bar Funk 1

258. 12-Bar Funk 1

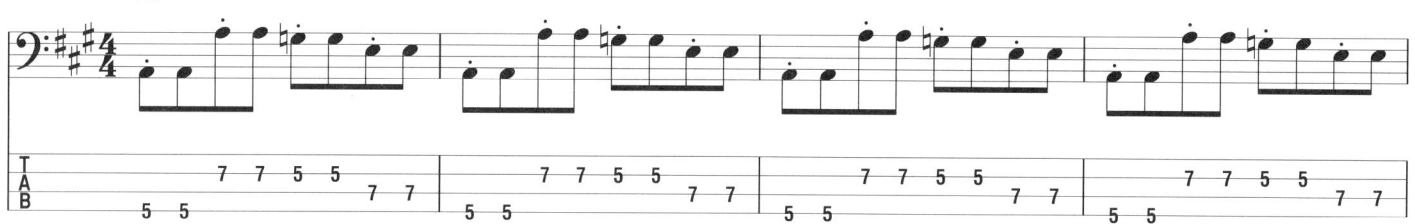
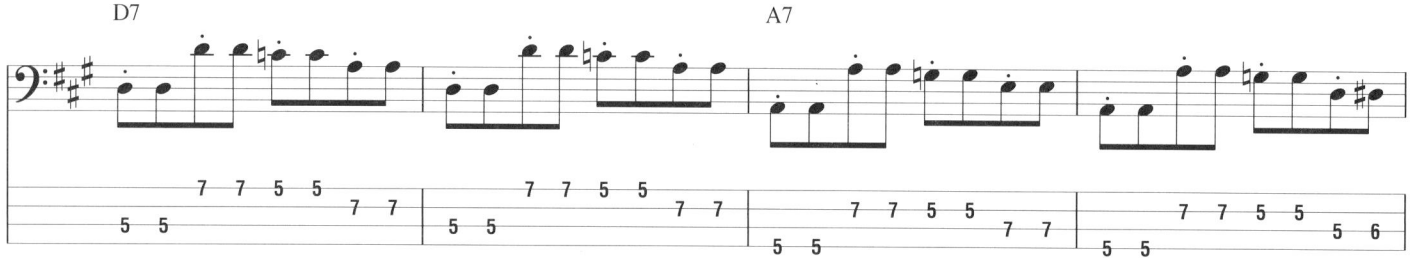
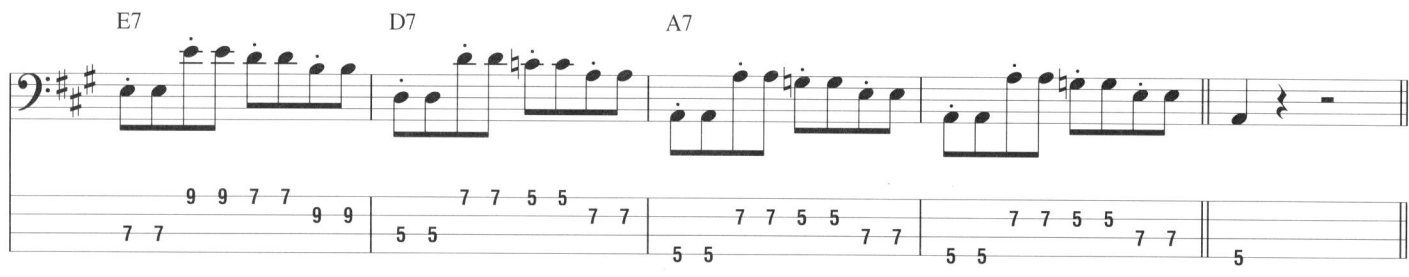

259. 12-Bar Straight Shuffle

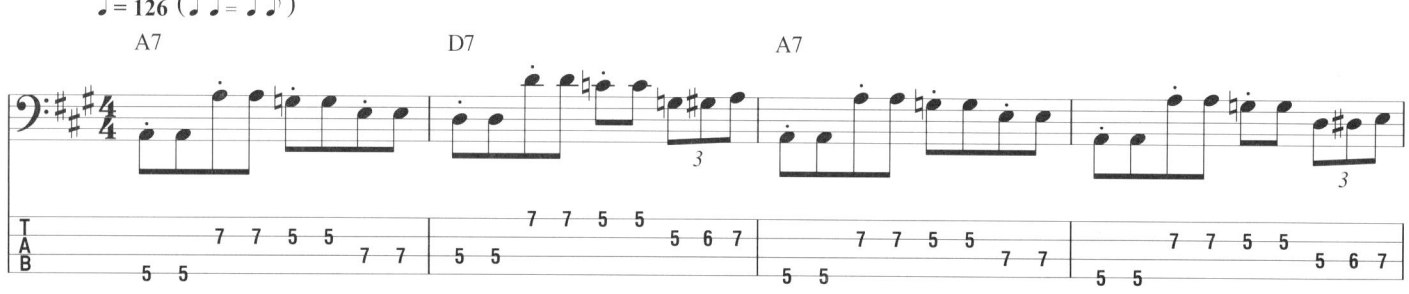
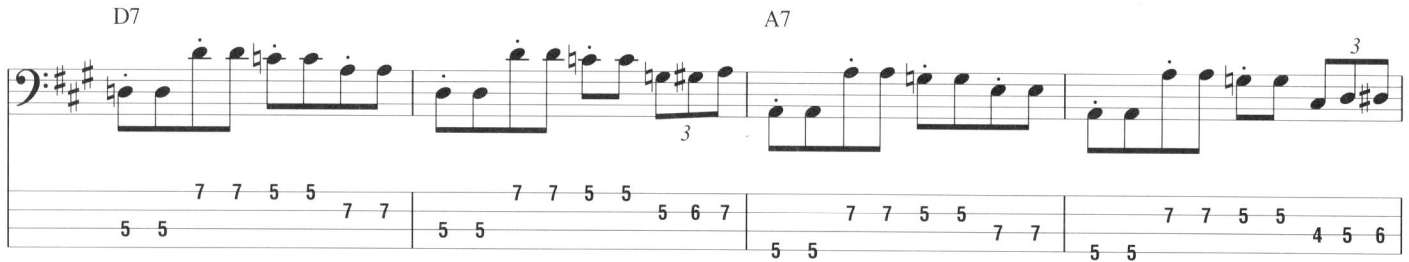
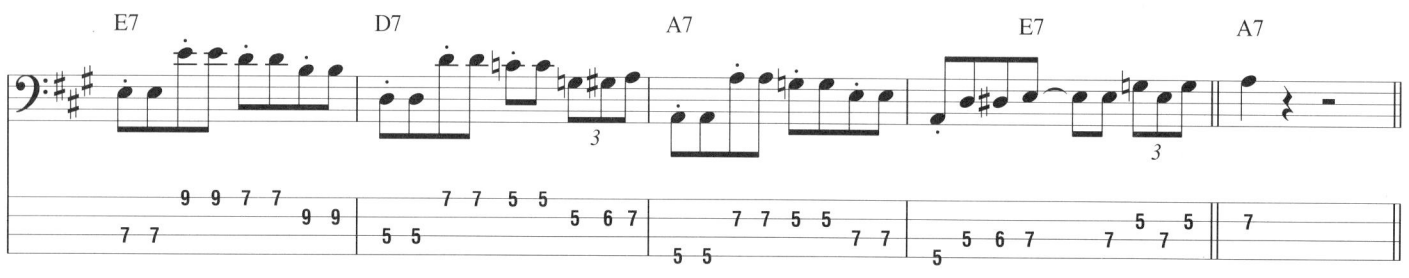

260. 12-Bar Rockabilly Shuffle

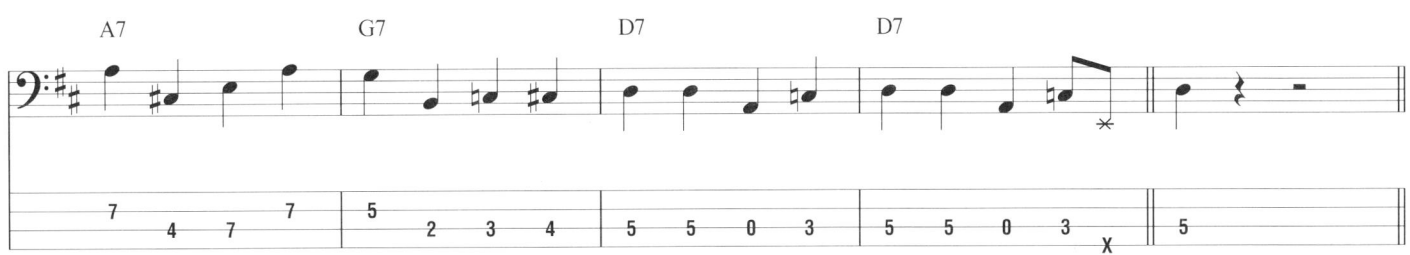

261. 12-Bar Blues Rhumba

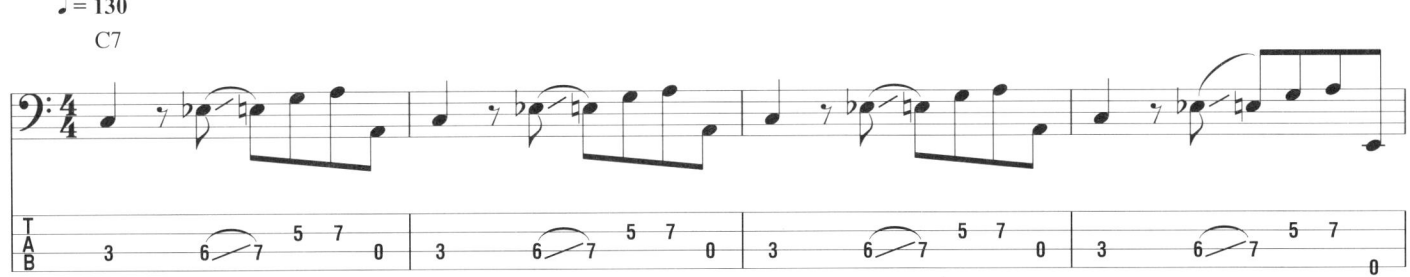

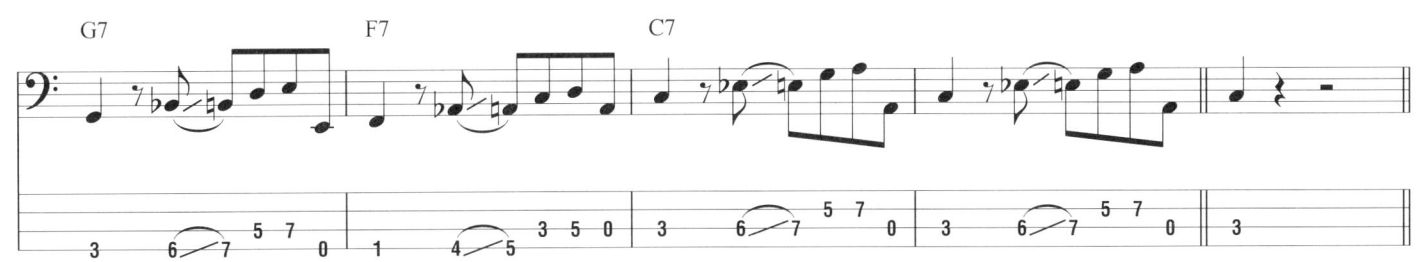

262. 12-Bar Walking Shuffle

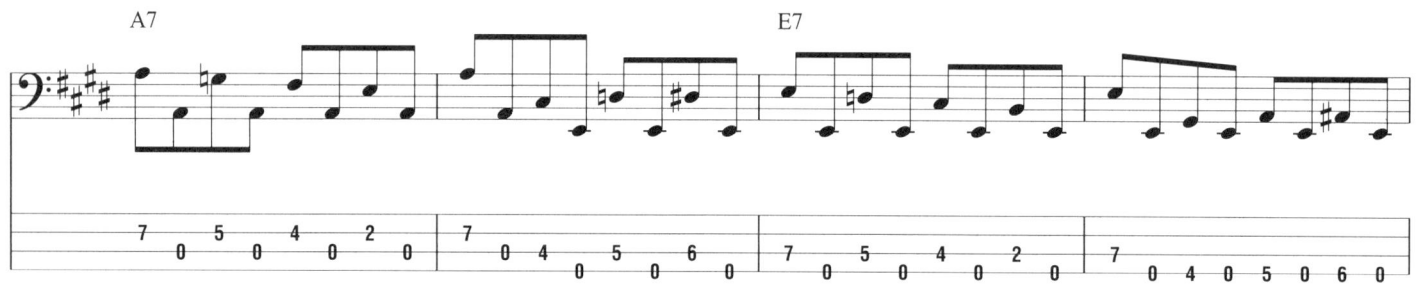

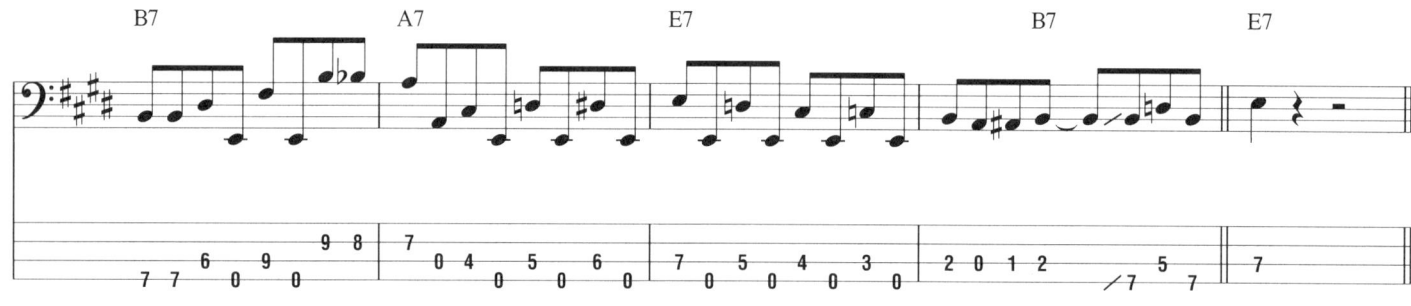

263. One-Chord Rock Blues Vamp

264. Fast Jazz Walk 1

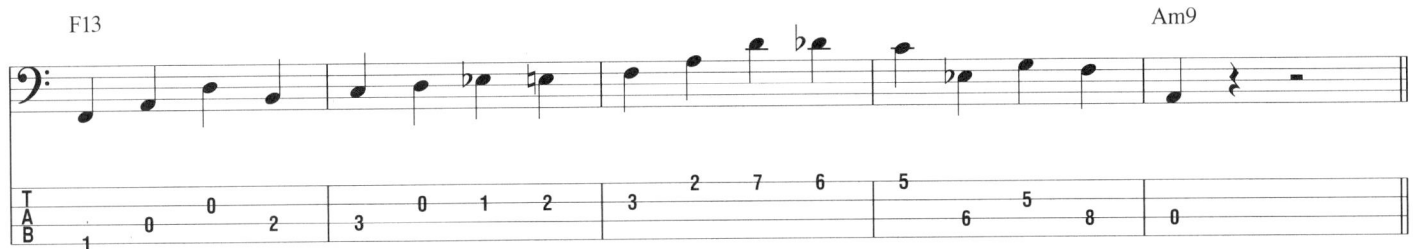

265. Fast Jazz Walk 2

266. Fast Gospel Walk

COUNTRY

267. Low-Down Bend

268. Rock It Out

269. Pop Country 1

270. Pop Country 2

271. Basic Country

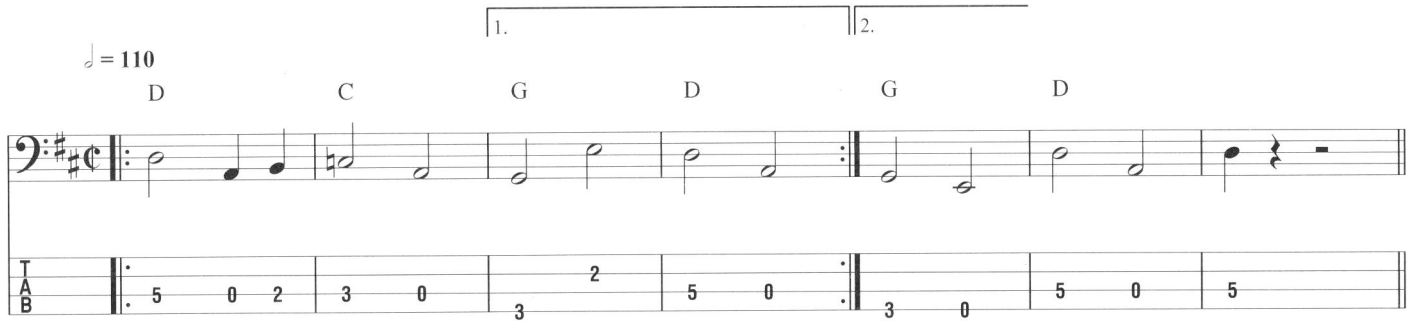

272. Dirty Saloon

273. Fast Train Rhythm

274. Seashore Country

275. Nashville Ballad

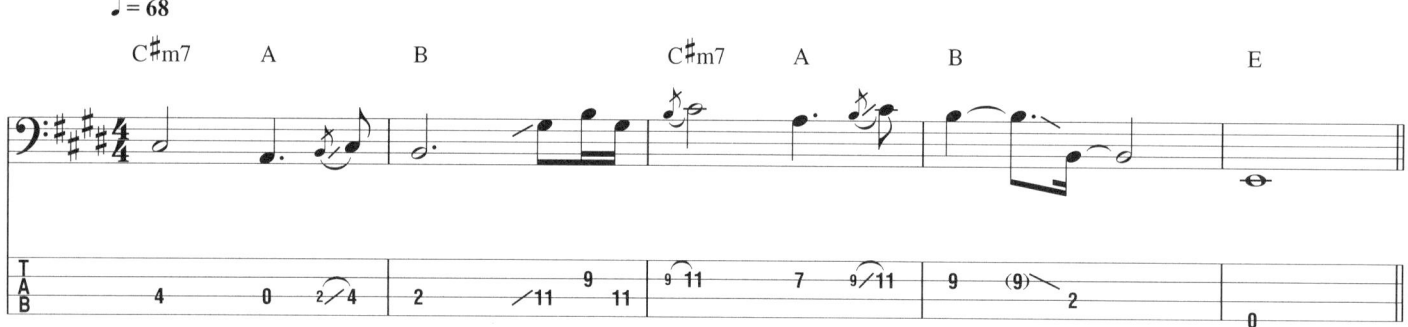

276. Nashville I-IV-V

ELECTRONIC DANCE MUSIC (EDM)

277. Dance Gallop

278. House 1

Drop D tuning:
(low to high) D-A-D-G

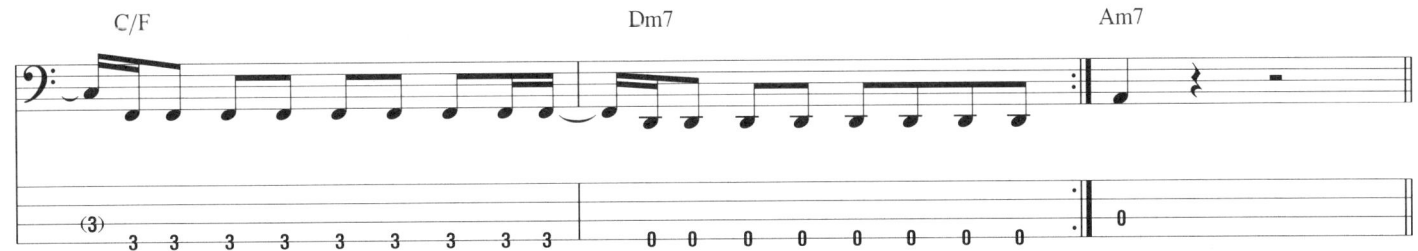

279. House 2

Drop D tuning:
(low to high) D-A-D-G

280. House 3

281. House 4

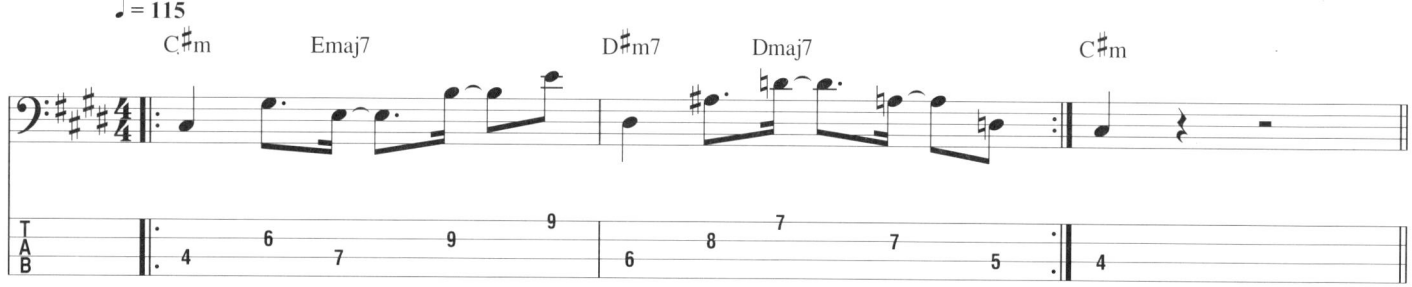

282. House 5

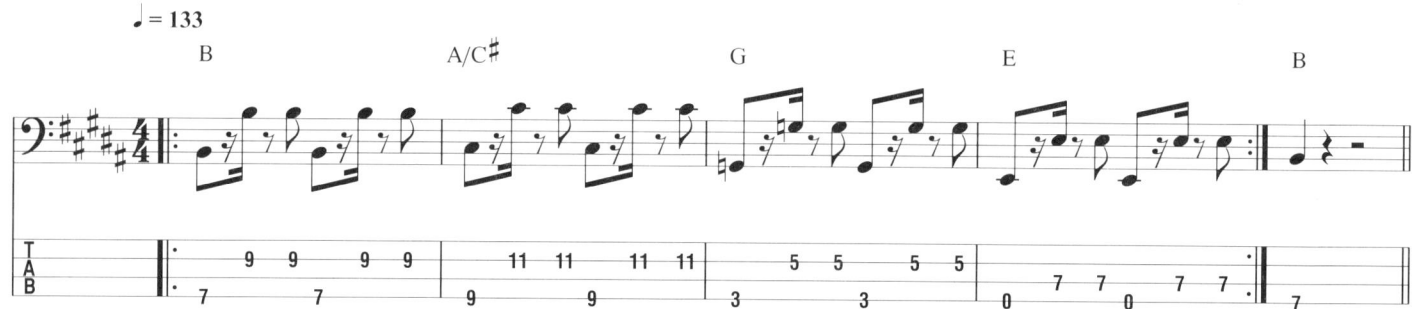

283. House 6

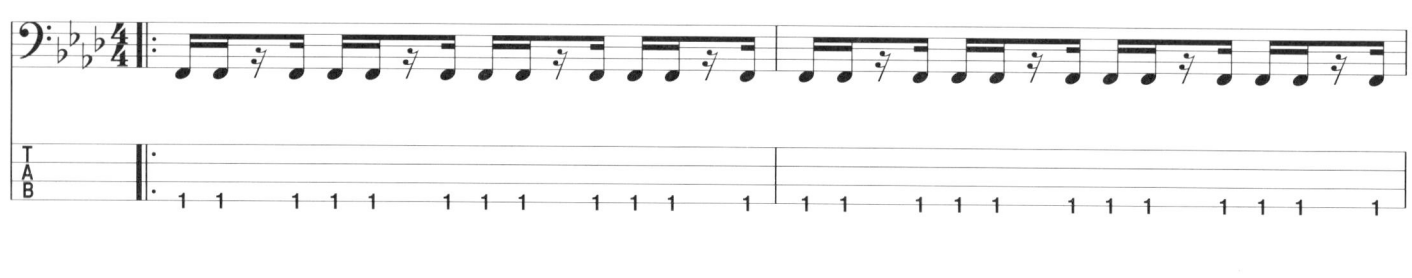

284. House 7

285. House 8

286. Off-beats

287. Basic Club Groove 1

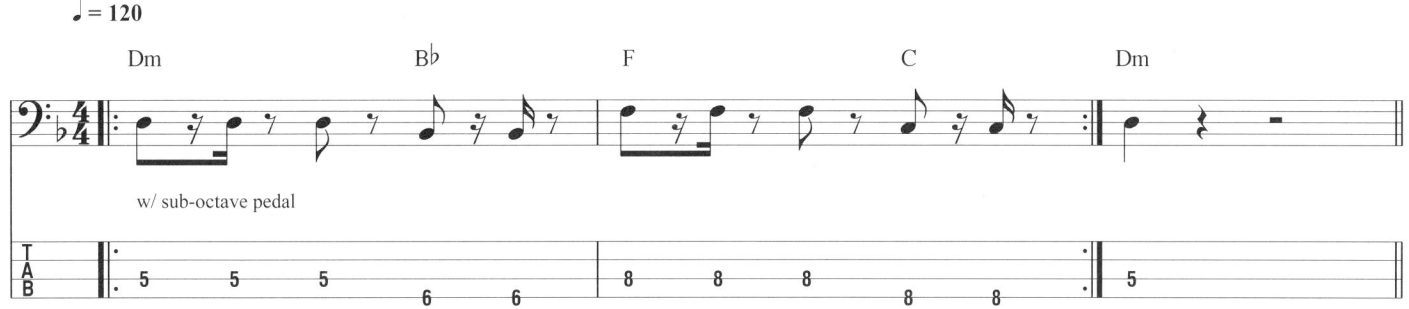

288. Basic Club Groove 2 (with Fills)

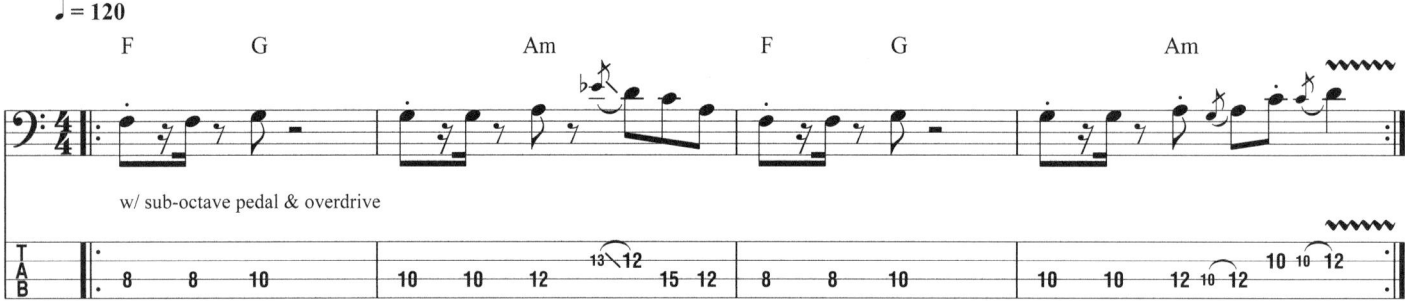

289. Basic EDM Groove

290. Basic EDM Groove with Octave Gallop

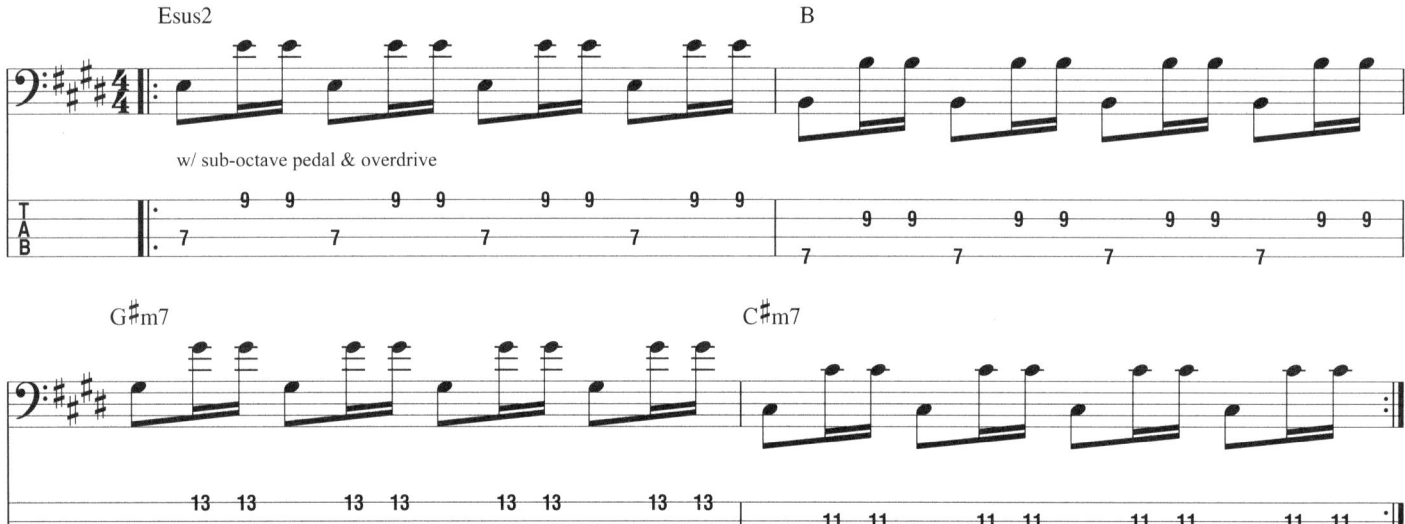

291. Melodic EDM

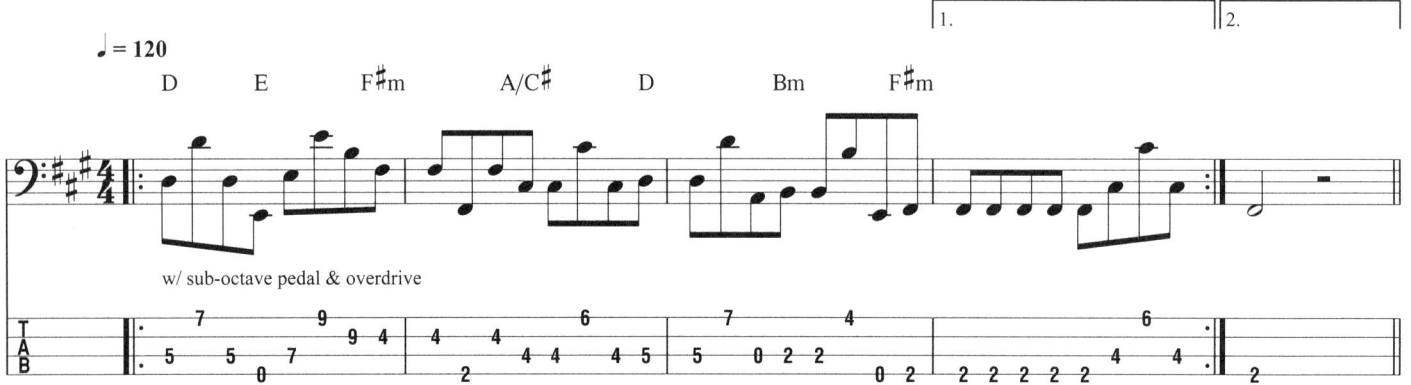

292. Andersong

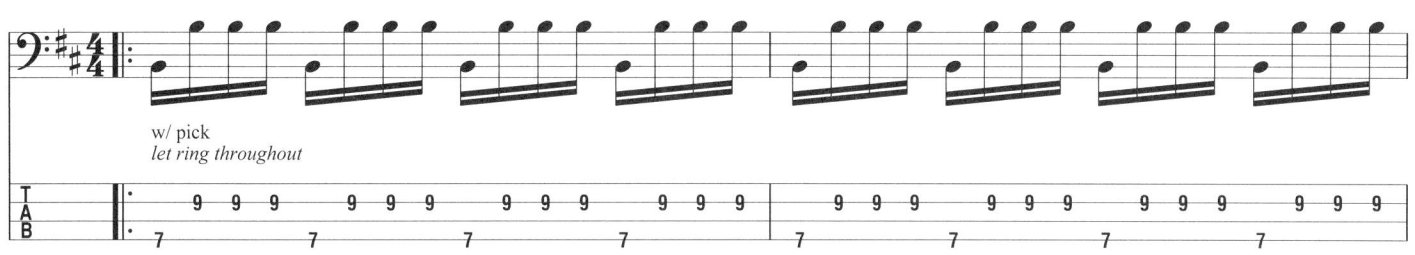

293. Trance 1

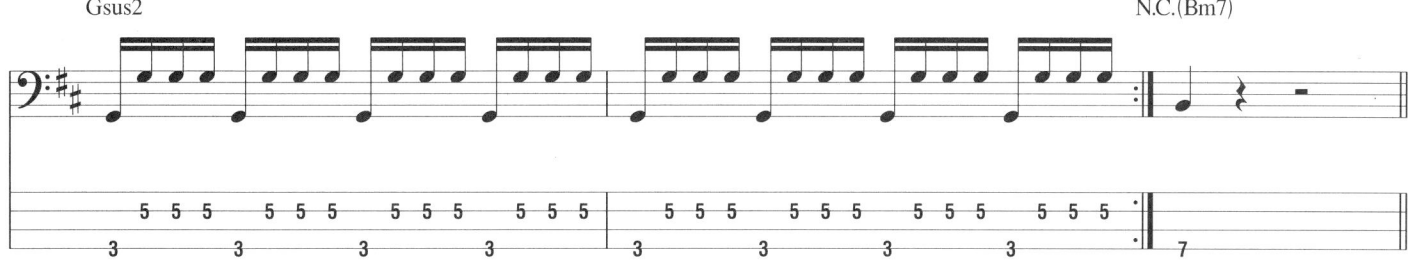

294. Trance 2

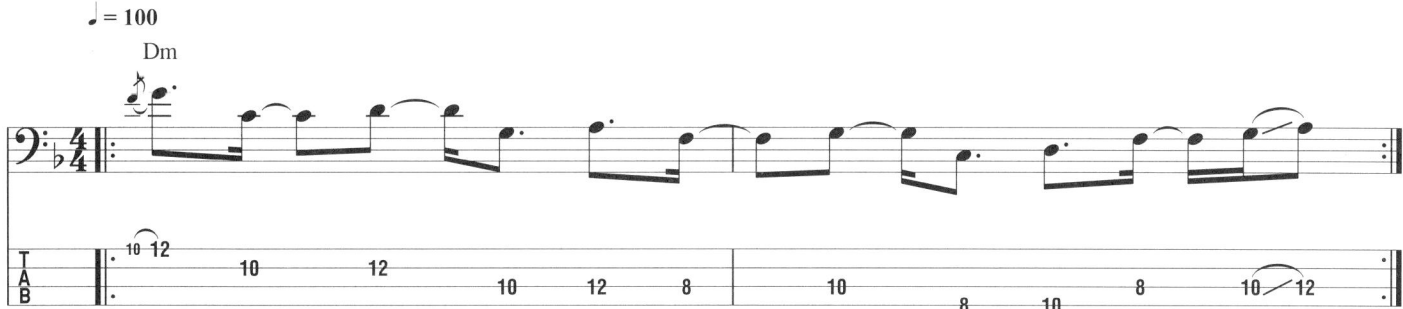

295. Chill 1

296. Chill 2

297. Chill Octaves

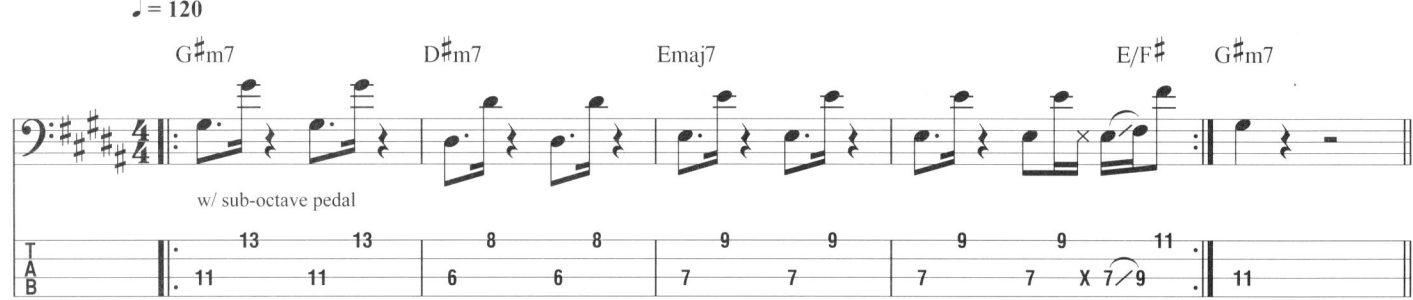

298. Sequencer Bass 2

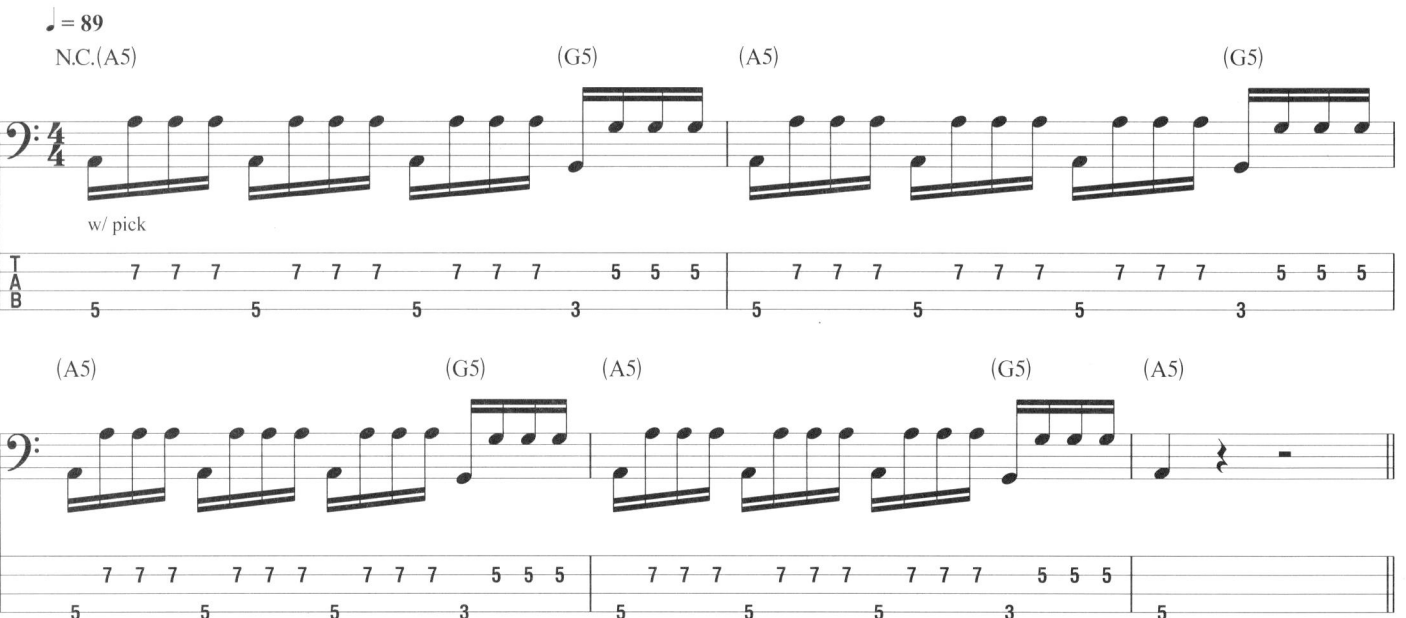

299. Sequencer Bass 3

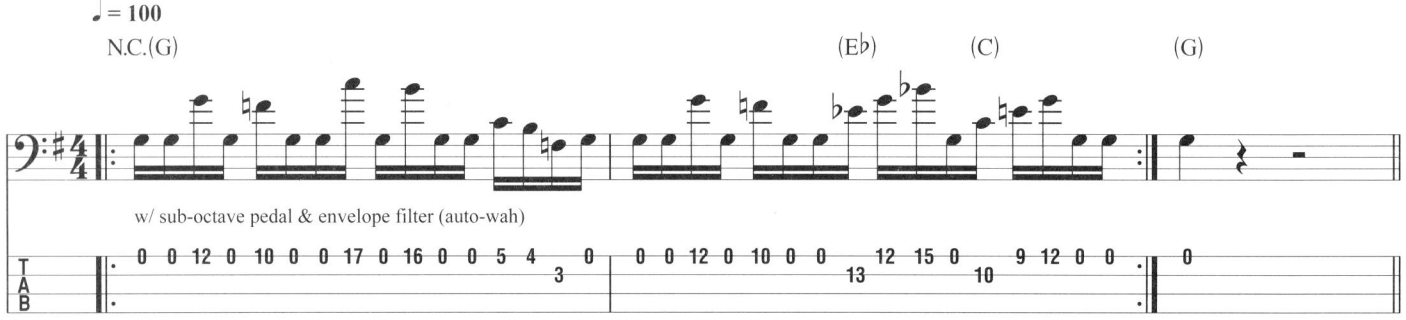

300. Electronica

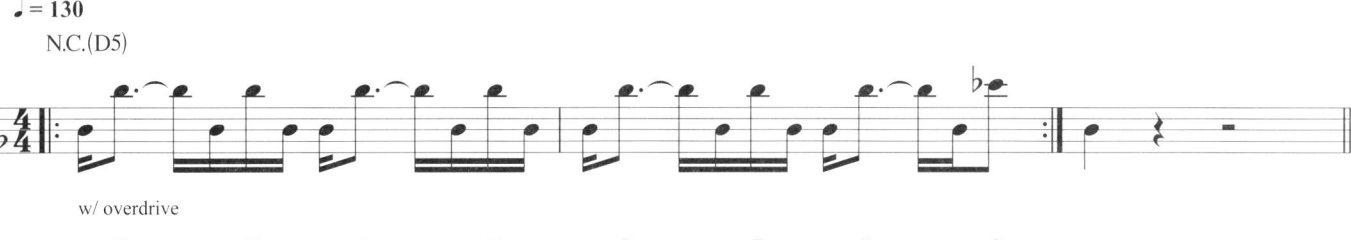

301. Groove From That Music They Play in European-Based Clothing Retail Chains 2

302. Dropping 5ths Walk

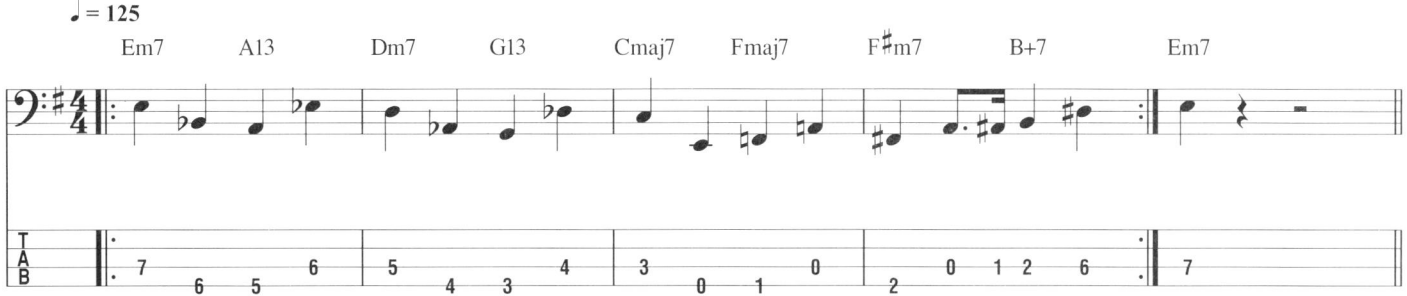

303. Get Your Phrygian On

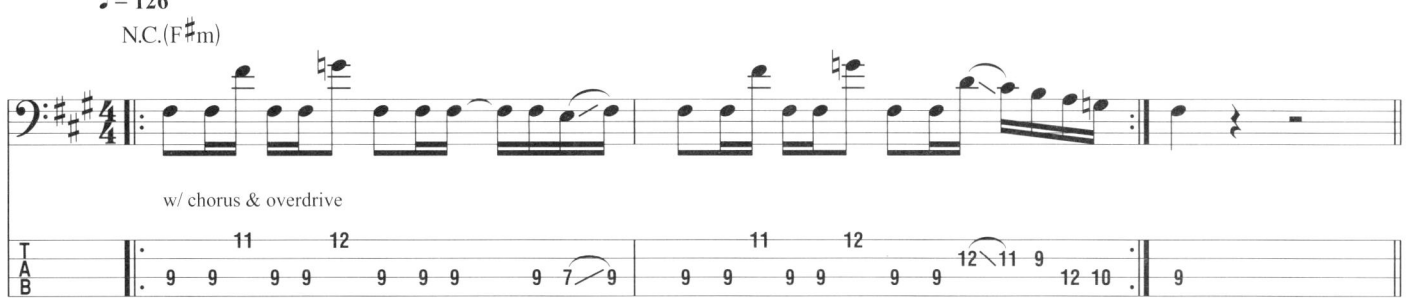

304. Holding it Down

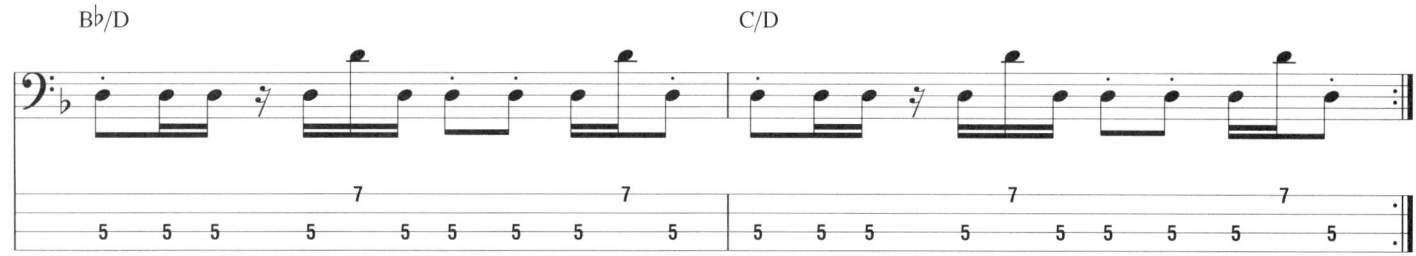

305. 80's Dance

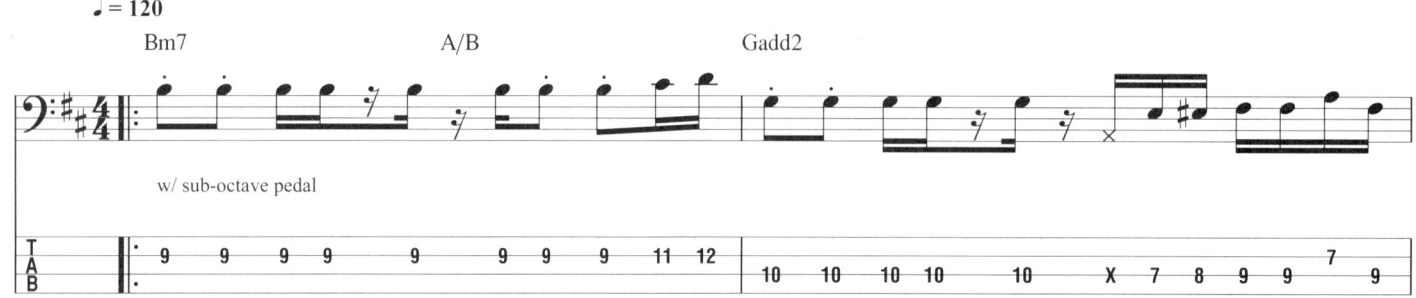

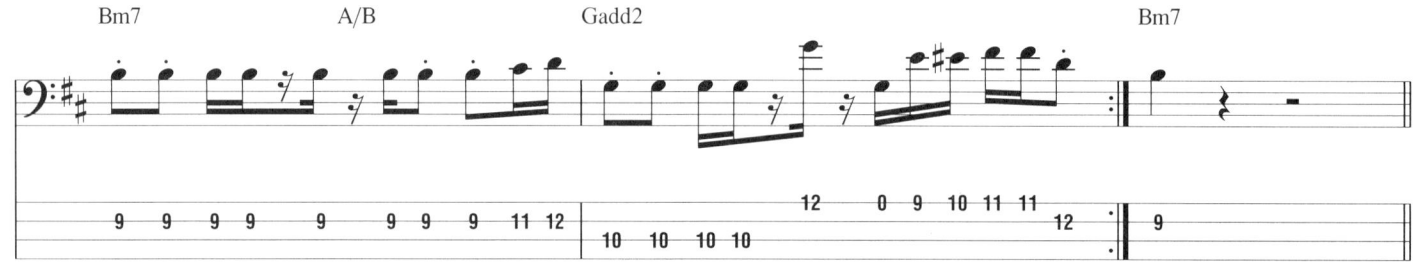

306. Elbows Out

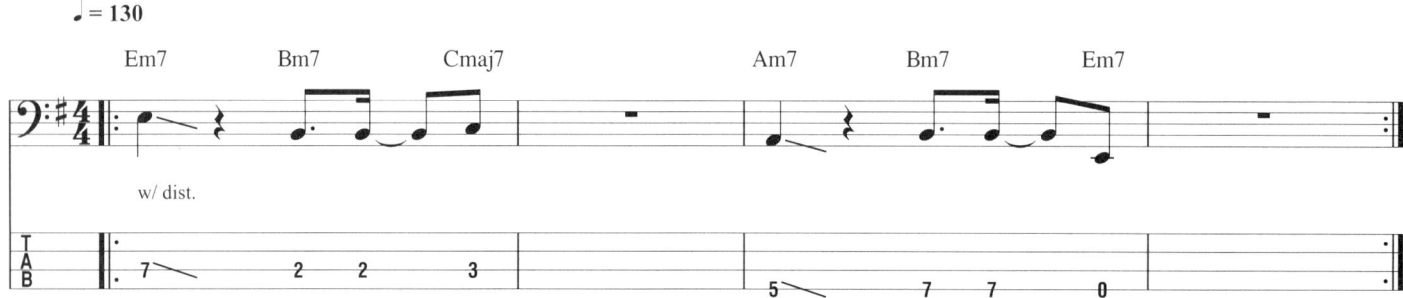

FUNK AND R&B

307. Funk Basics 1

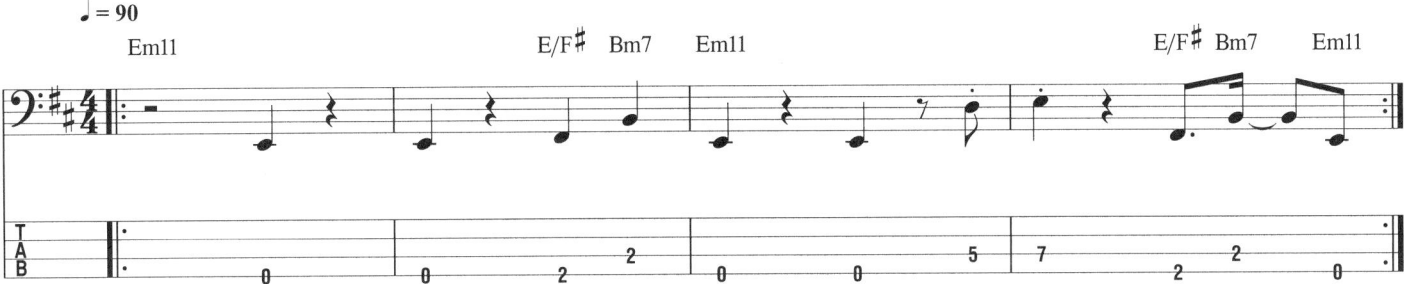

308. Funk Basics 2

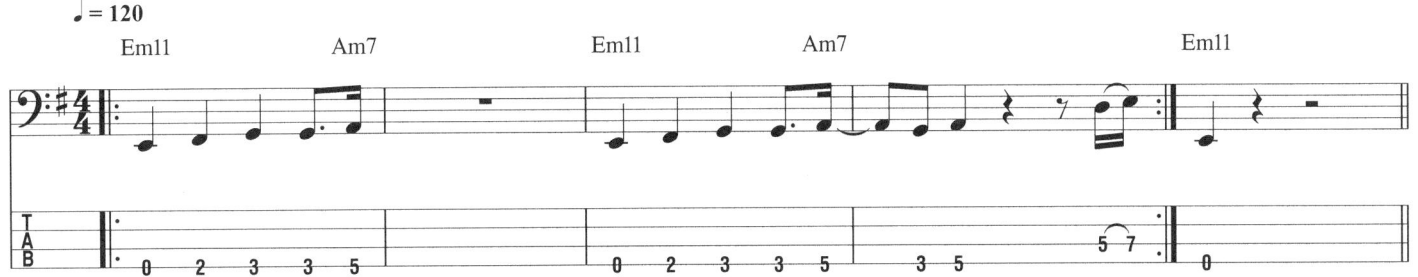

309. Funk Basics 3

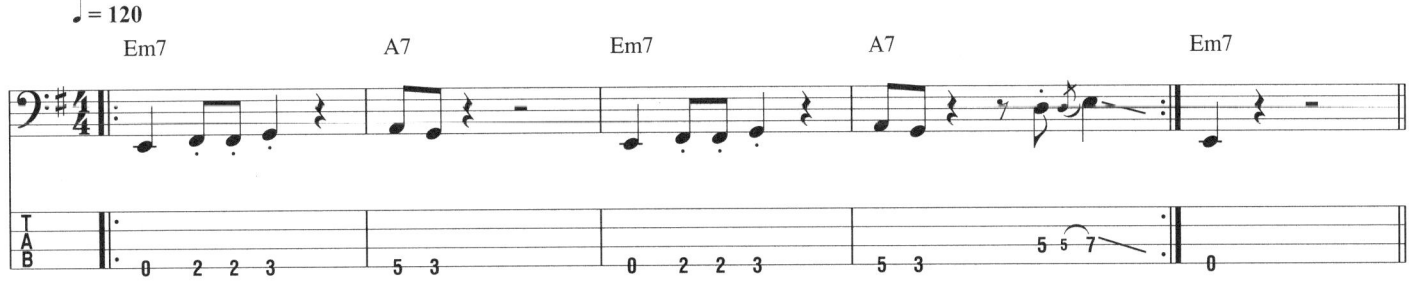

310. Funk Basics 4

311. Nice and Simple 1

312. Nice and Simple 2

313. Nice and Simple 3

314. Funky Octaves

315. Sliding Octaves

316. Lowdown Ninth

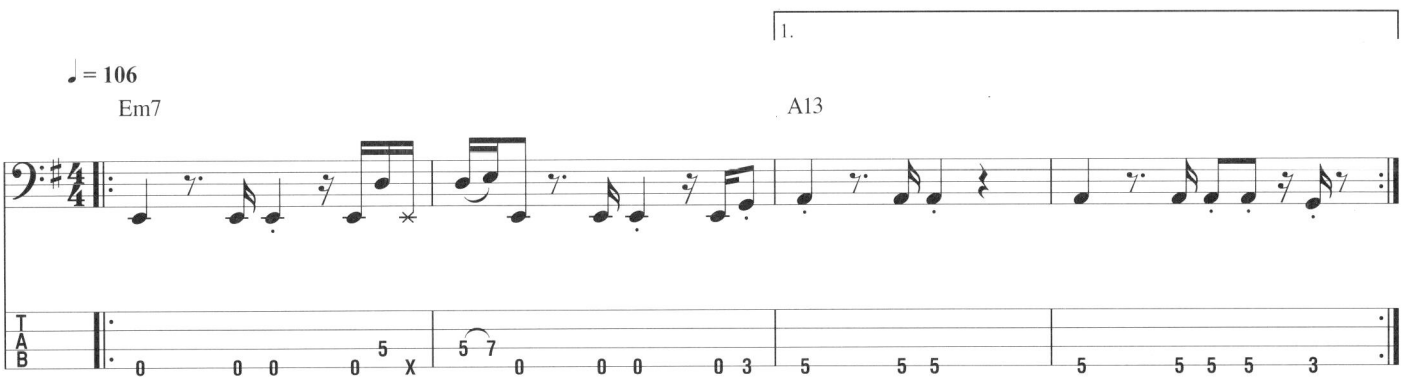
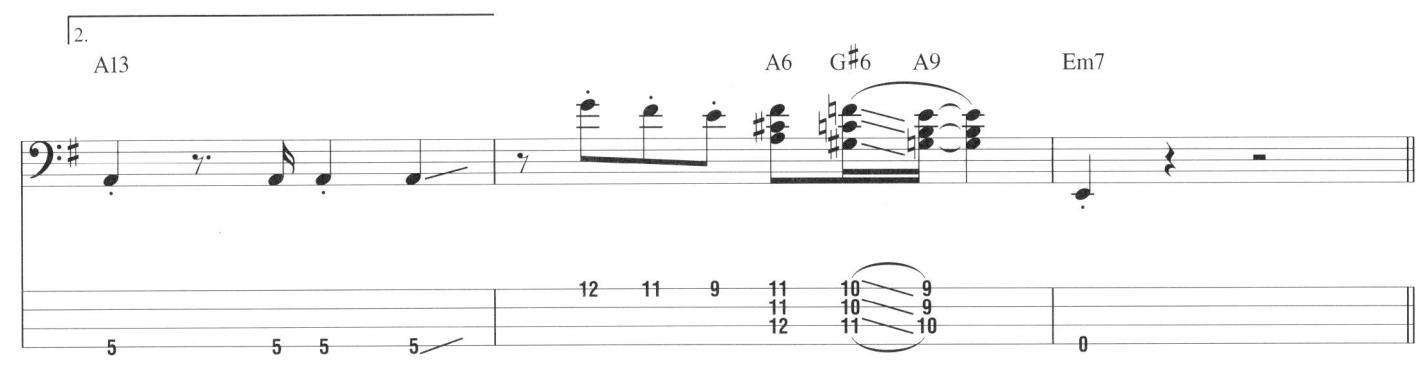

317. Slick 1

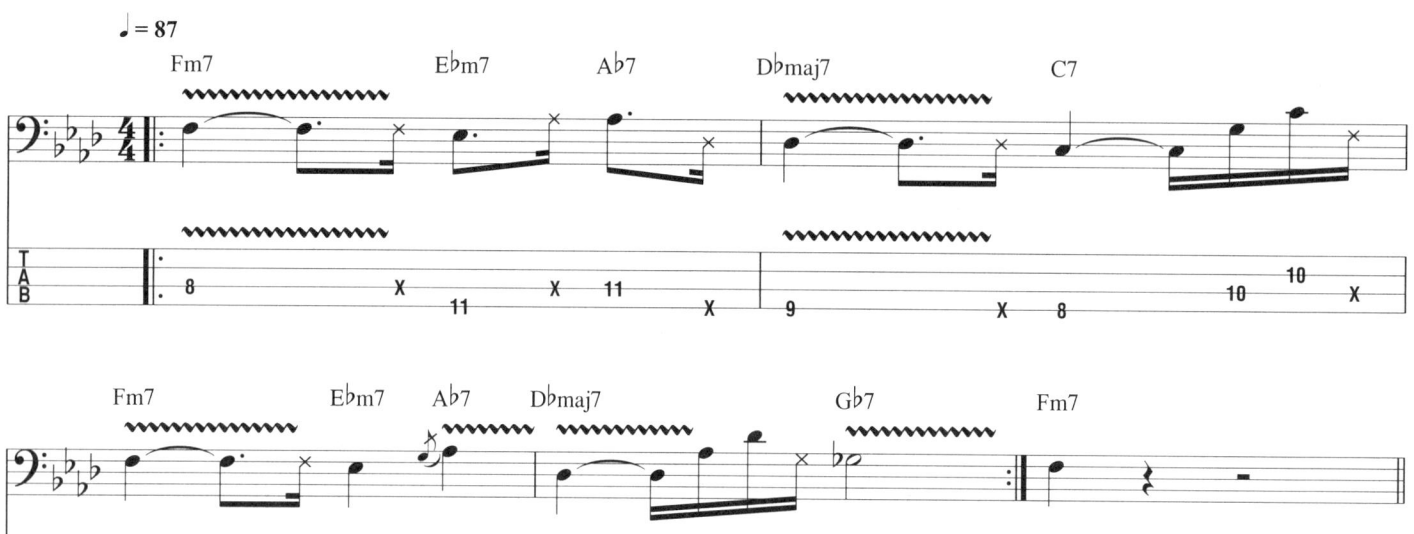

318. Slick 2

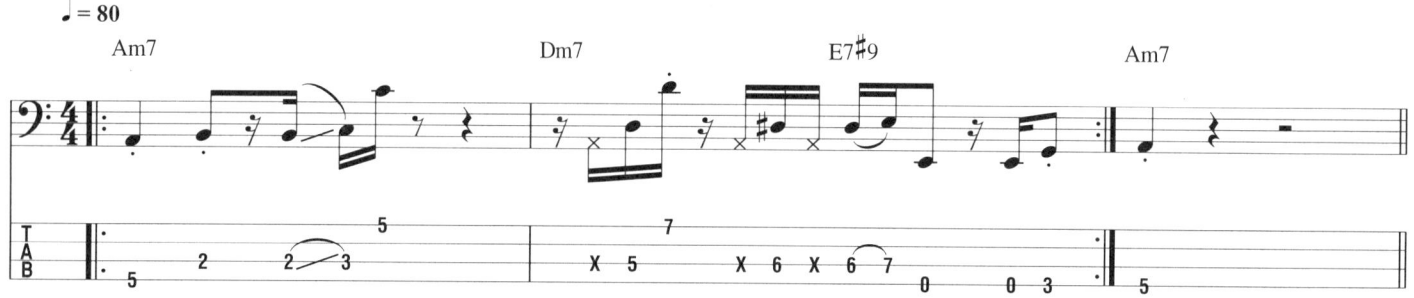

319. Slick 3

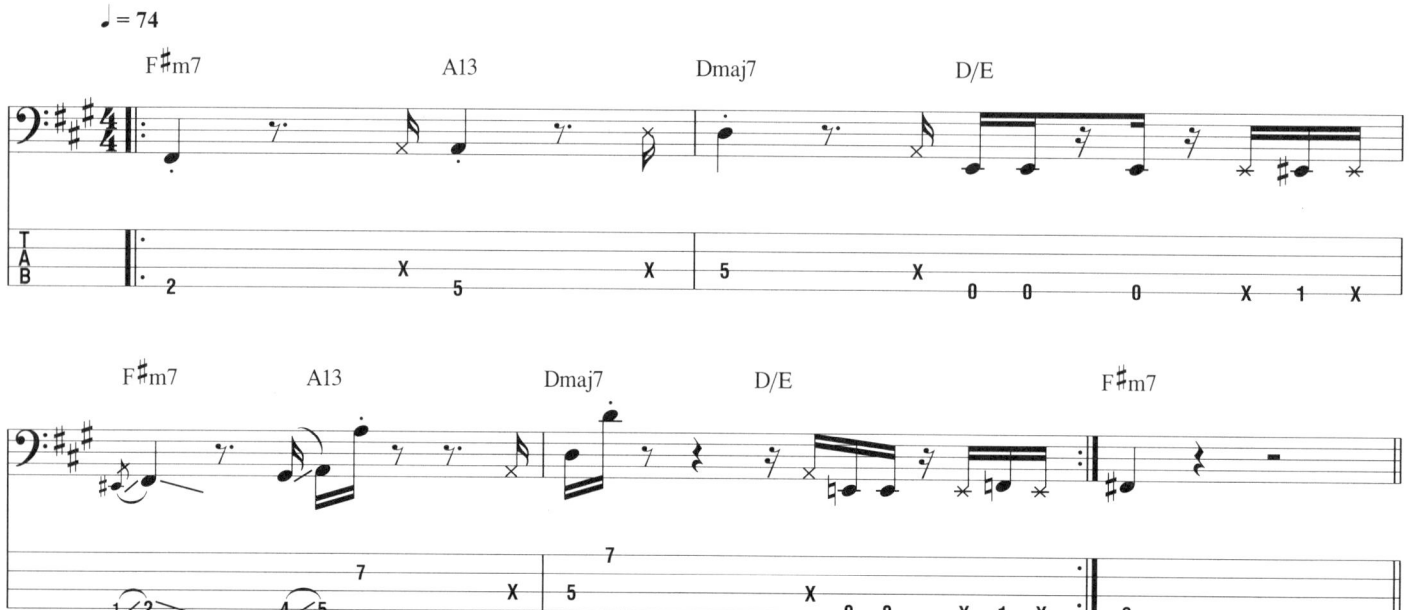

320. Slick 4

321. Slick 5

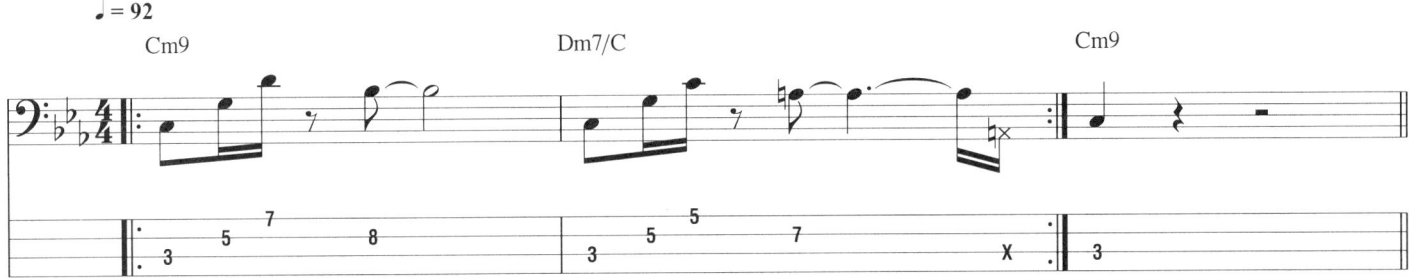

322. JPJ-ish 1

323. JPJ-ish 2

324. Slow Palm-Mute Funk

325. Palm-Muted Motown (Variation 1)

326. Palm-Muted Motown (Variation 2)

327. Groove for Weeks

328. Rocco-ish

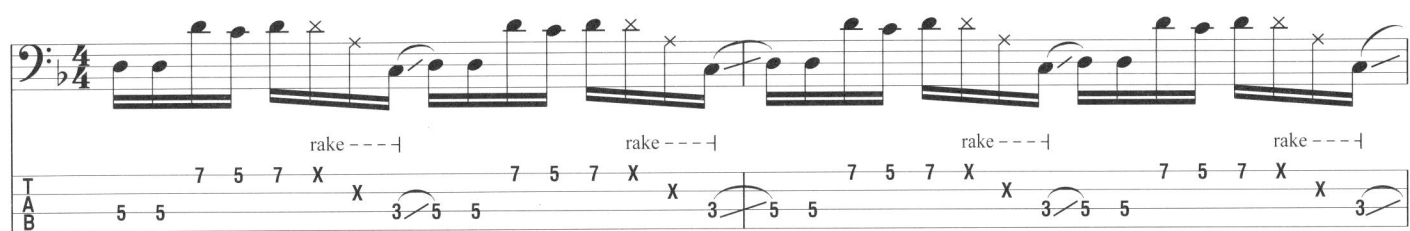

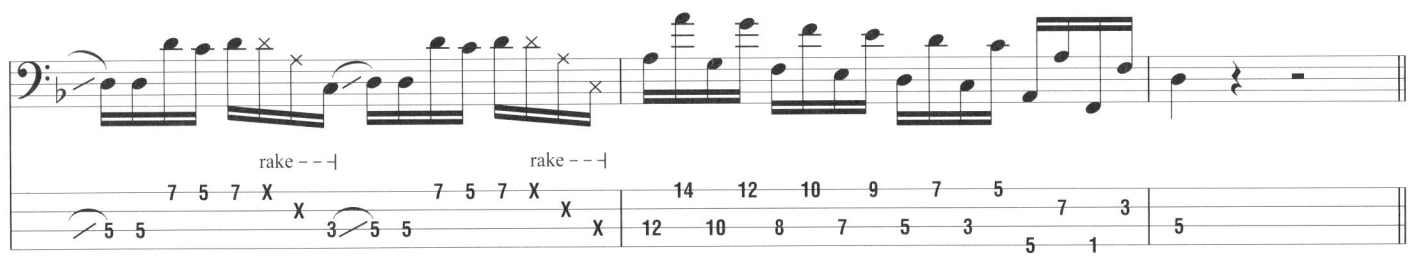

329. Jaco-ish

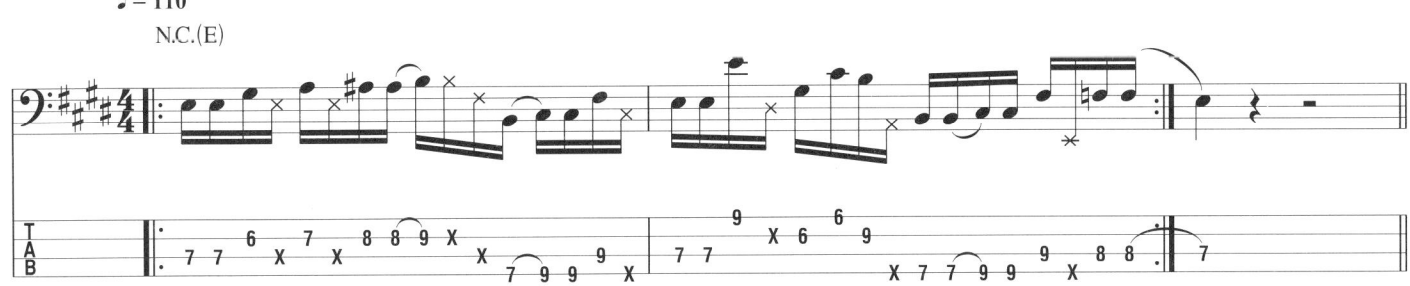

330. Chill 3

93

331. Chill 4

332. Chill 5

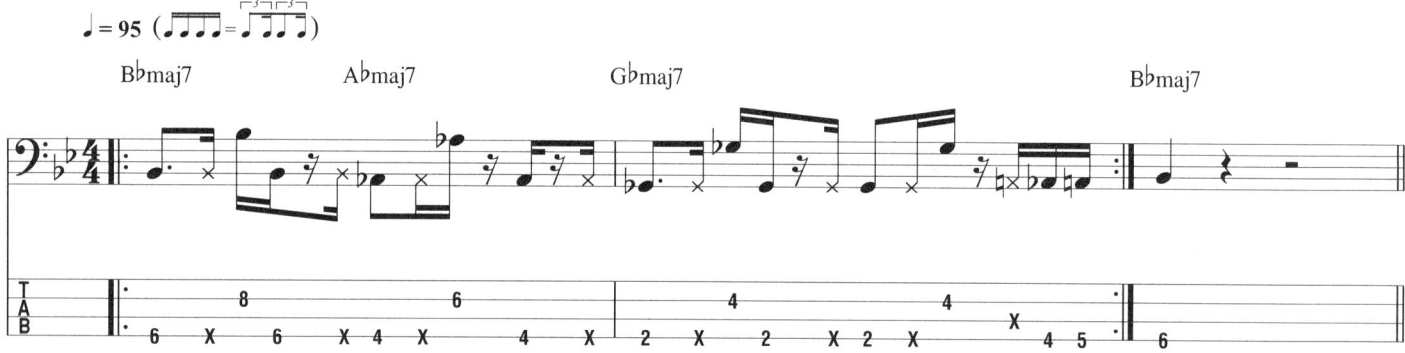

333. Chill 6

334. Smooth Motown Groove

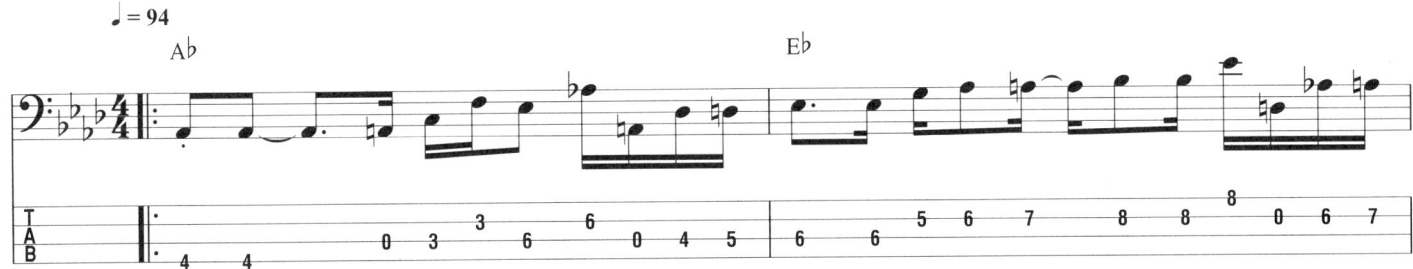

335. Smooth Jazz 1

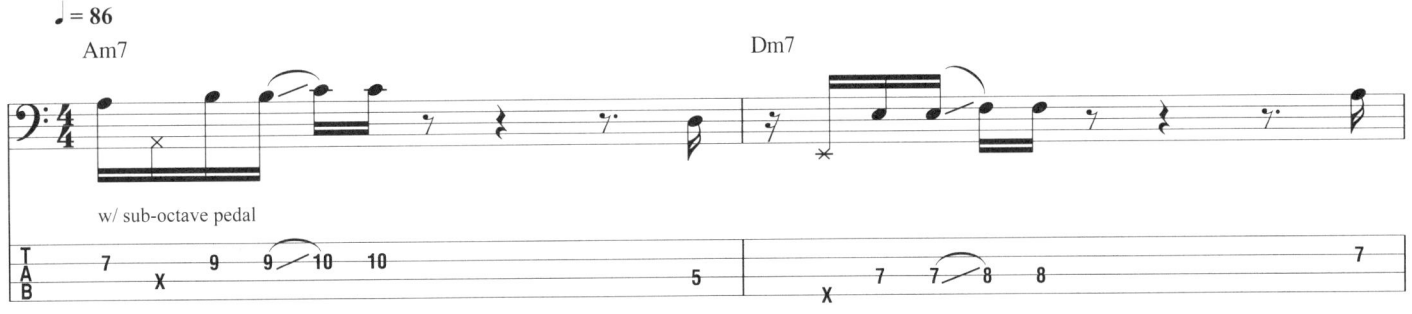

336. Smooth Jazz 2

337. Smooth Jazz 3

338. One-Chord Motown Groove

339. i-IV Groove Variation 1: Laid-Back with Funky Fills

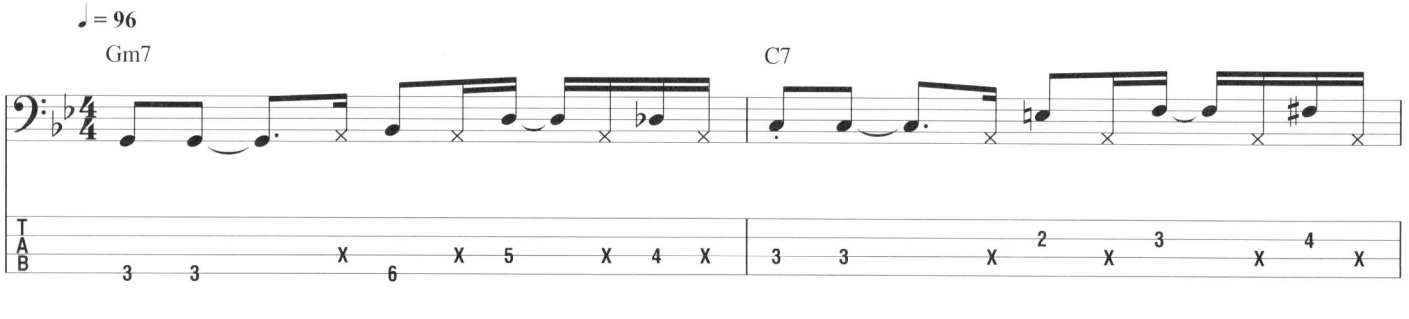
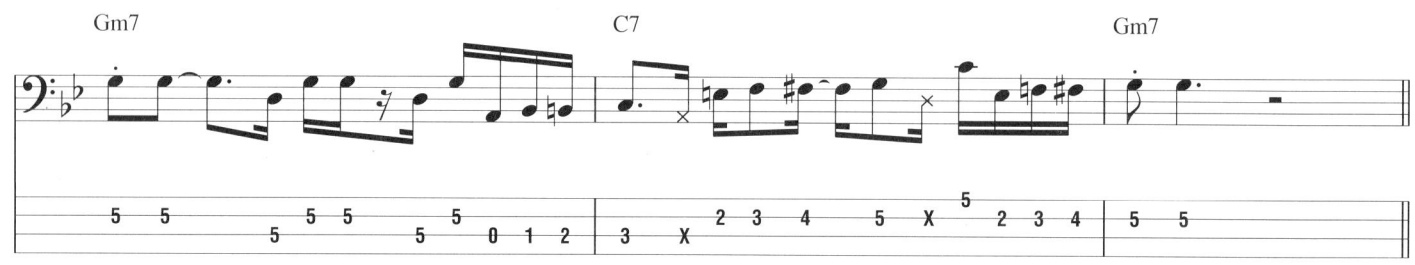

340. i-IV Groove Variation 2: Mid-Tempo

341. i-IV Groove Variation 3: Mid-Tempo

342. i-IV Groove Variation 4: Mid-Tempo

343. R&B Rave-up

344. Dropping 5ths

345. Finger Funk 1

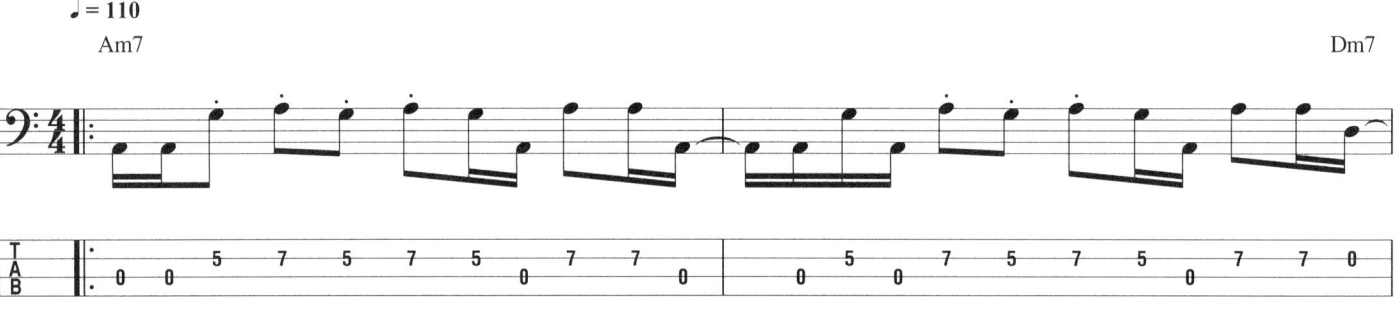

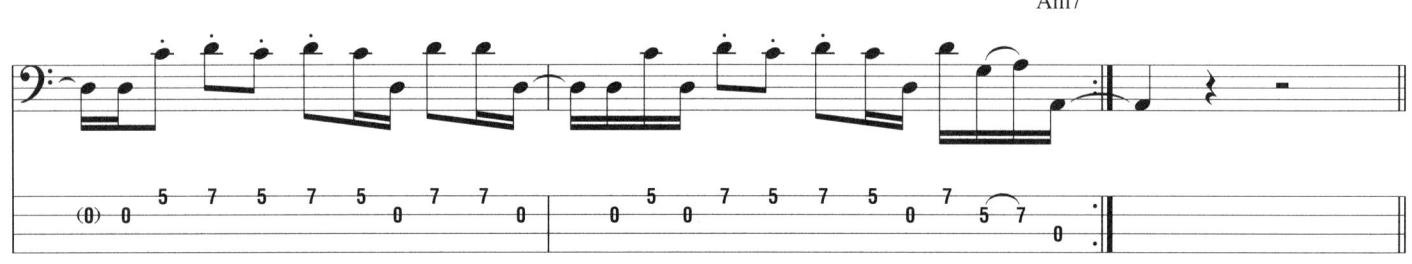

346. Finger Funk 2

347. Finger Funk 3

348. Finger Funk 4

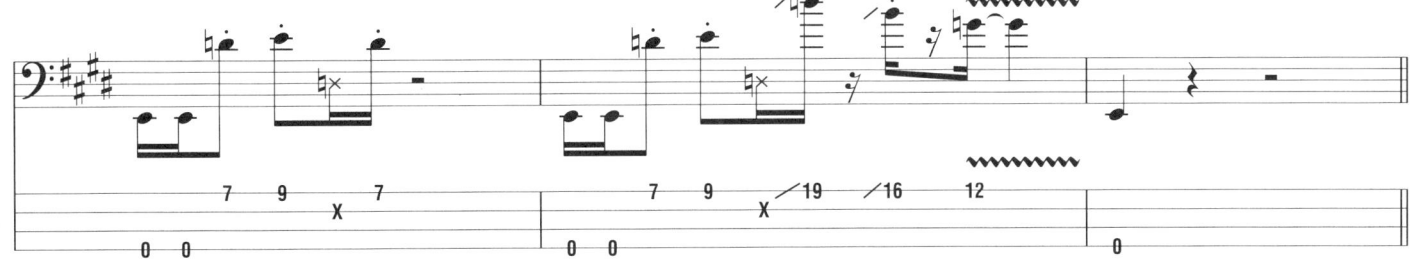

349. Finger Funk 5

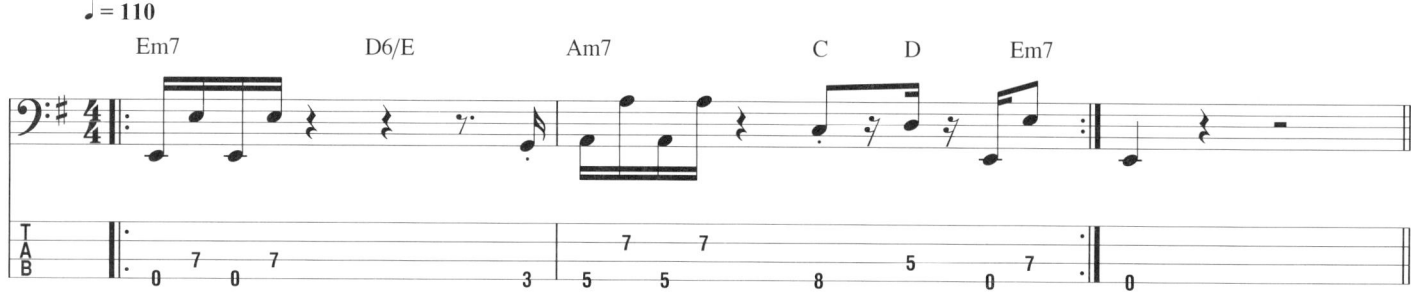

350. Finger Funk 6

351. Finger Funk 7

352. Finger Funk 8

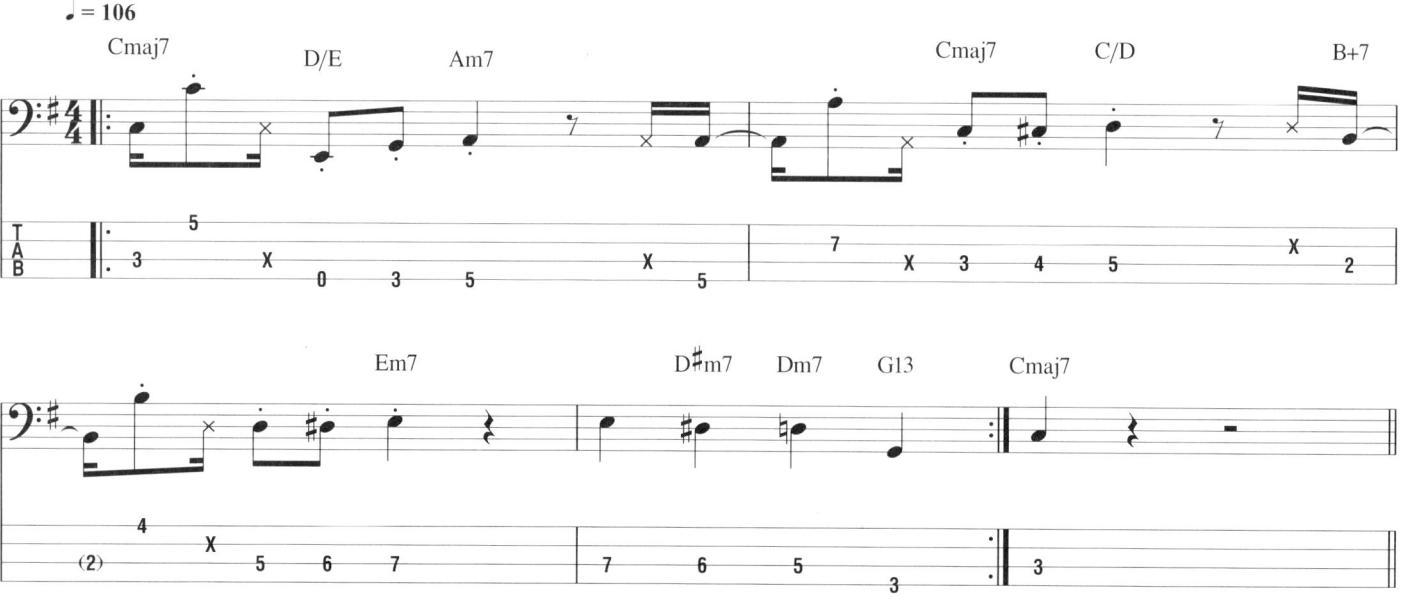

353. Finger Funk 9

354. Finger Funk 10

Drop D tuning:
(low to high) D-A-D-G

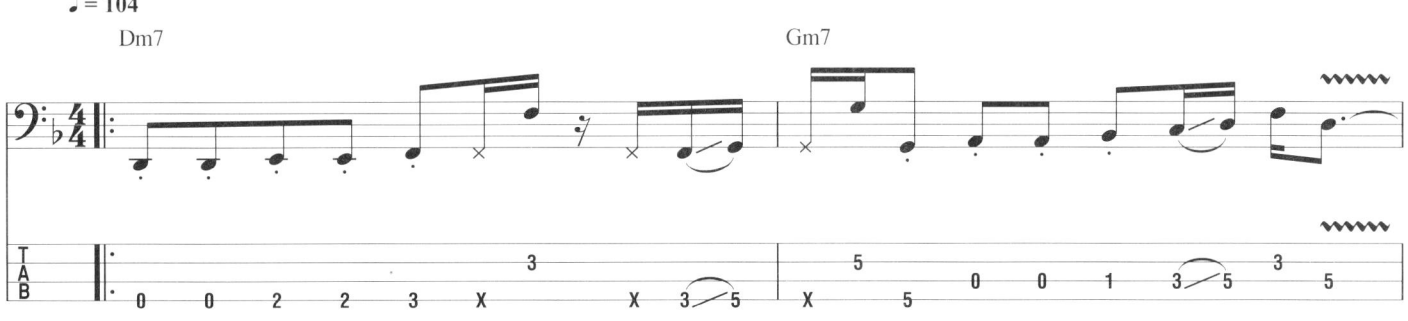

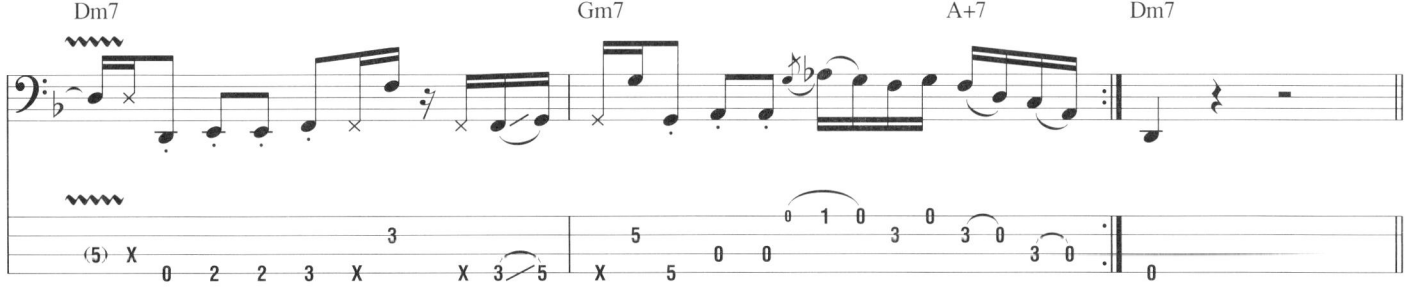

355. Finger Funk 11

356. Finger Funk 12

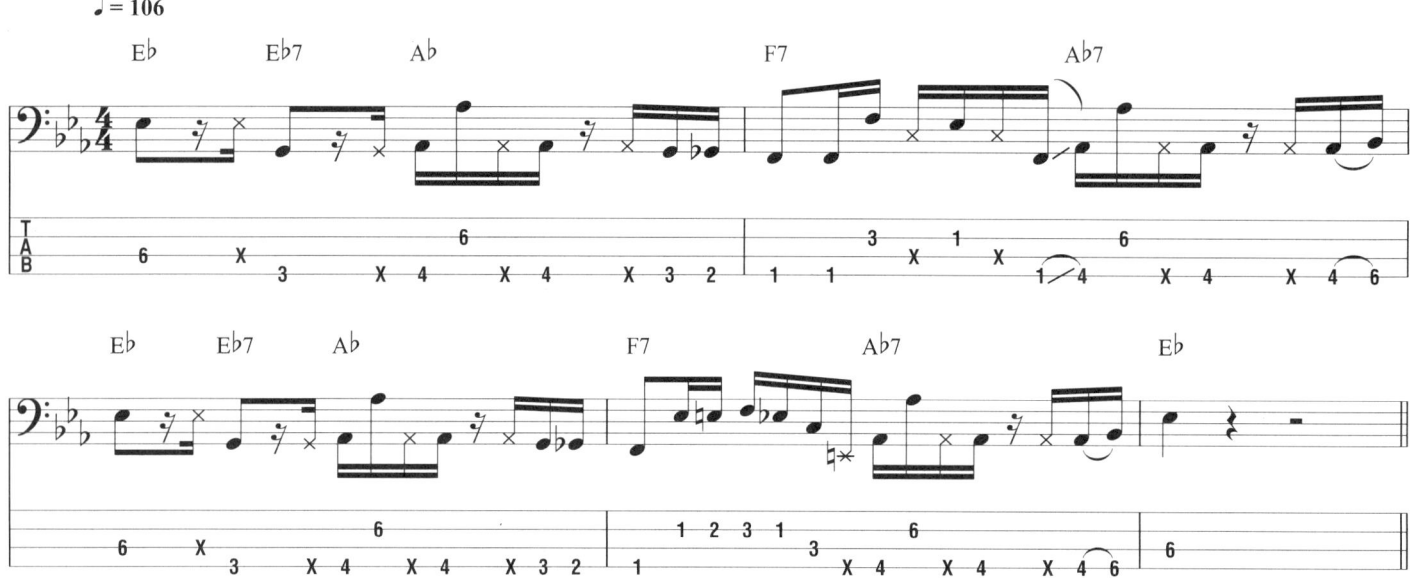

357. Finger Funk 13

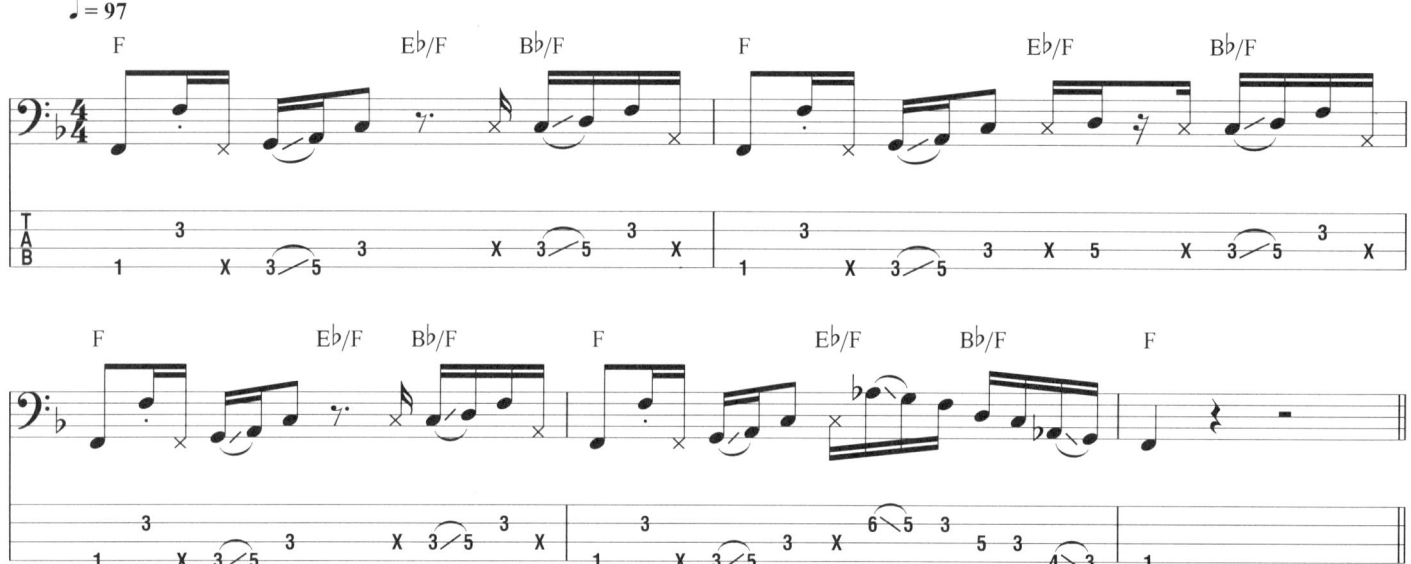

358. Finger Funk 14

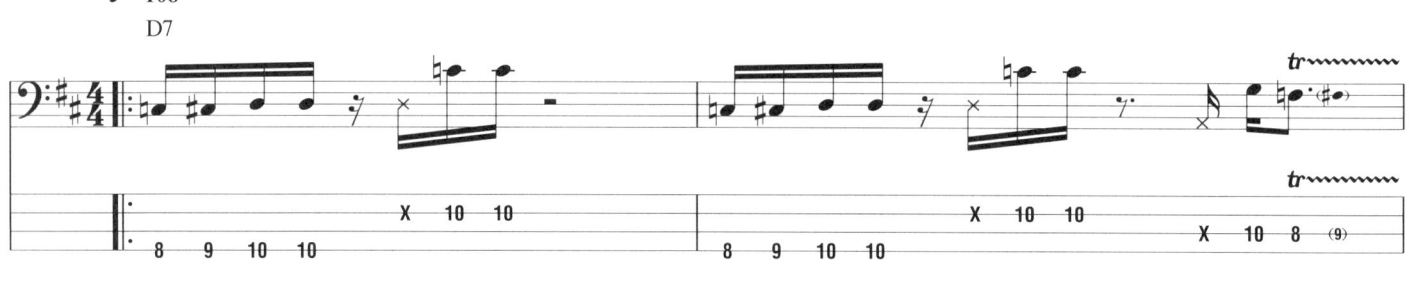

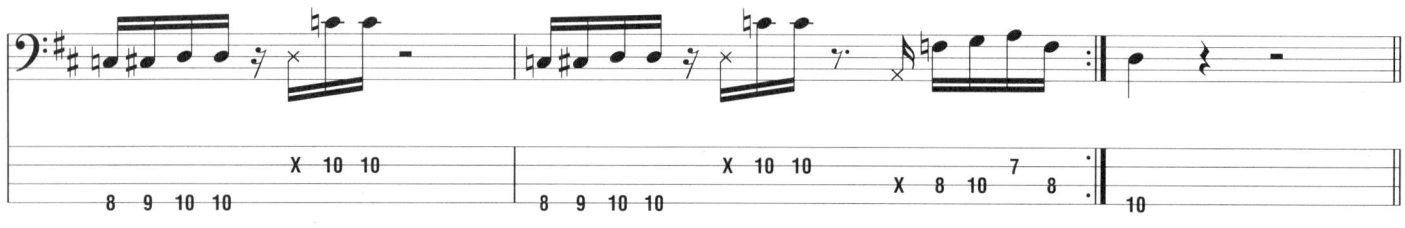

359. Finger Funk 15

Drop D tuning:
(low to high) D-A-D-G

360. Slow Funk

361. Babymakin' Bass

362. Aww Yeaaahhh

363. Bendy Soul

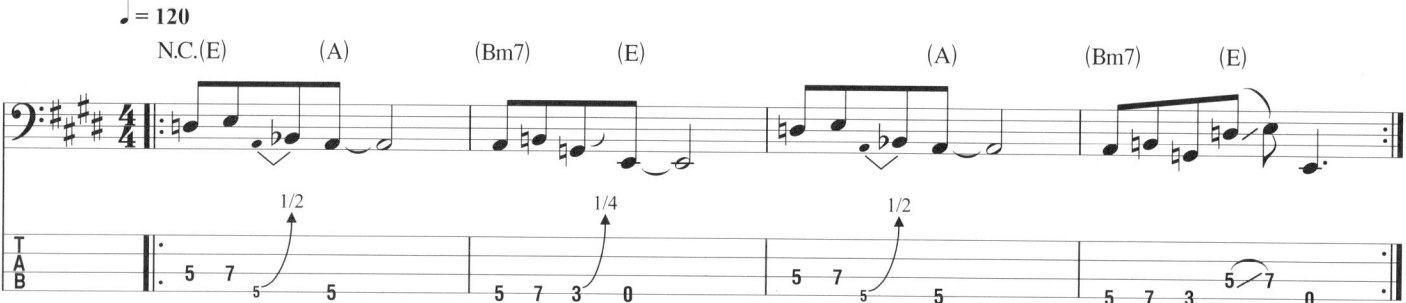

364. Old School 1

365. Old School 2

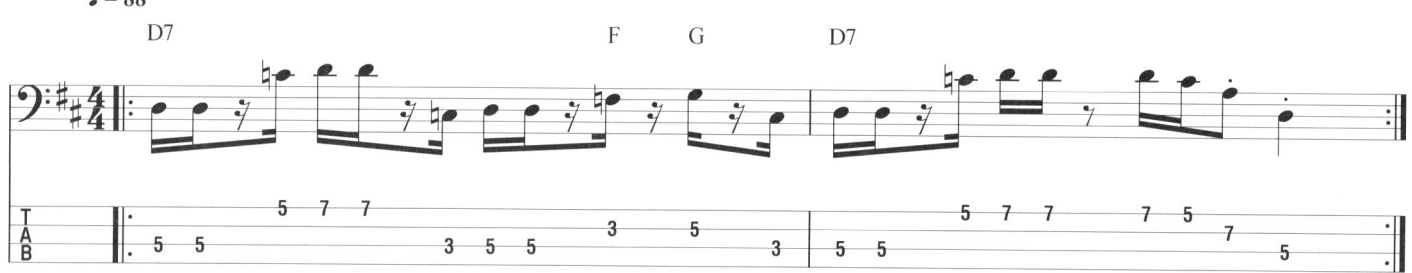

366. Old School Motown

367. One-Chord Funk 1

368. One-Chord Funk 2

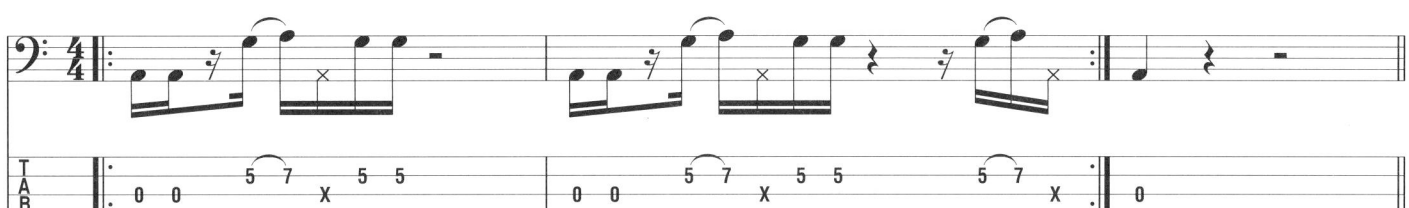

369. One-Chord Funk 3

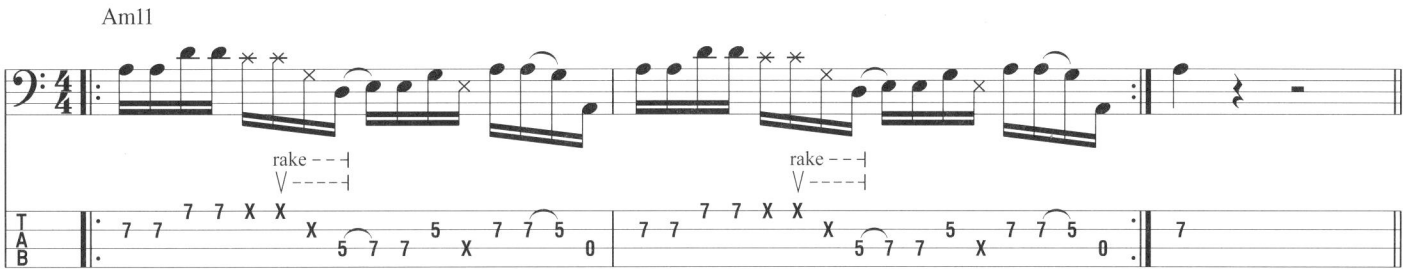

370. Simple Disco Groove

371. Not-As-Simple Disco Groove

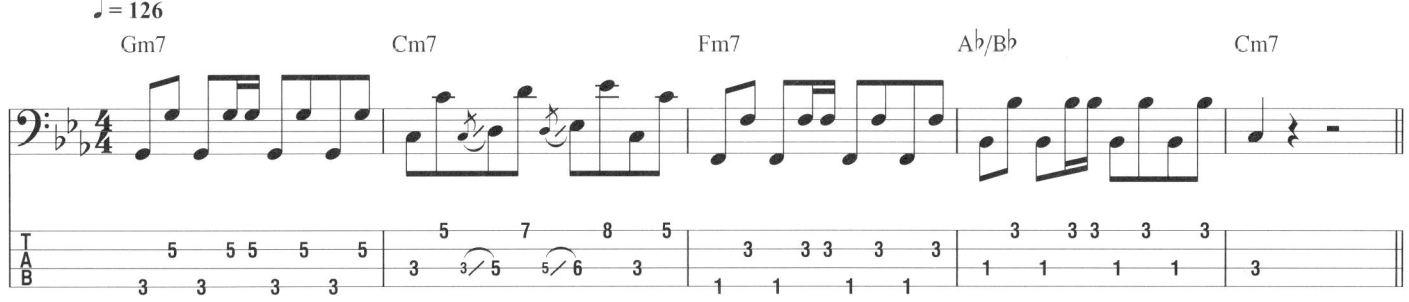

372. Disco Rules

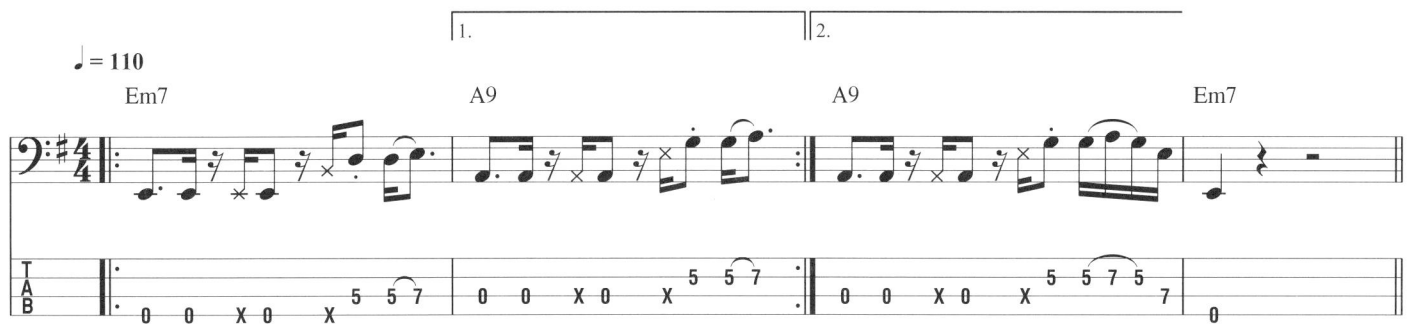

373. Stax-ish 2

374. Stax-ish 3
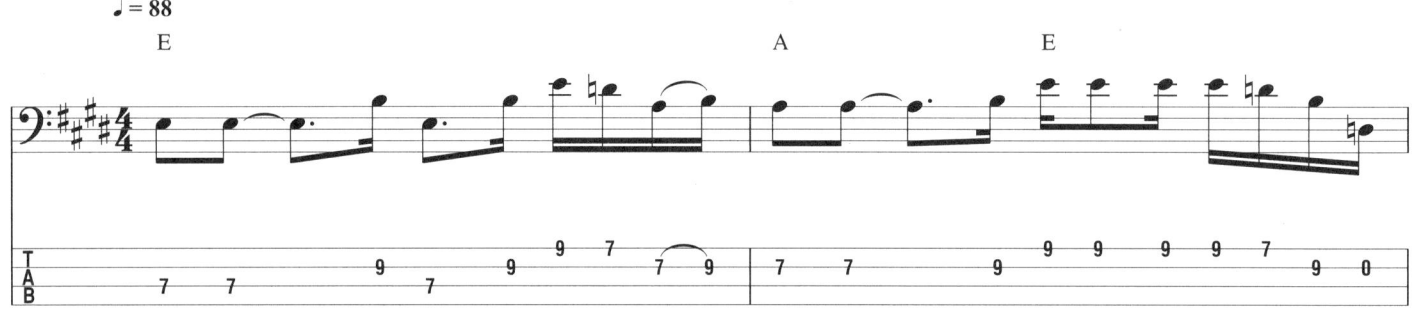
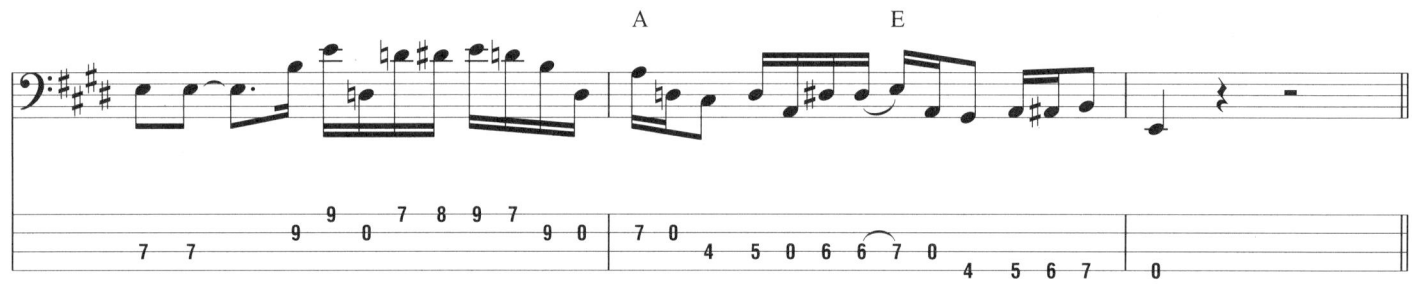

375. Stax-ish 4

376. You Don't Need Thumbs to Be Funky

377. Double Stops

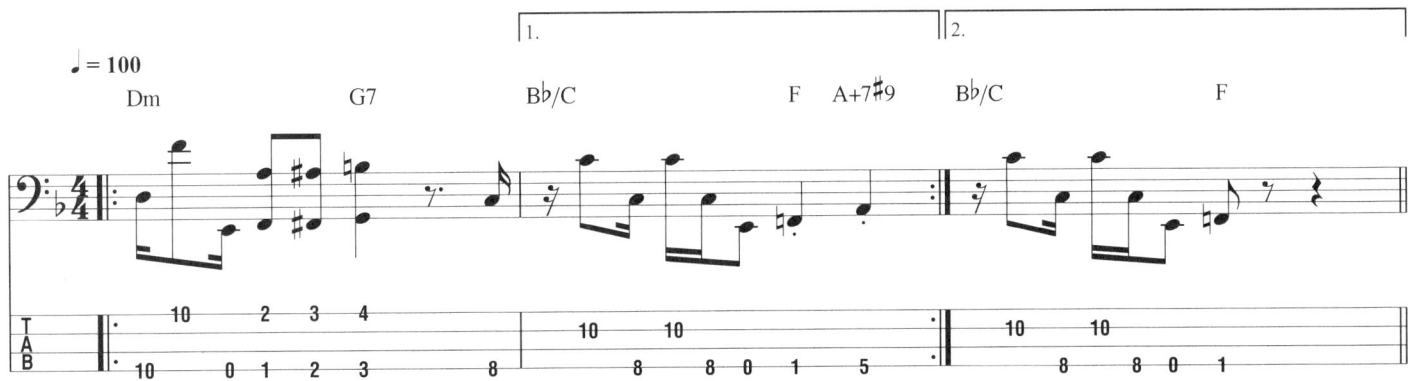

378. Two-Fret Funk

379. Don't Be a Stick in the Mud, Get Up and Dance 1

380. Don't Be a Stick in the Mud, Get Up and Dance 2

381. Don't Be a Stick in the Mud, Get Up and Dance 3

382. The Notes You *Don't* Play Are Just as Important 4

383. Groove with a Side of Open Strings 4

384. Groove with a Side of Open Strings 5

385. Pocket, Pocket, Pocket

386. Backbeat 5

387. Bounce

388. Motown Stomp

389. Cupcake Soul Jam

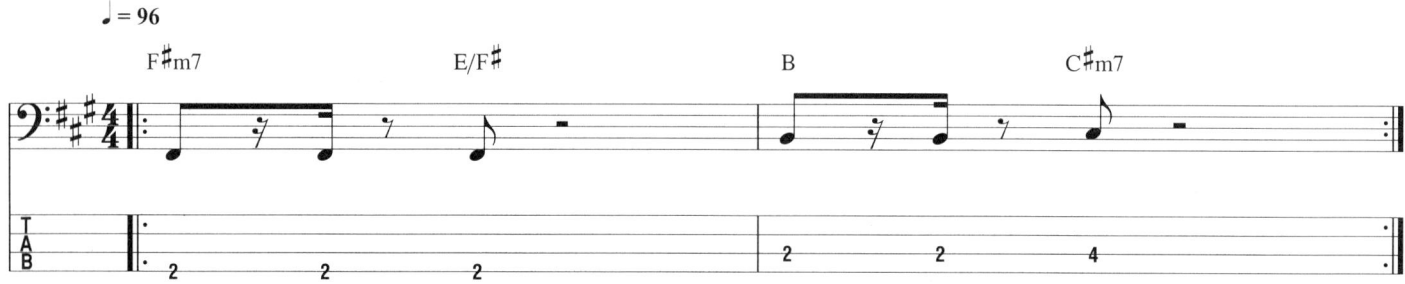

390. '80s

391. ElectroFunk 1

392. ElectroFunk 2

SLAP

T = Slap w/ thumb
P = Pull or snap w/ index finger
F = Fret-hand slap

393. Slappy Rock

394. Funk-Rock Slap 1

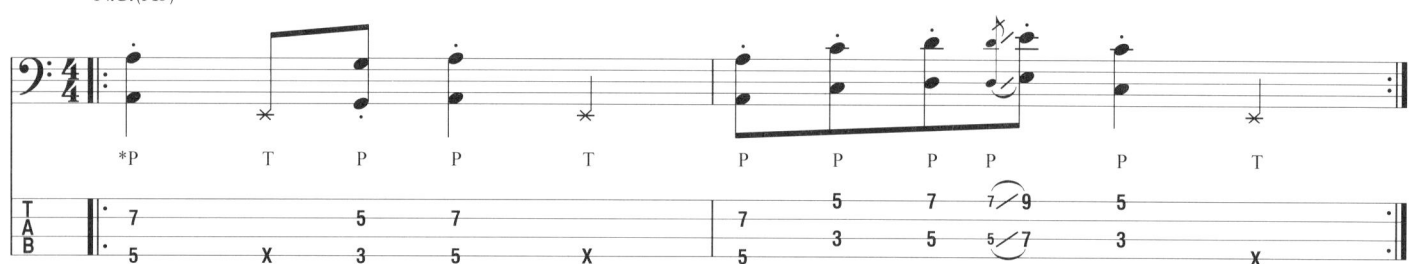

*Pull strings with thumb and index finger.

395. Funk-Rock Slap 2

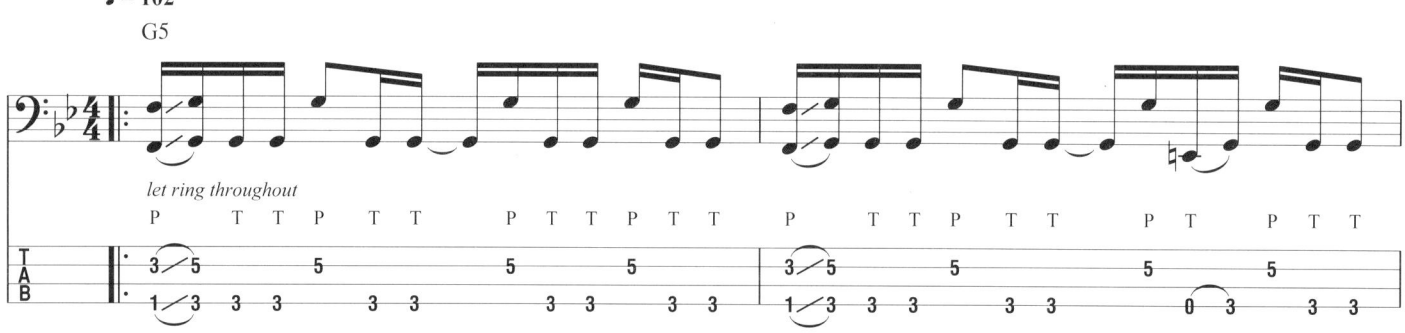

396. Slap 101

397. Slappa da Octaves

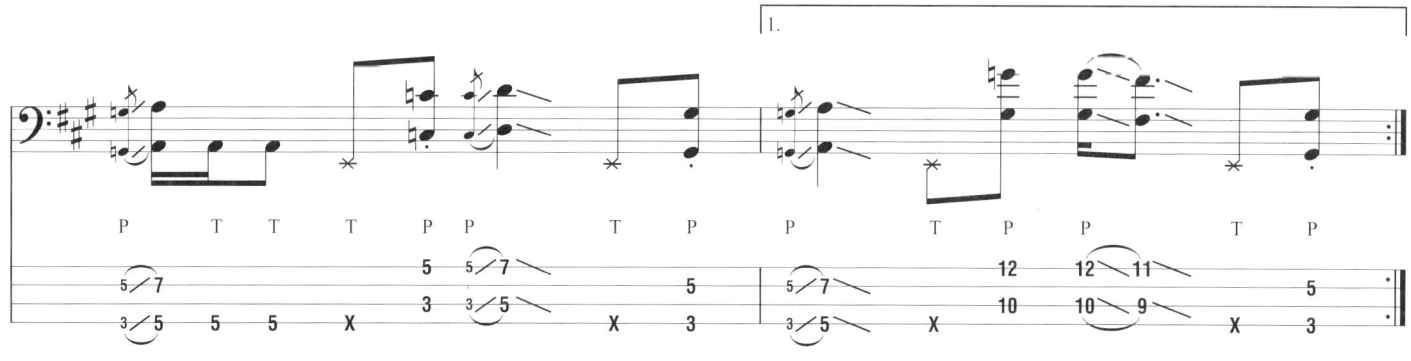

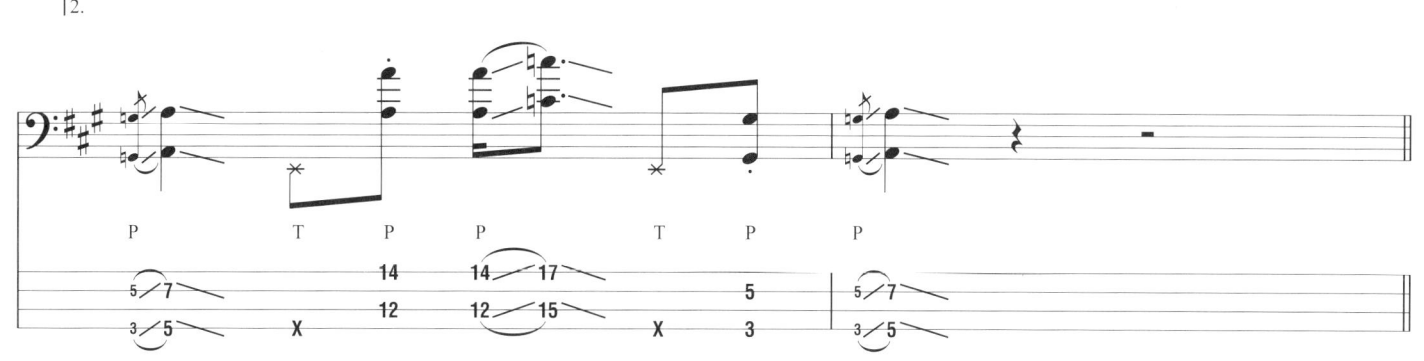

398. I Dare You Not to Bob Your Head to This

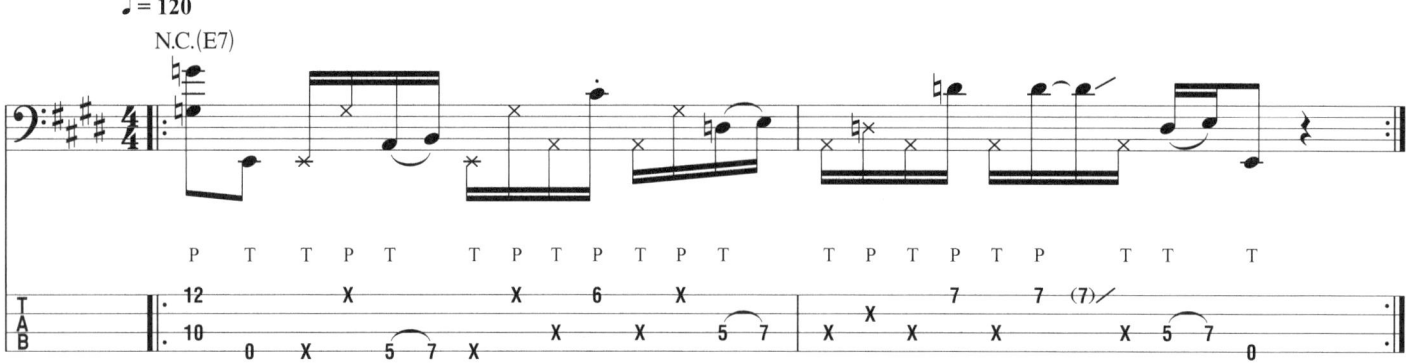

399. No, Seriously

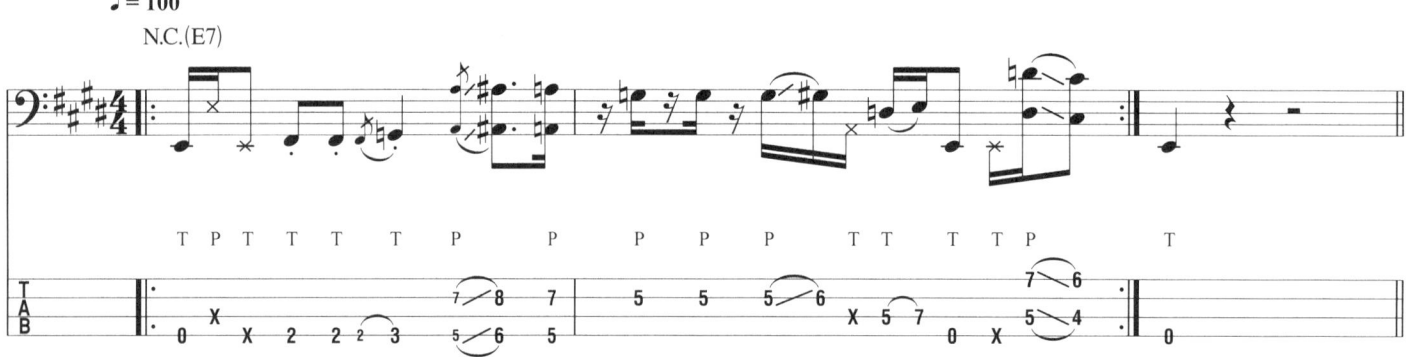

400. Basic Slap Climb

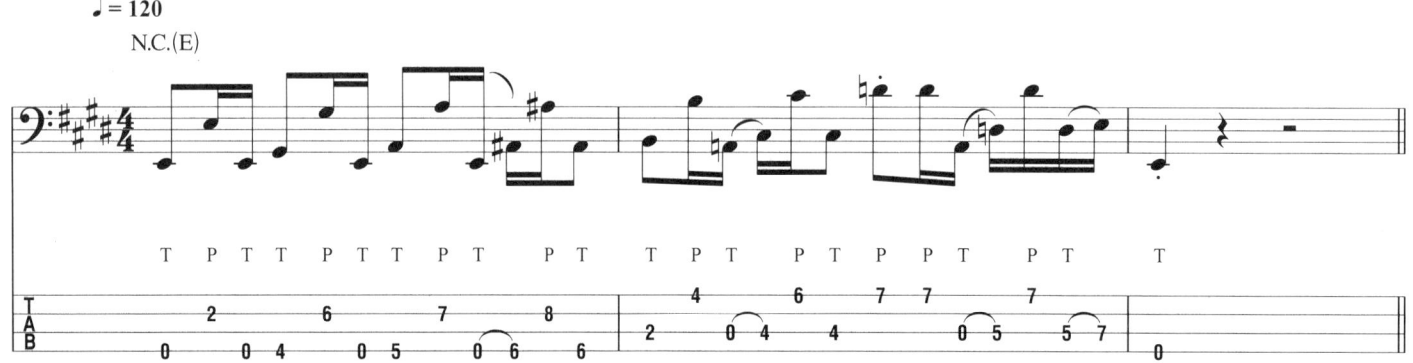

401. Fast Slap Groove with Fills

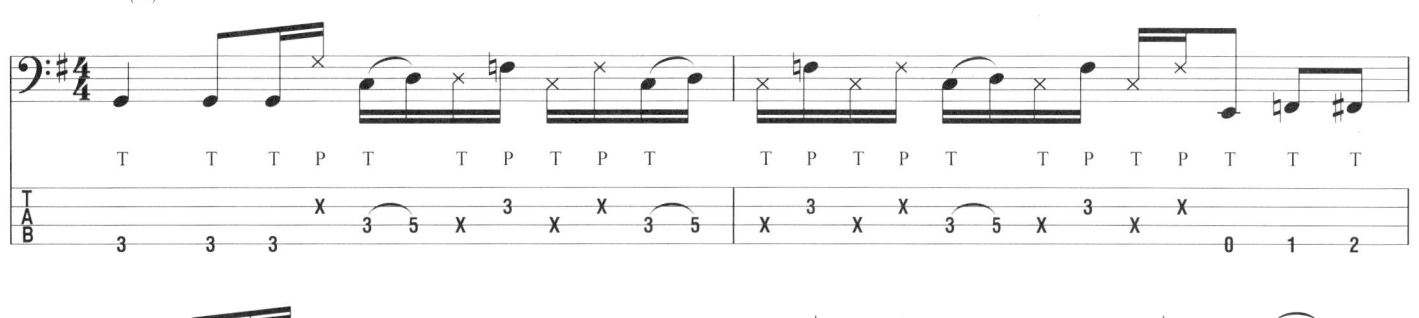
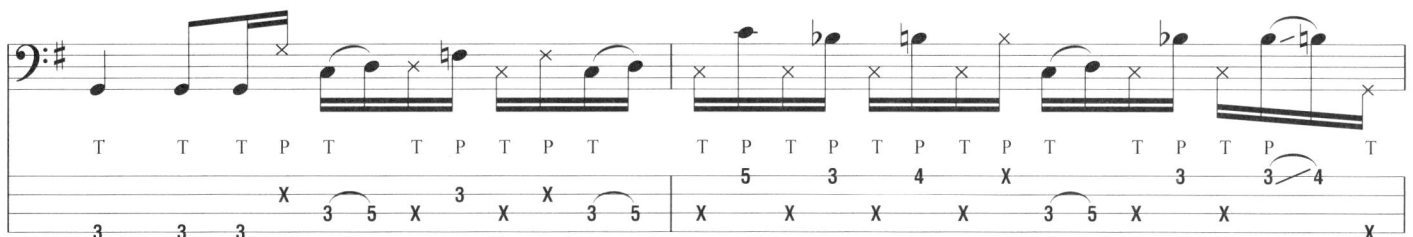
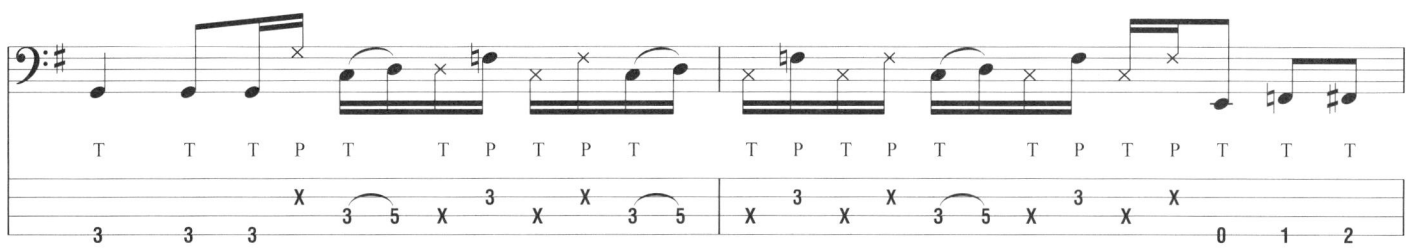
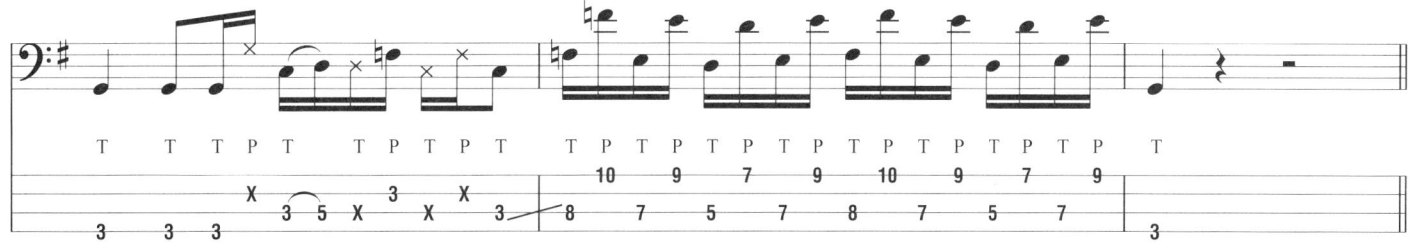

402. Slap with 16th-Note Triplets 1

403. Slap with 16th-Note Triplets 2

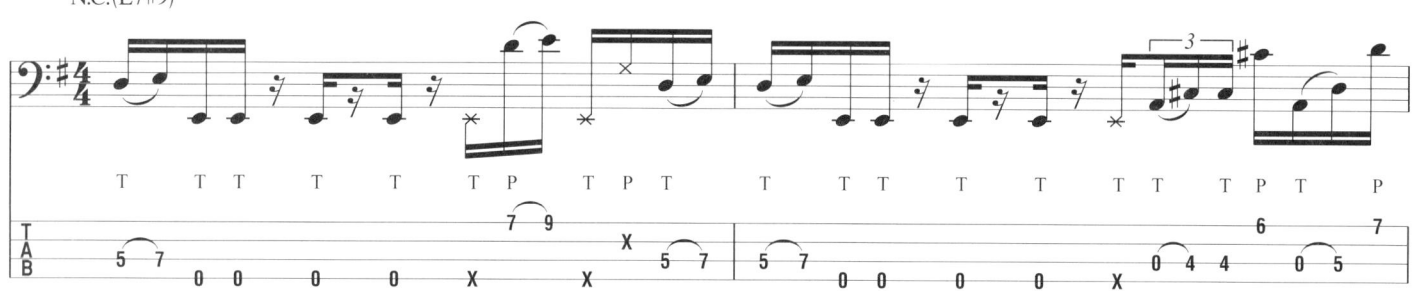

404. Two-Handed Breakdown

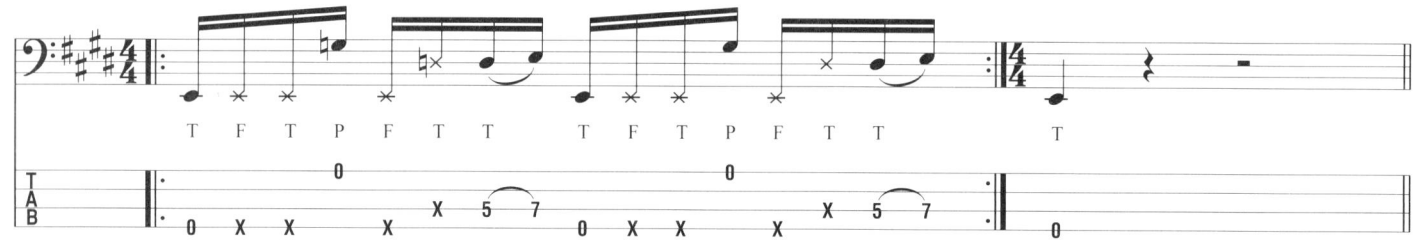

405. Slap Groove with Two-Handed 16th-Note Triplet Fill

406. Slap Groove with Sliding Octave Fill

407. Slap Call and Response

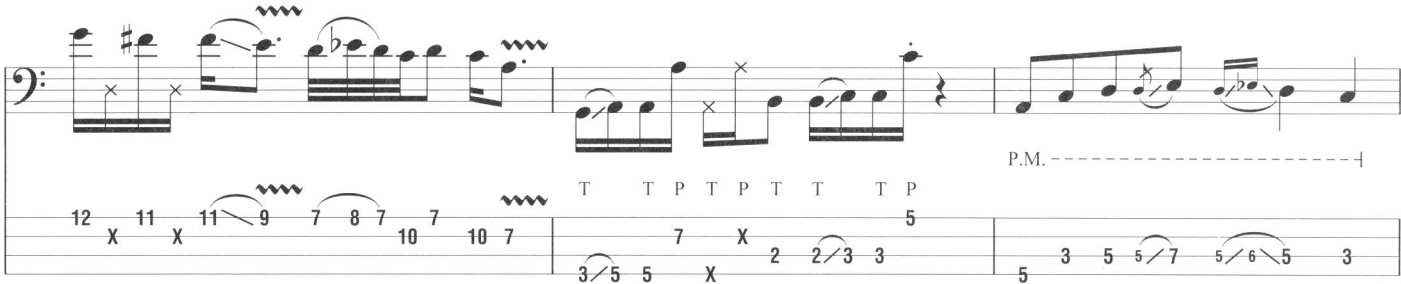

408. Basic Slapped Octave Groove

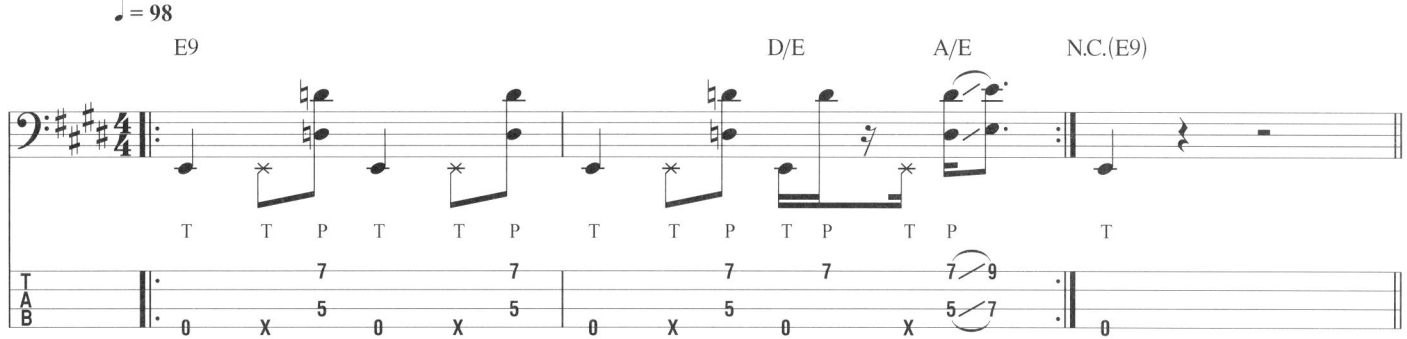

409. Melodic Pop/R&B Slap Line

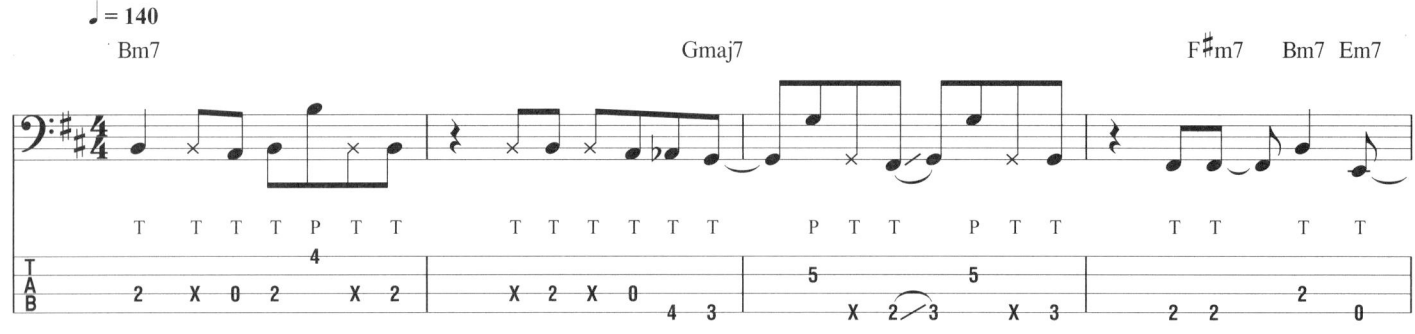

410. Mid-Tempo Slap Over Chord Changes 1

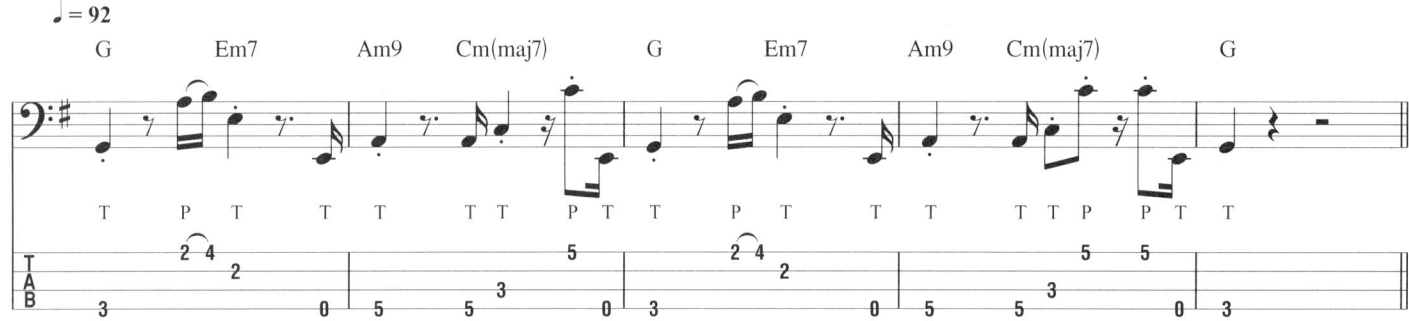

411. Mid-Tempo Slap Over Chord Changes 2

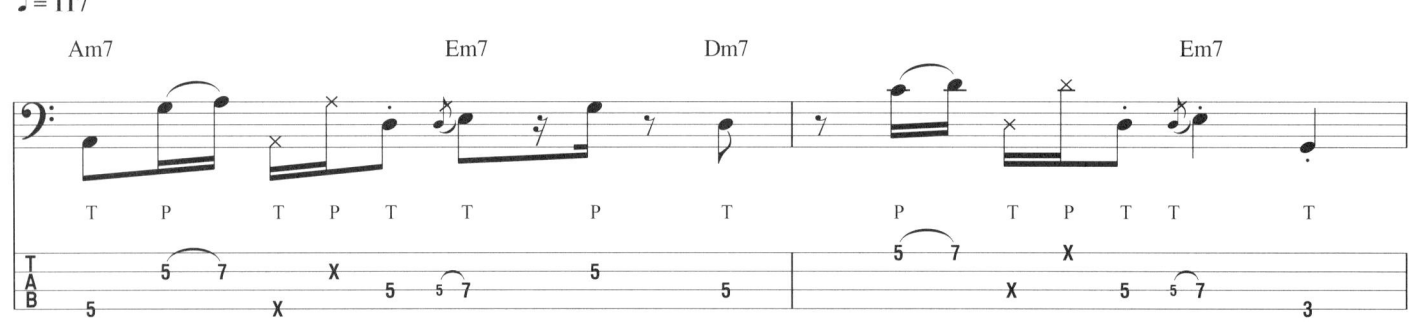

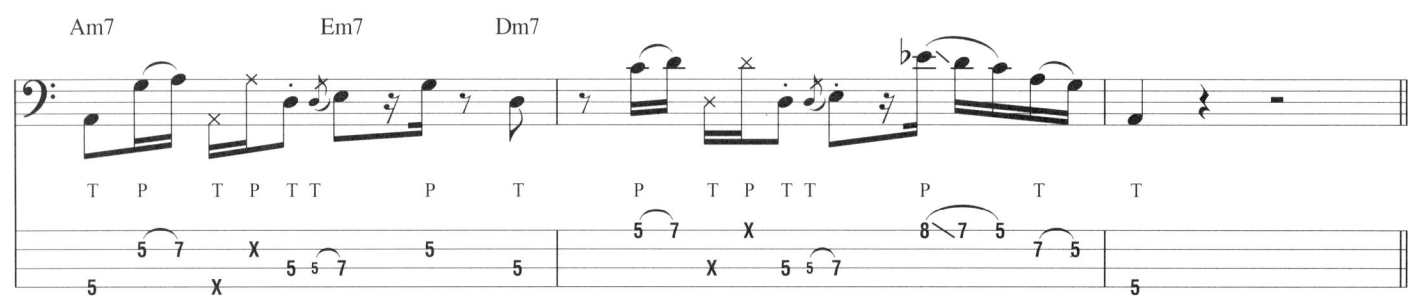

412. Mid-Tempo Slap Over Chord Changes 3

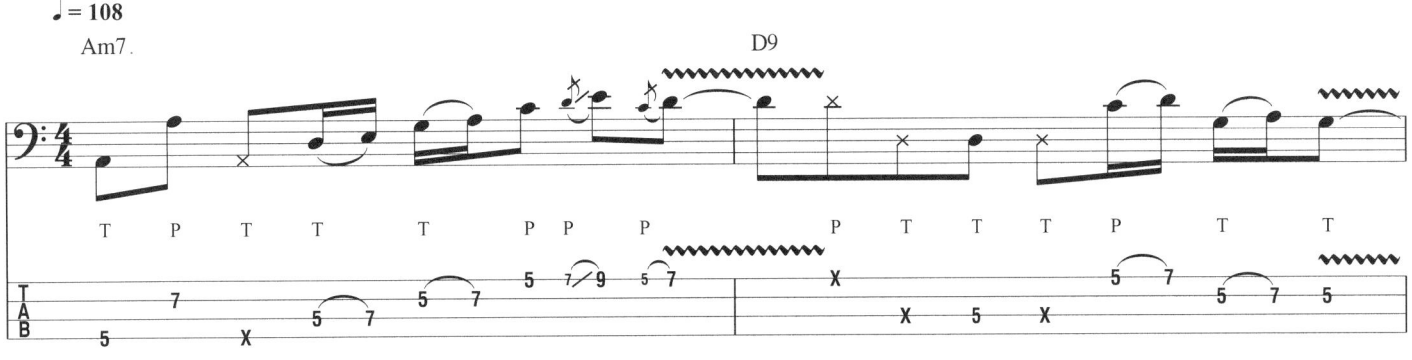
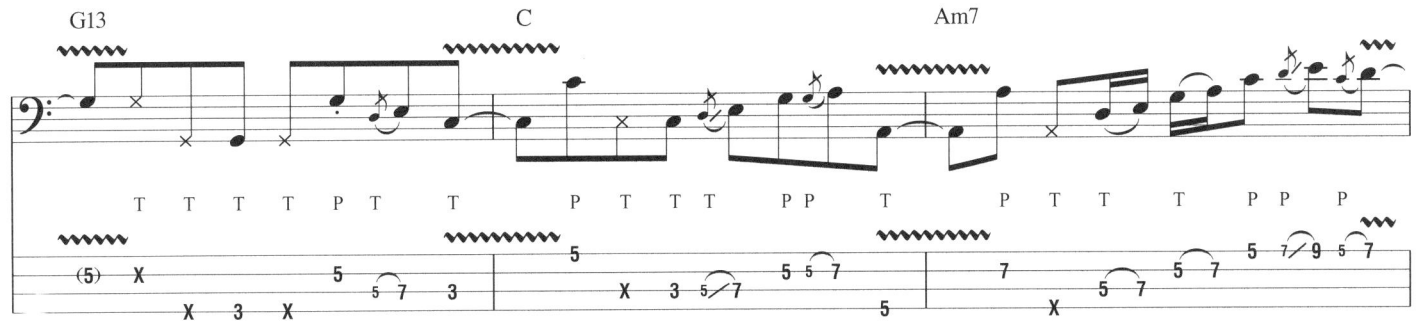
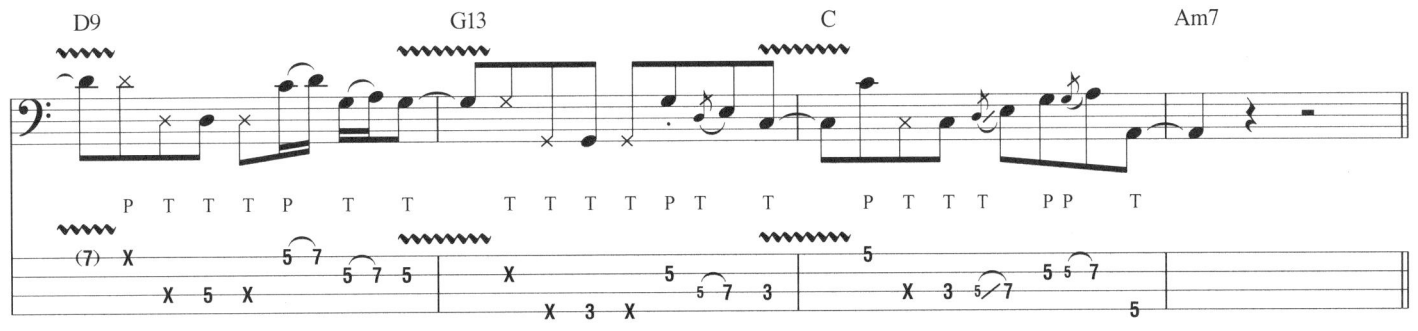

413. Slap with Spaces

414. Weird Slap Rock Groove

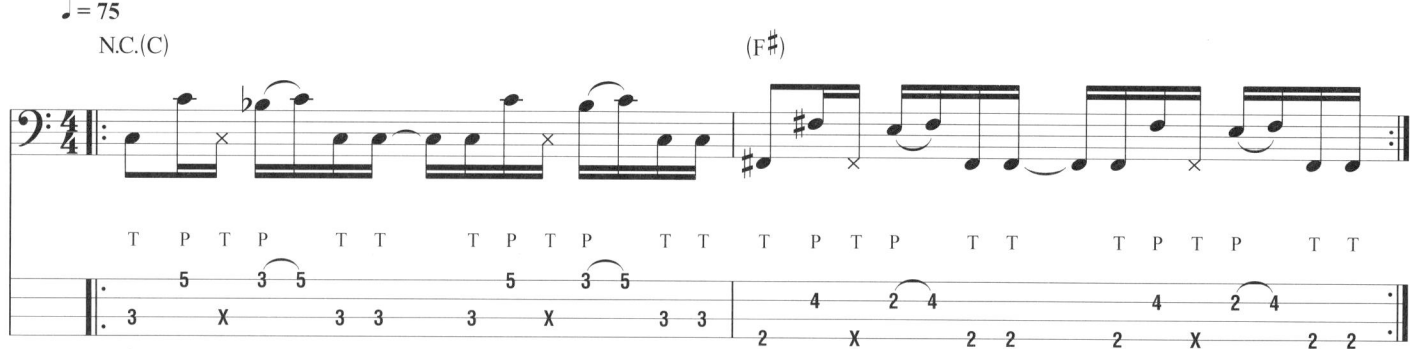

415. Pop Slap 1

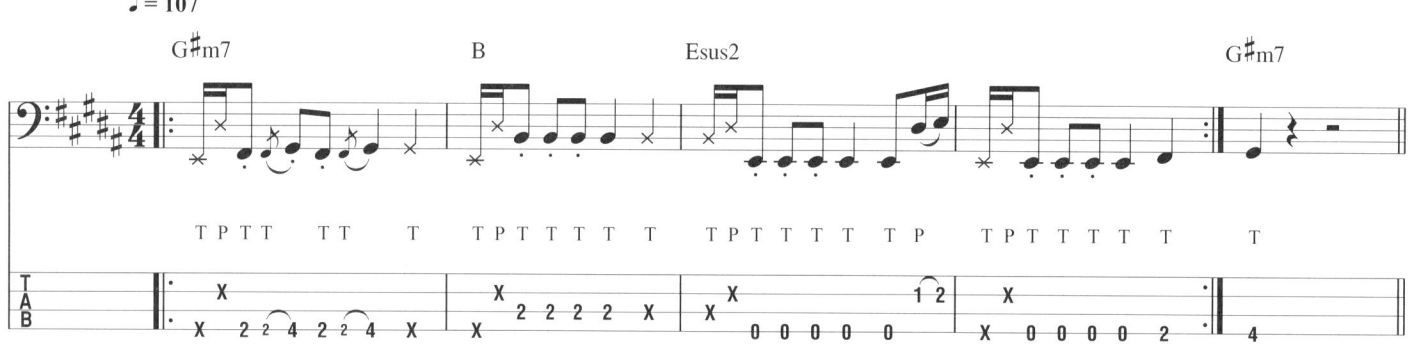

416. Pop Slap 2

417. Don't Be a Stick in the Mud, Get Up and Dance 4

418. Slaps of Fury

419. All Thumbs

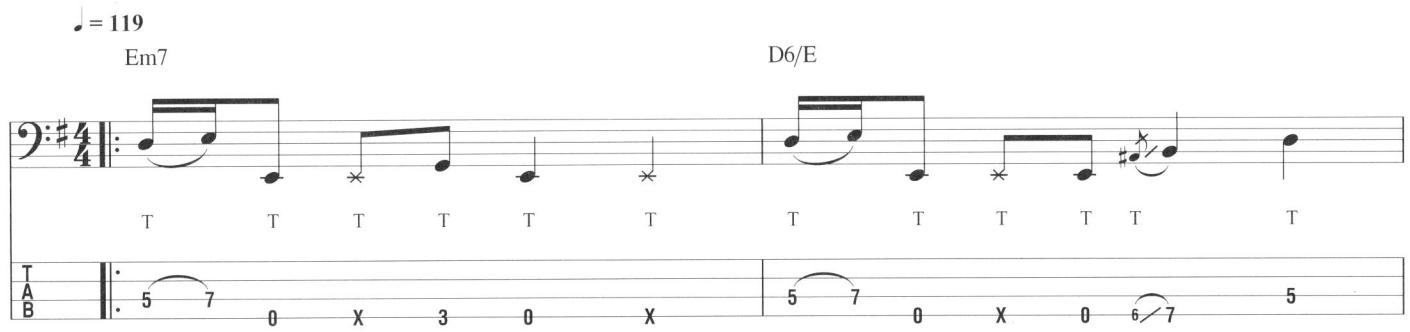

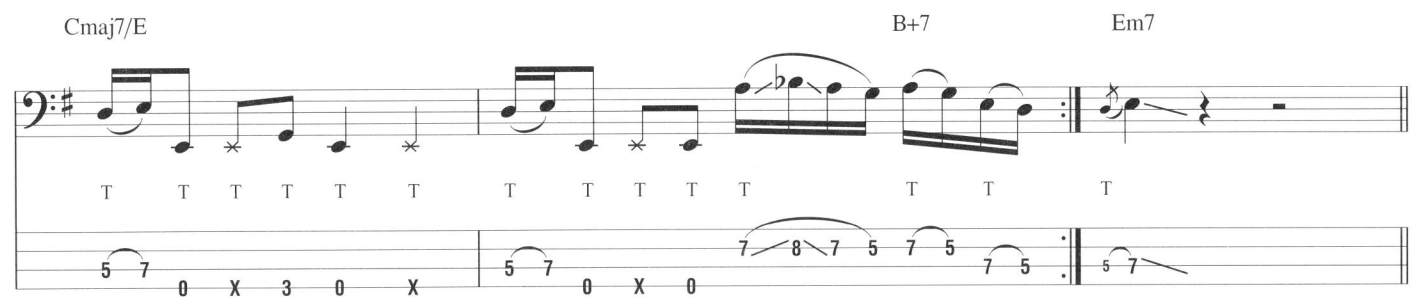

METAL

420. Heavy Palm-Mute

421. Rattlesnake Suitcase

Drop D tuning:
(low to high) D-A-D-G

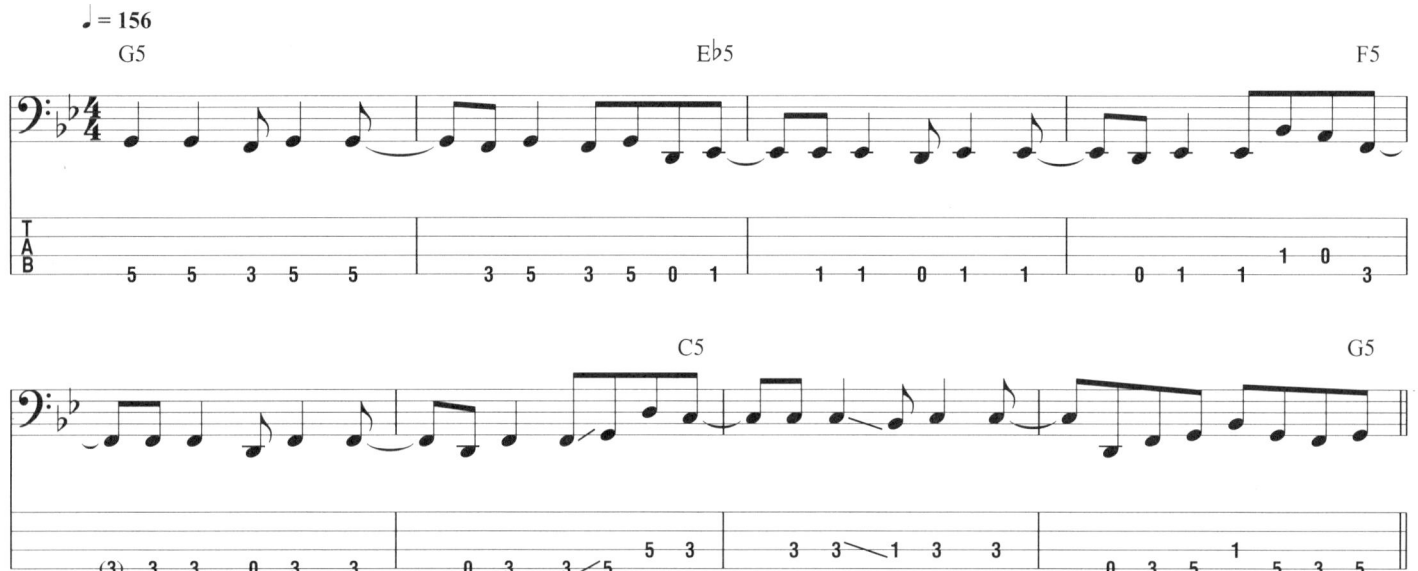

422. Watch Those Turns

Drop D tuning:
(low to high) D-A-D-G

423. Thunder Riff

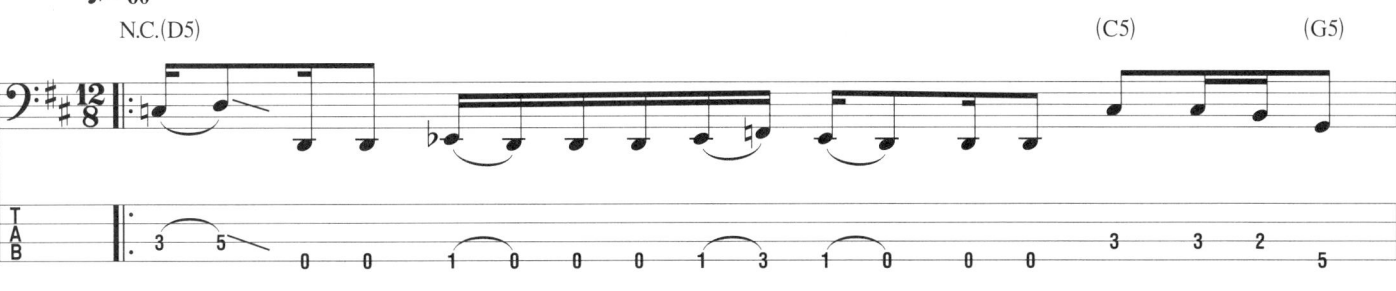

424. Rock Your World

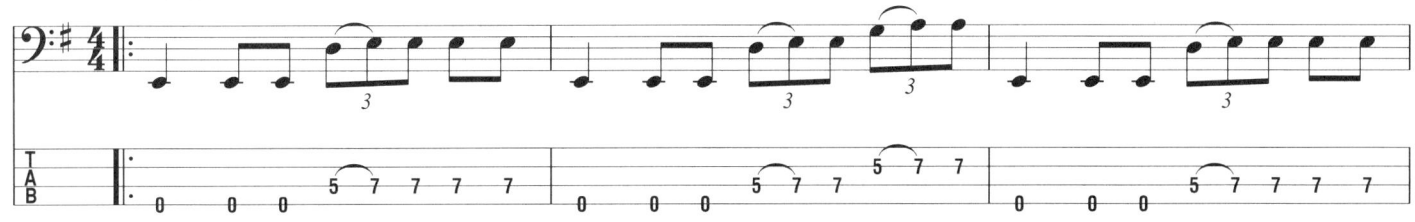

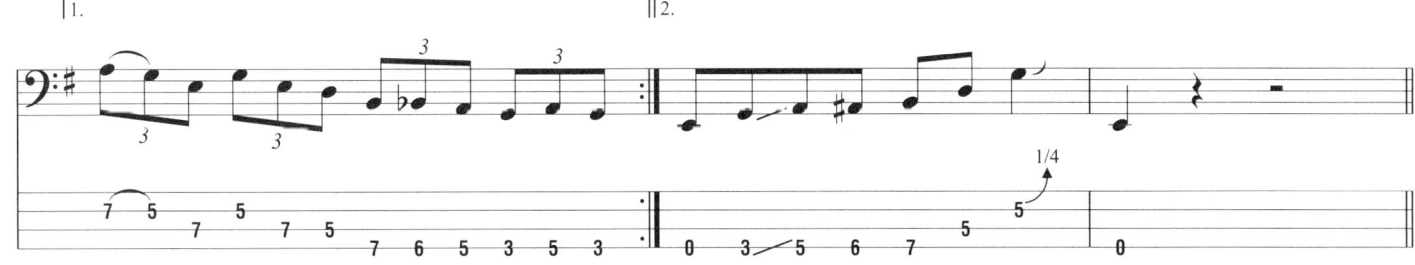

425. Heavy Locrian Groove

426. Harmonic Minor

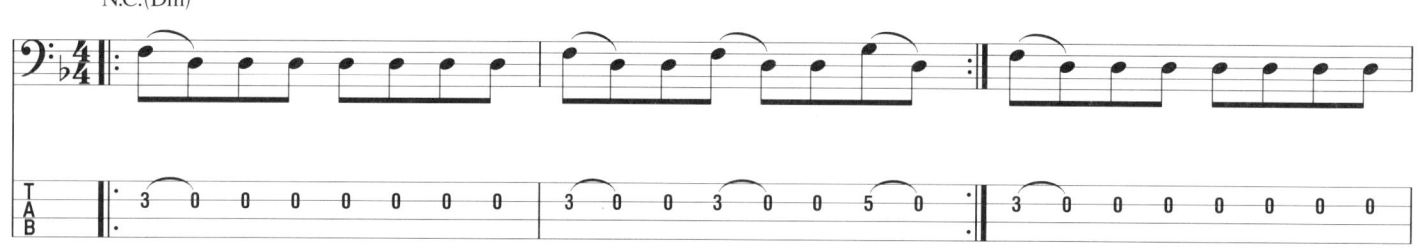

427. Pedal Metal

428. Phrygian Metal 1

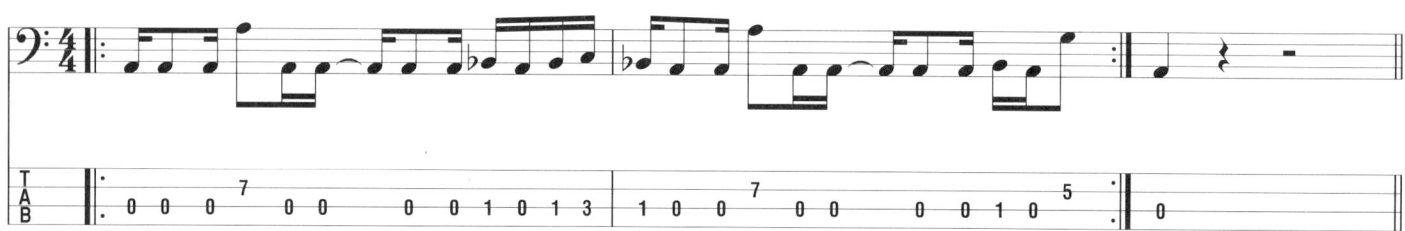

429. Phrygian Metal 2

430. Phrygian Metal 3

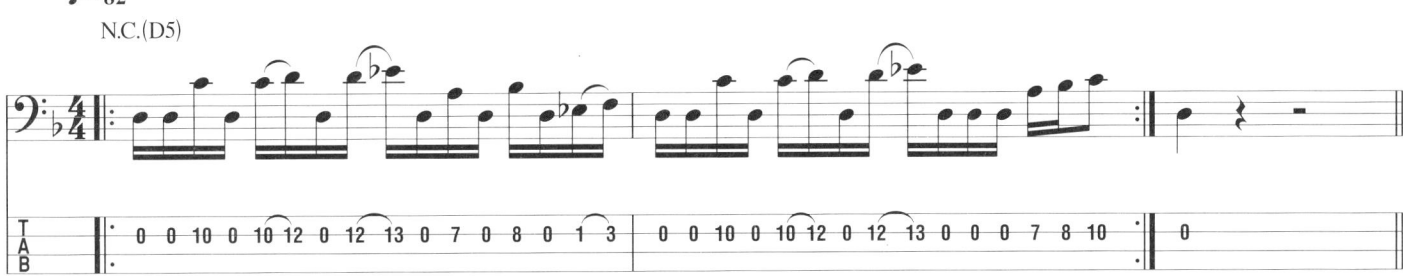

431. Phrygian Metal 4

432. Phrygian Metal 5

433. Moving Minor 3rds

434. Angular Riff 3

435. Angular Riff 4

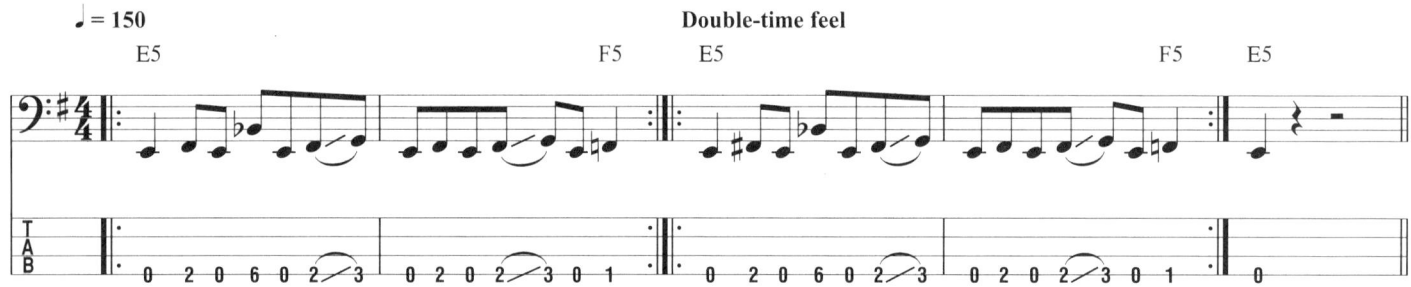

436. Angular Riff 5

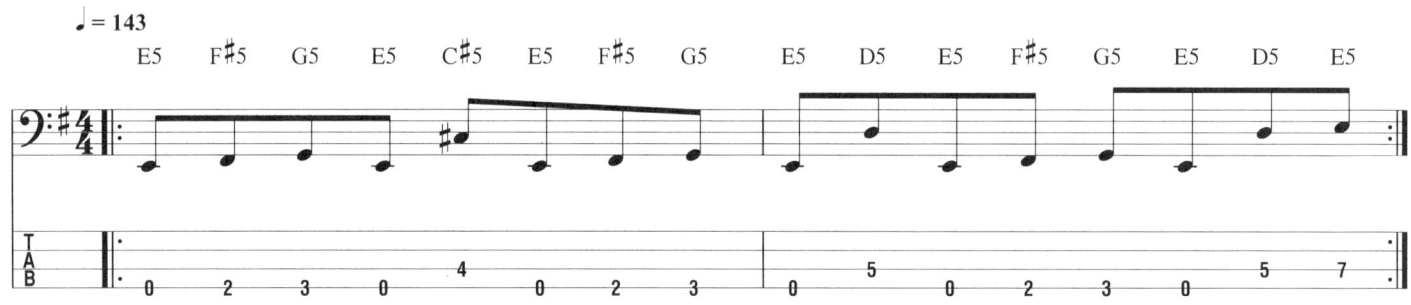

437. Baroque 2

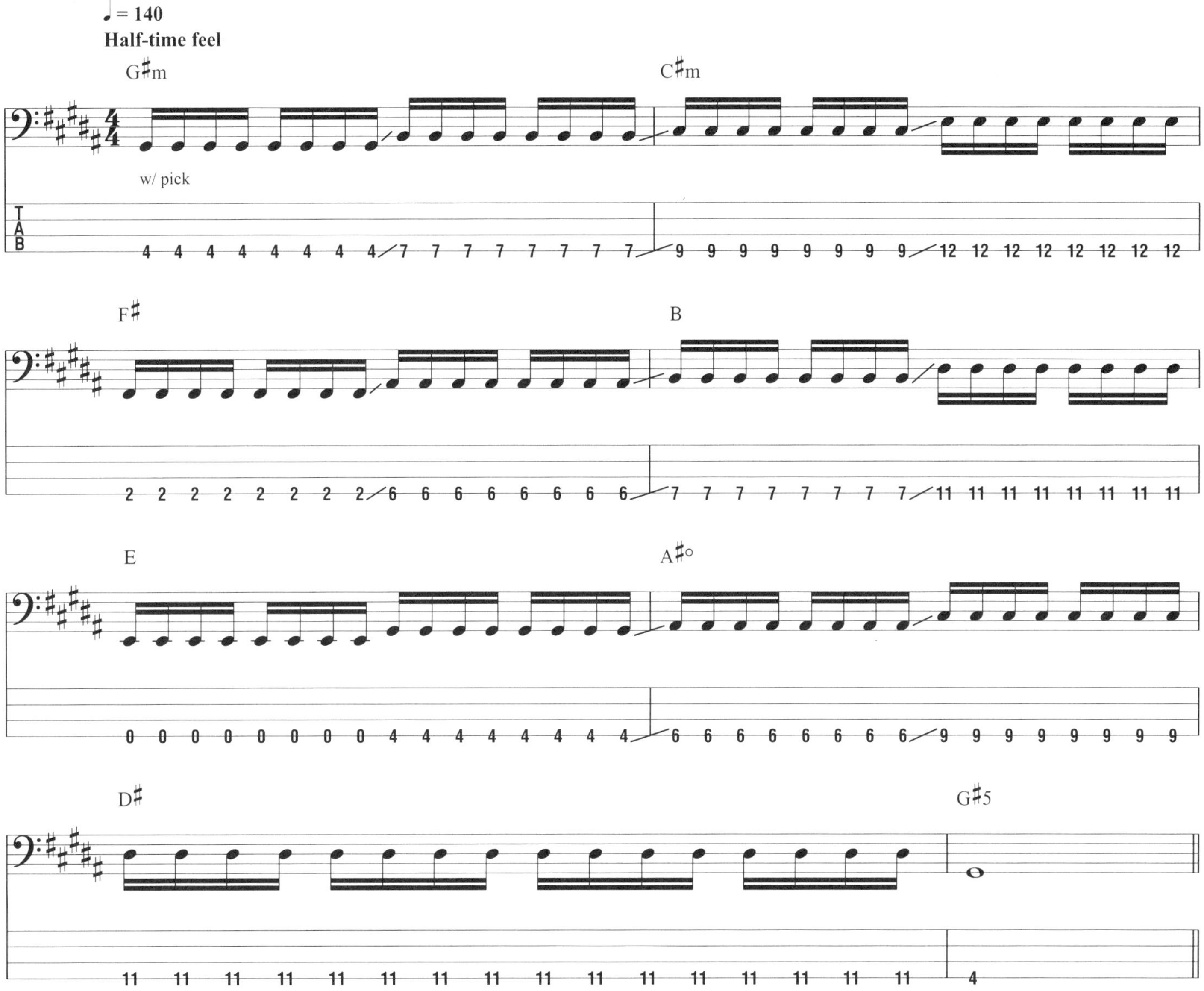

438. Baroque 3

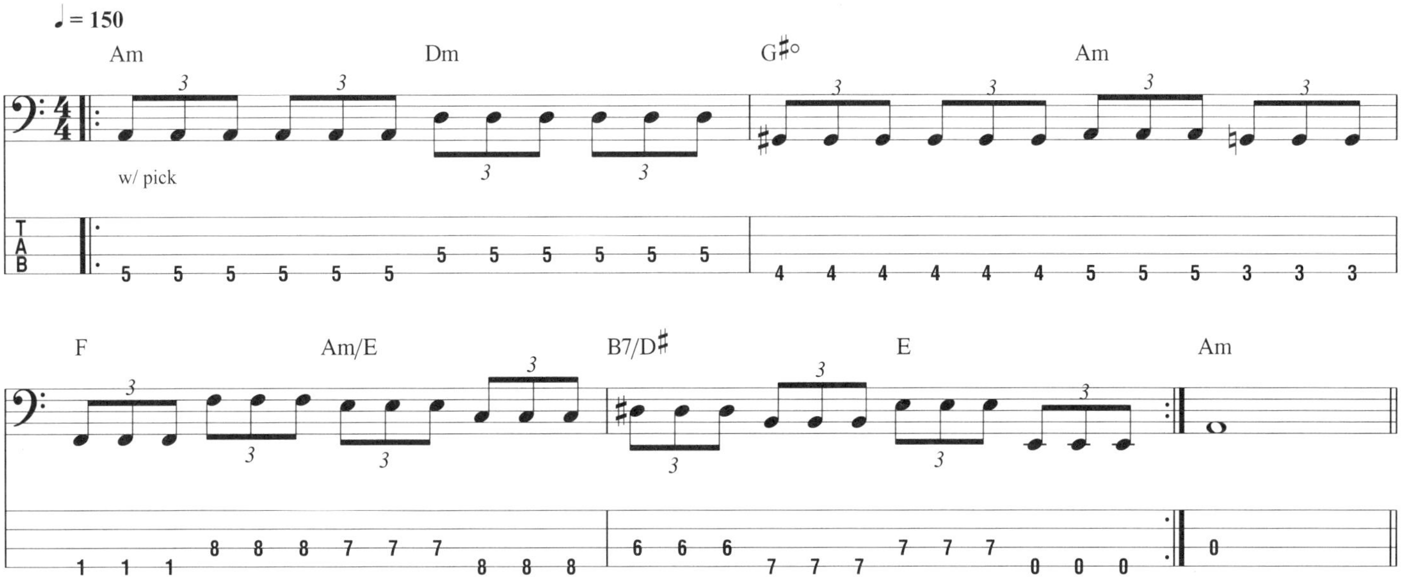

439. Baroque 4

440. Metal Major 3rds

441. Maidenish 1

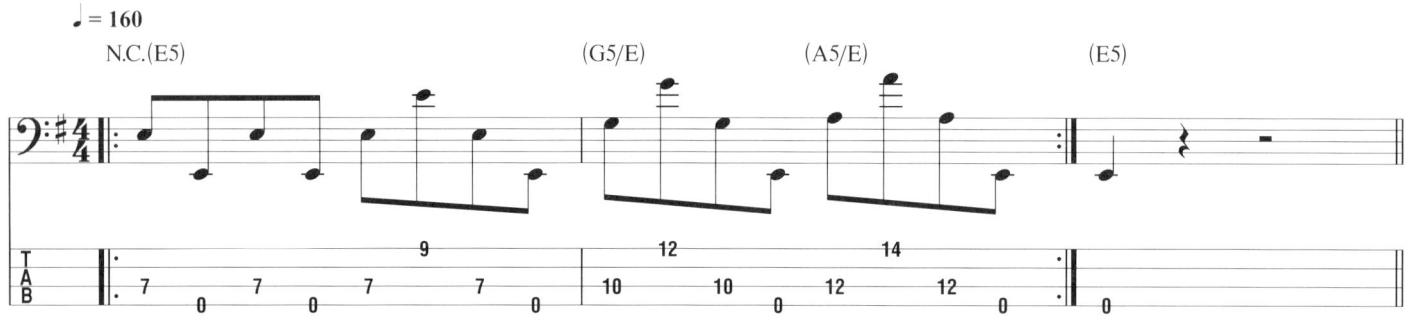

442. Maidenish 2

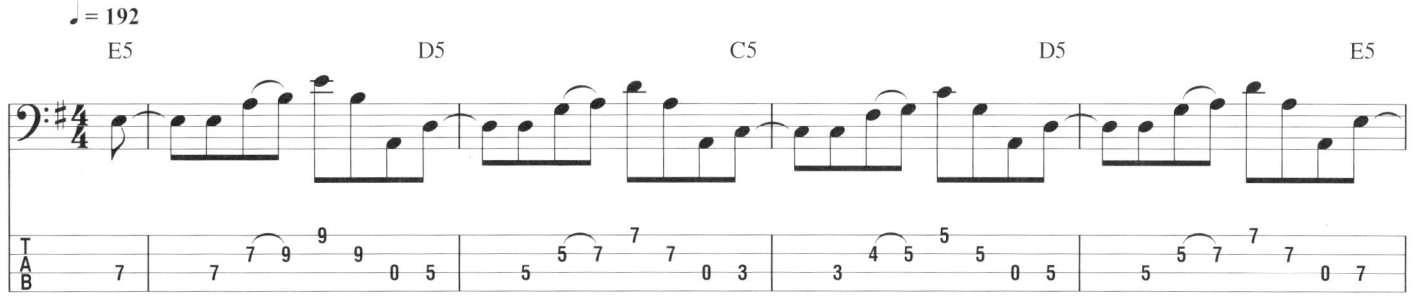

443. Pull-offs 1

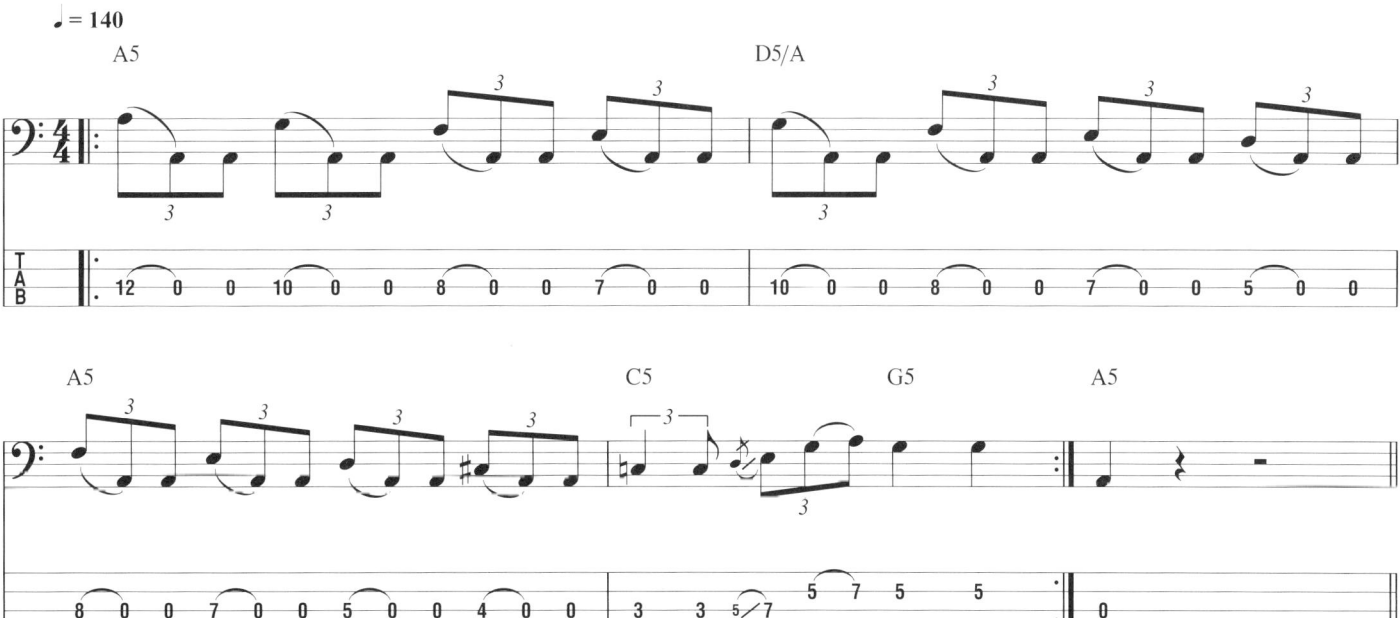

444. Stoner Metal 1

Drop D tuning:
(low to high) D-A-D-G

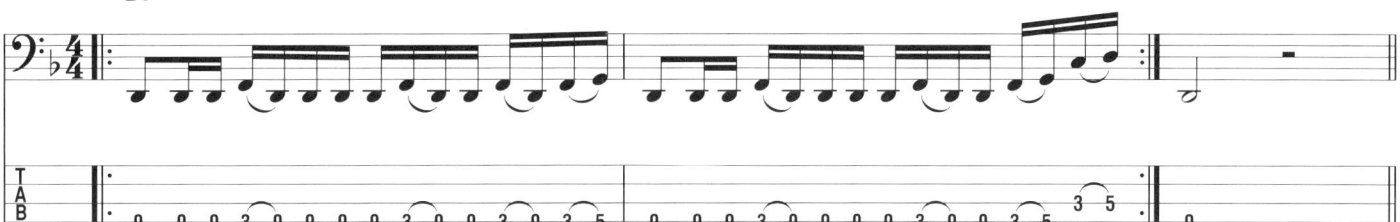

445. Pull-offs 2

Drop D tuning:
(low to high) D-A-D-G

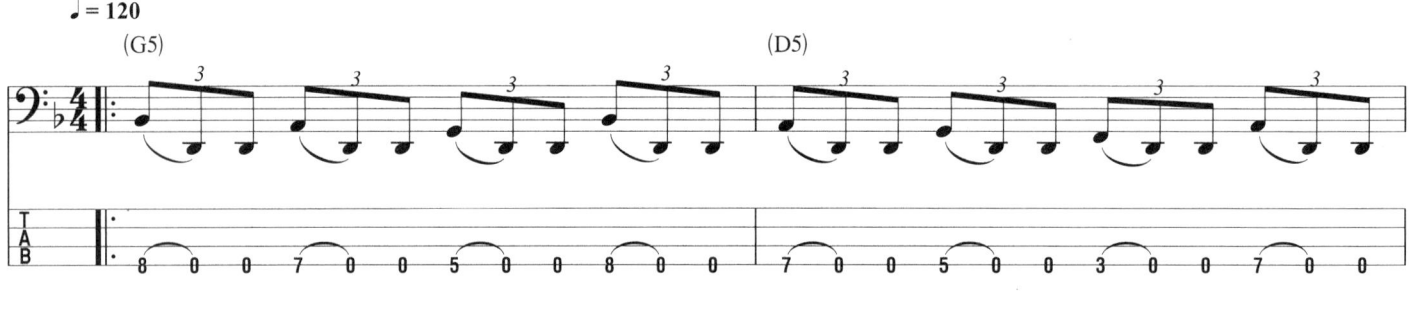
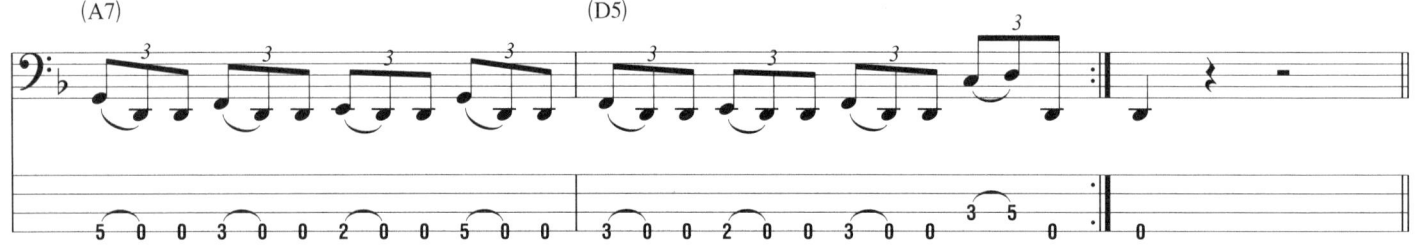

446. Stoner Metal 2

Drop D tuning:
(low to high) D-A-D-G

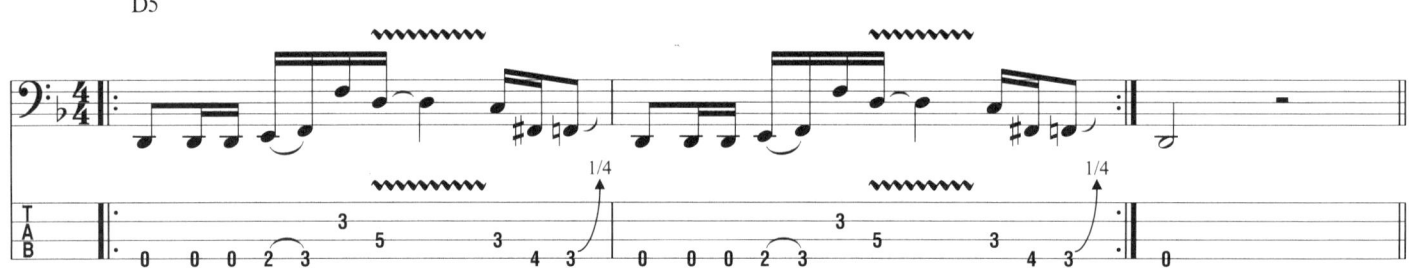

447. Stoner Metal 3

Drop D tuning:
(low to high) D-A-D-G

448. Stoner Metal 4

449. Aggro

Drop D tuning:
(low to high) D-A-D-G

450. Triplets of Doom 1

Drop D tuning:
(low to high) D-A-D-G

451. Triplets of Doom 2

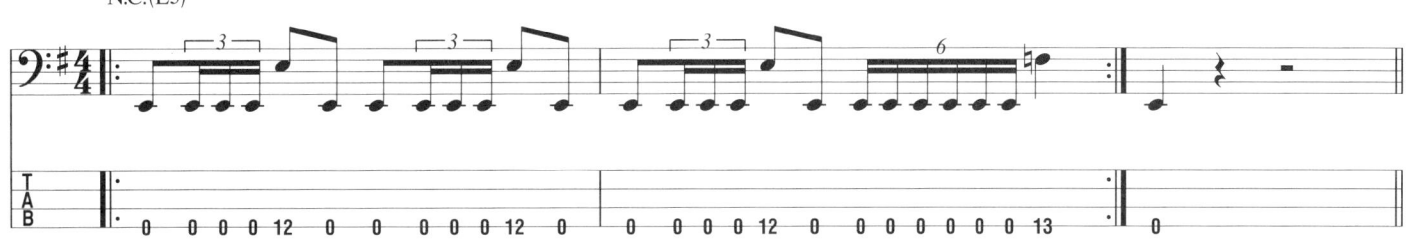

452. Triplets of Doom 3

Drop D tuning:
(low to high) D-A-D-G

♩ = 113

453. Ascending Line Cliché with Pedal Tone

Drop D tuning:
(low to high) D-A-D-G

♩ = 100

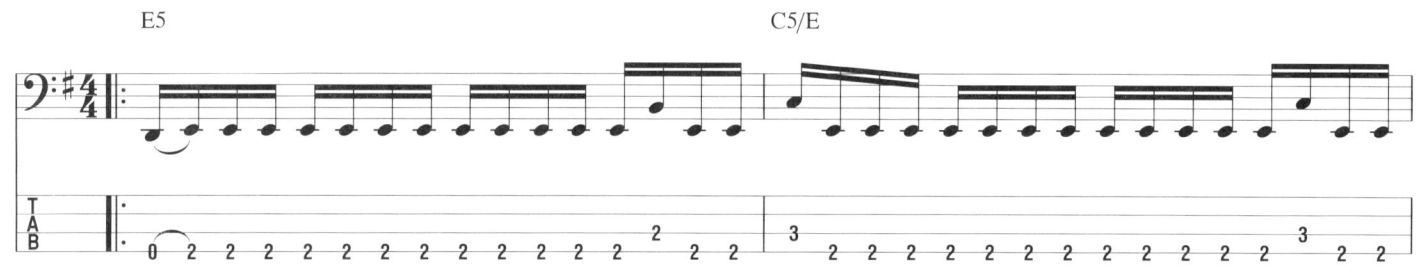

454. Half-Time

Drop D tuning:
(low to high) D-A-D-G

♩ = 100
Half-time feel

WORLD MUSIC

455. Reggae 1

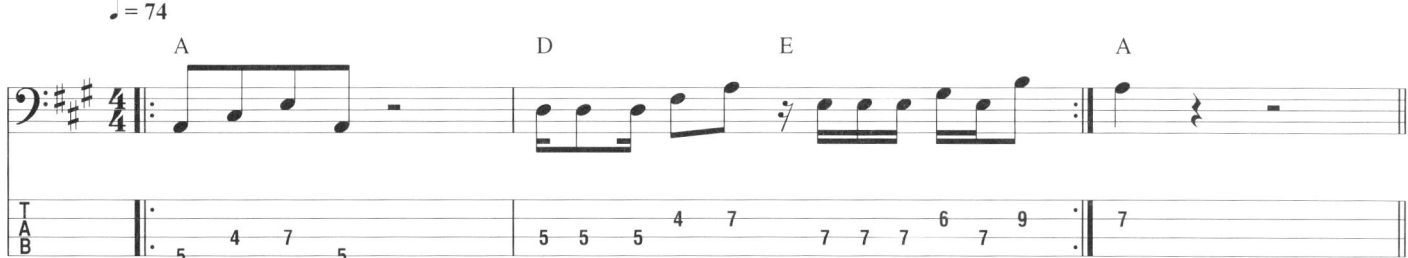

456. Reggae 2

457. Reggae 3

458. Reggae 4

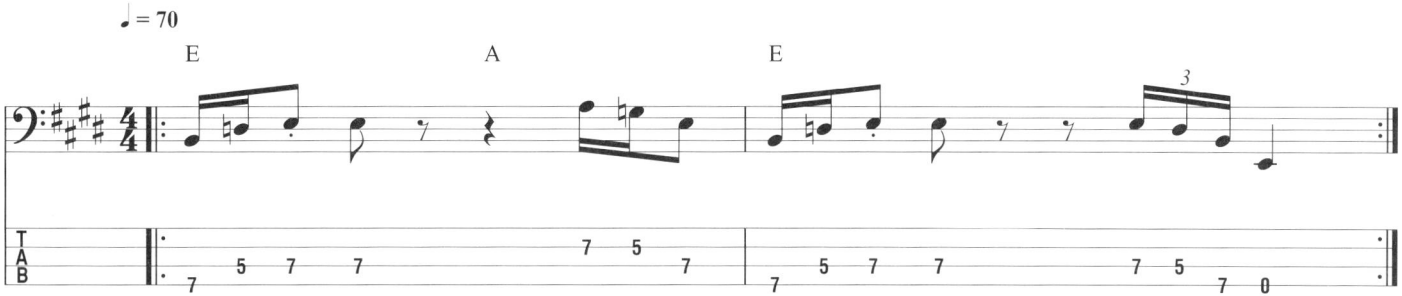

459. Reggae 5

460. Reggae 6

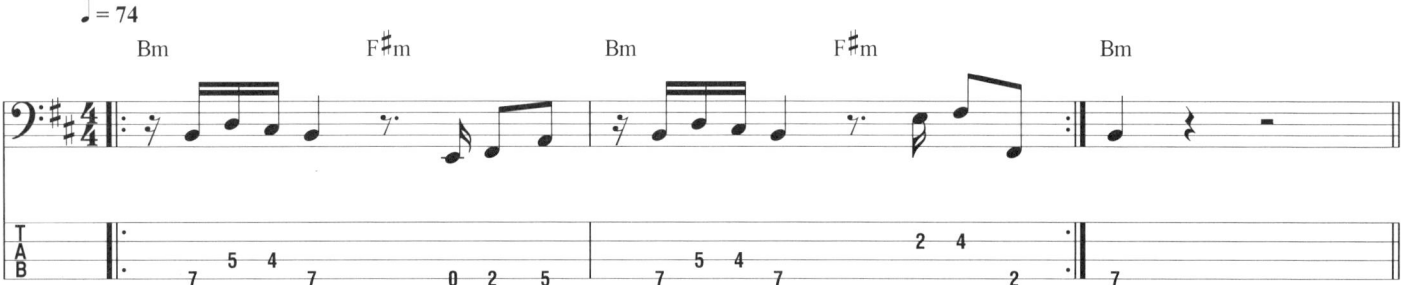

461. Reggae 7

462. Funky Reggae Break

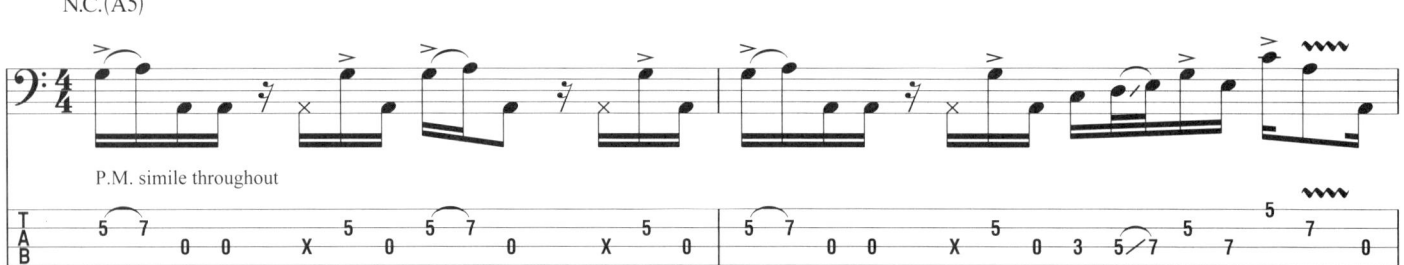
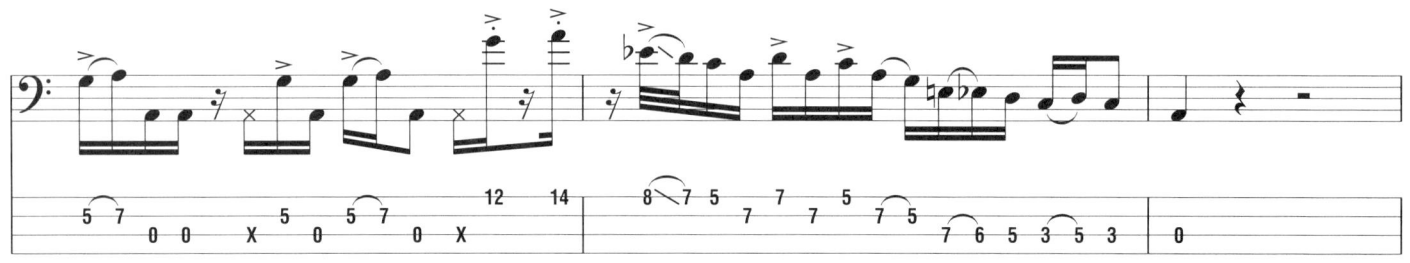

463. Busy Reggae Groove

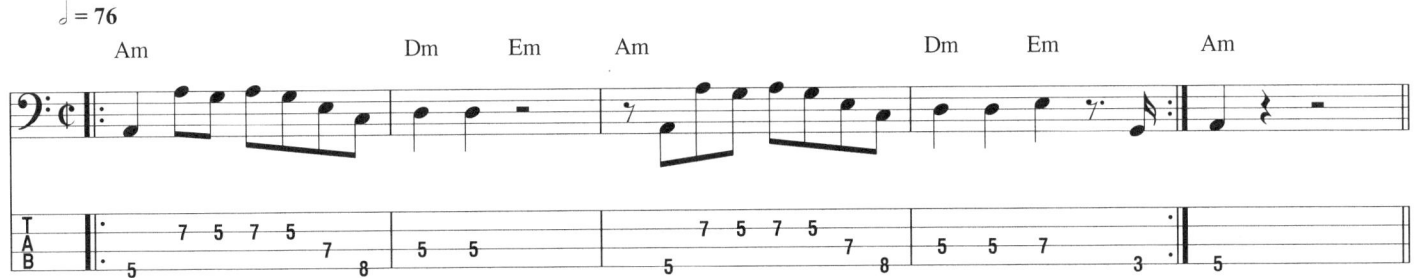

464. Shaky Octaves

465. Basic Latin Groove

466. Funky Samba 1

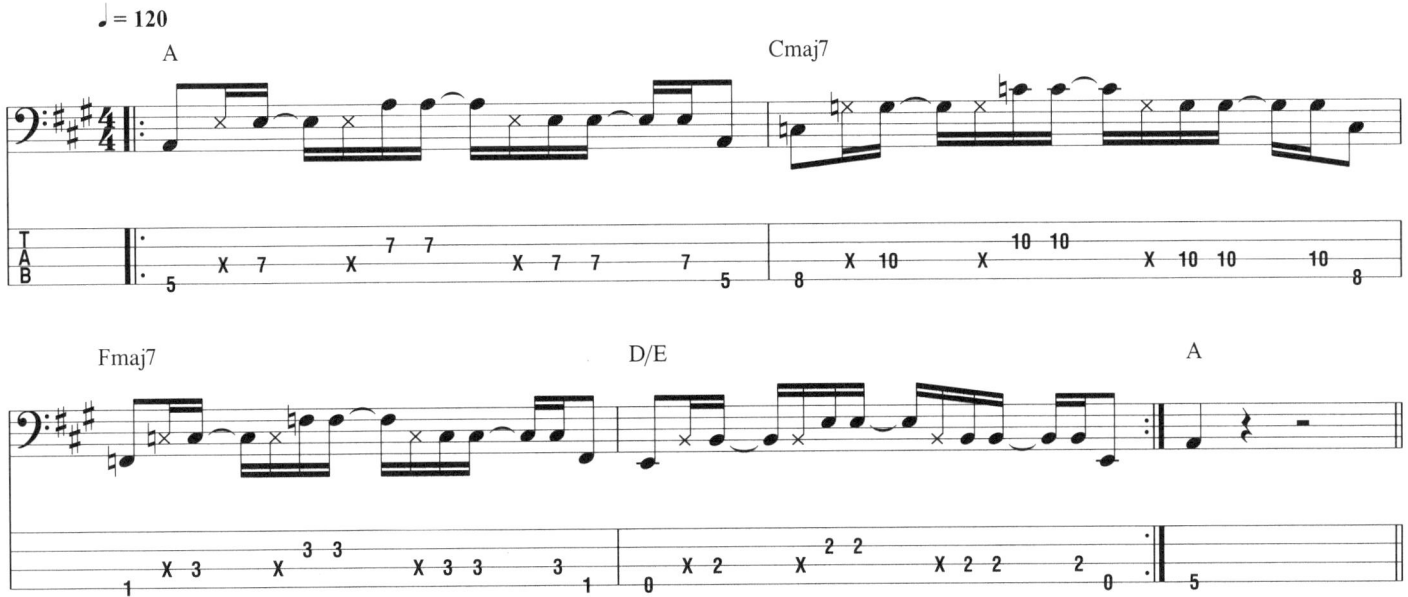

467. Funky Samba 2

468. Funky Samba 3

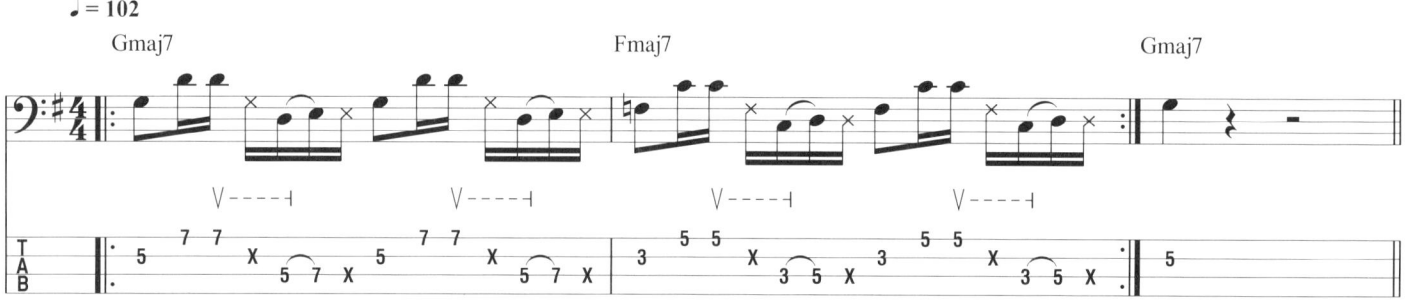

469. Funky Samba 4

470. Funky Latin

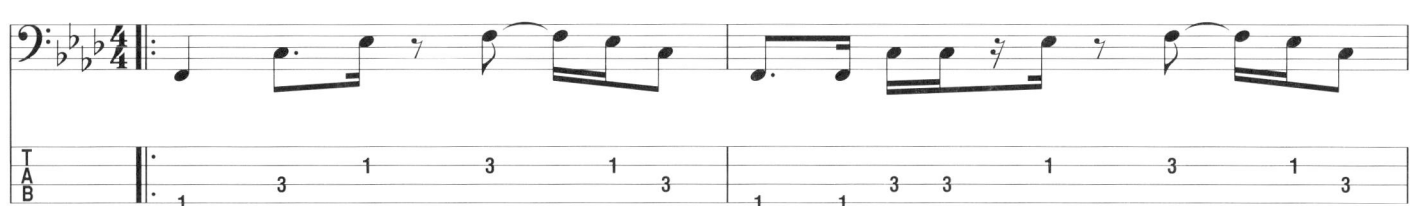

471. Fast Samba 1

472. Fast Samba 2

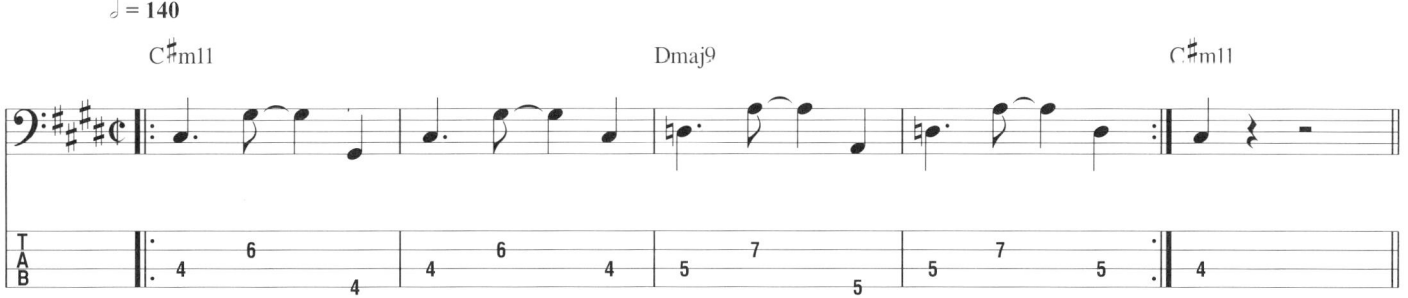

473. Fast Samba 3

474. Fast Samba 4

475. Fast Samba 5

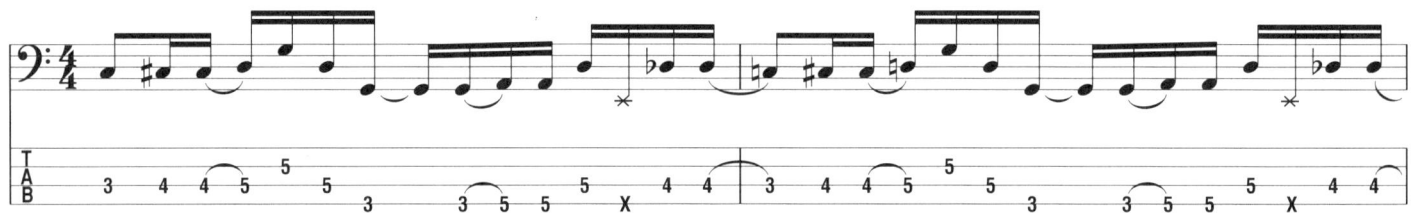

476. Fast Samba 6

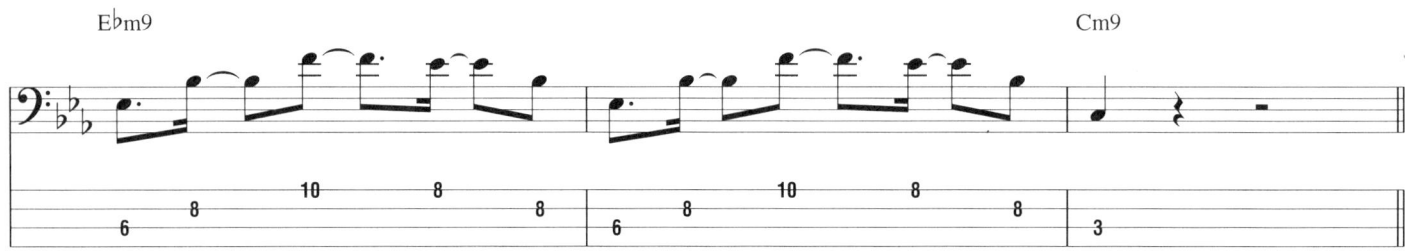

477. Samba Pull-offs and Rakes

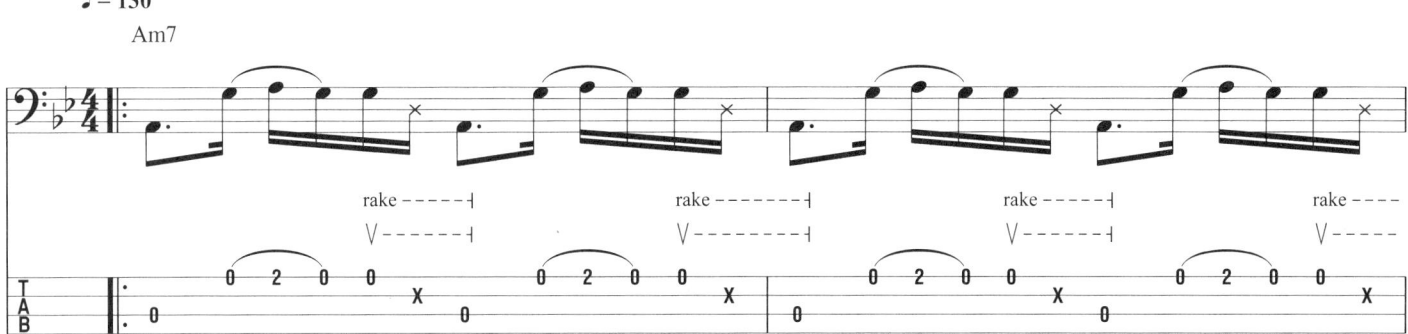

478. Box Pattern Latin

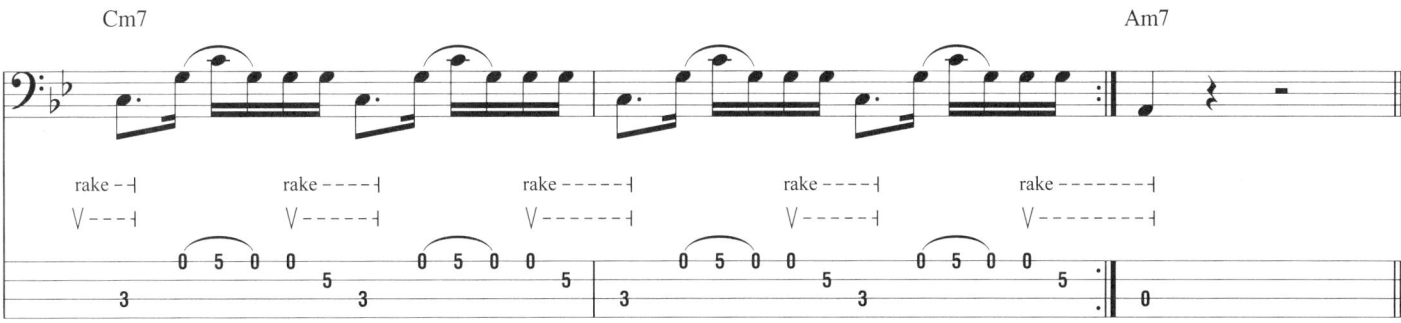

479. Latin Dance Groove 1

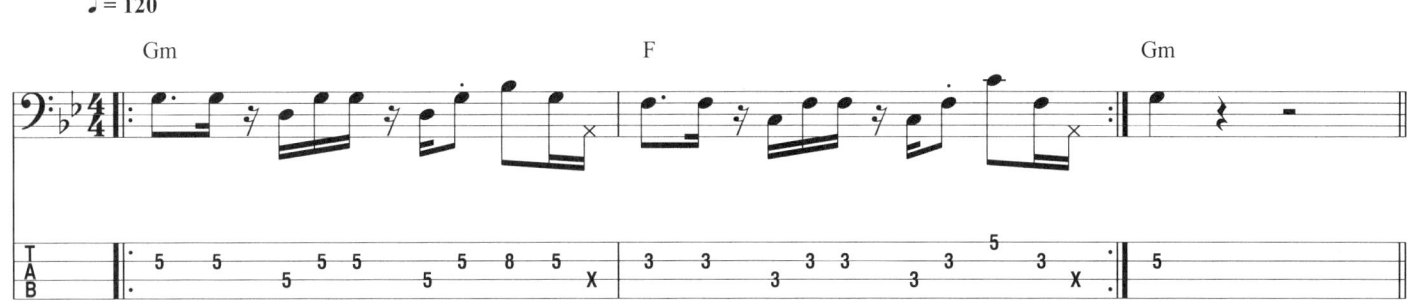

480. Latin Dance Groove 2

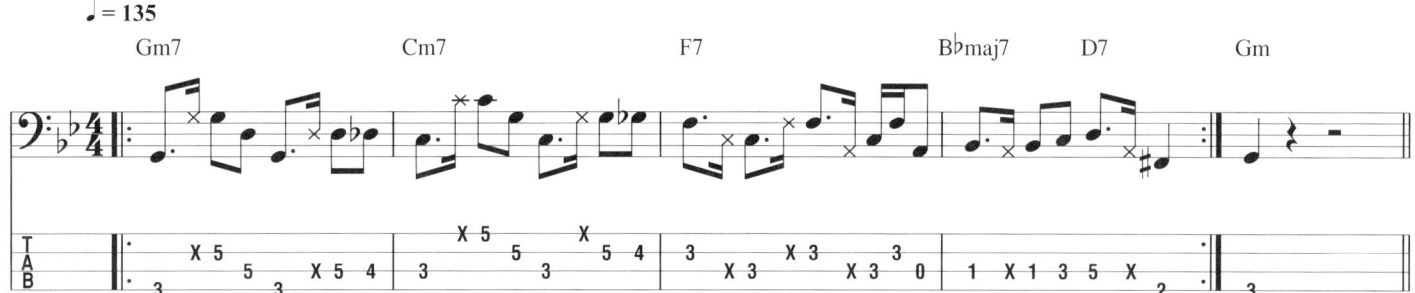

481. The Notes You *Don't* Play Are Just as Important 5

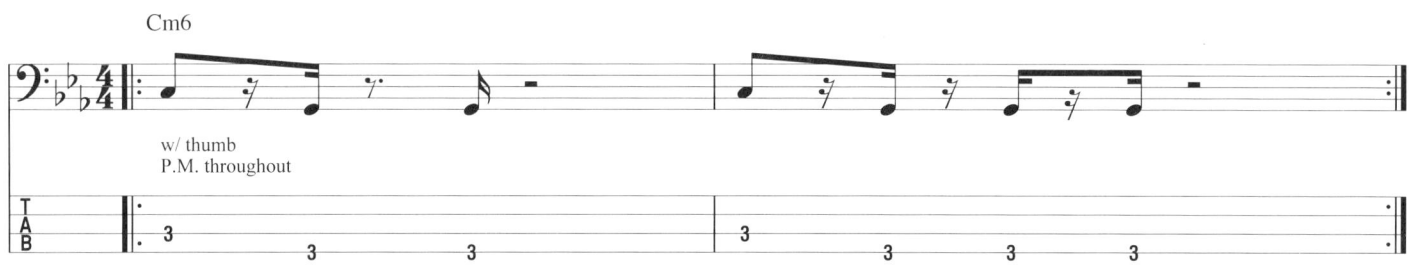

482. Calypso 1

483. Calypso 2

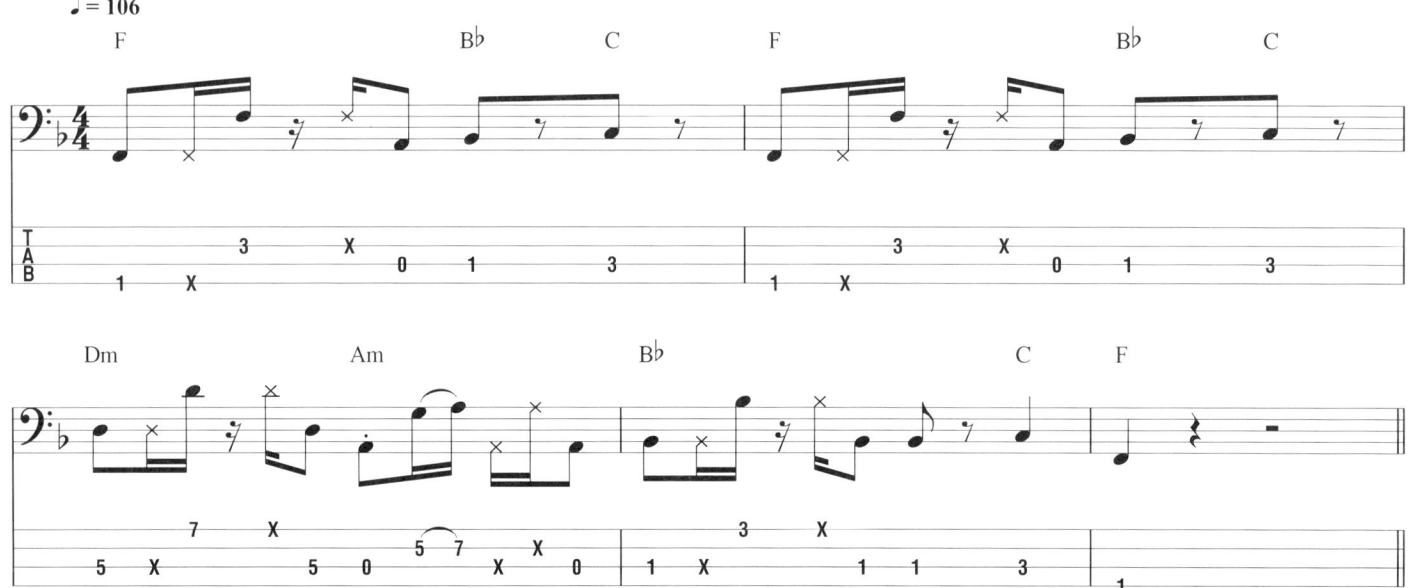

484. Calypso 3

485. Simple Montuno

486. Not-So-Simple Montuno 1

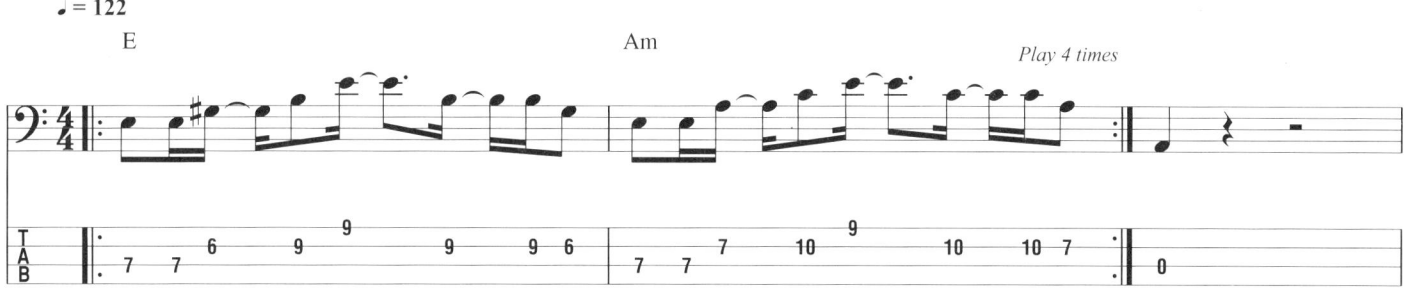

487. Not-So-Simple Montuno 2

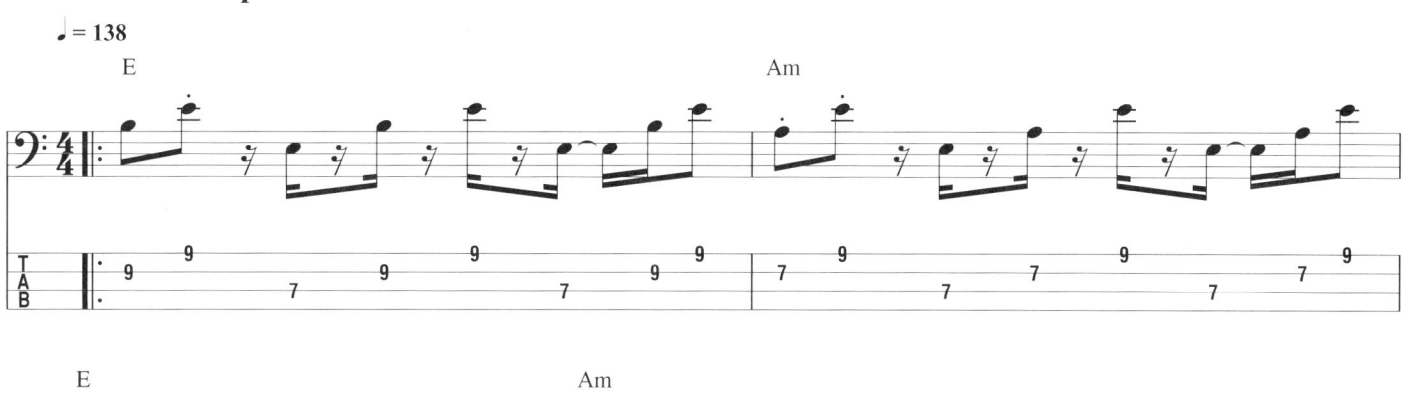

488. It's Montuno Boy 1

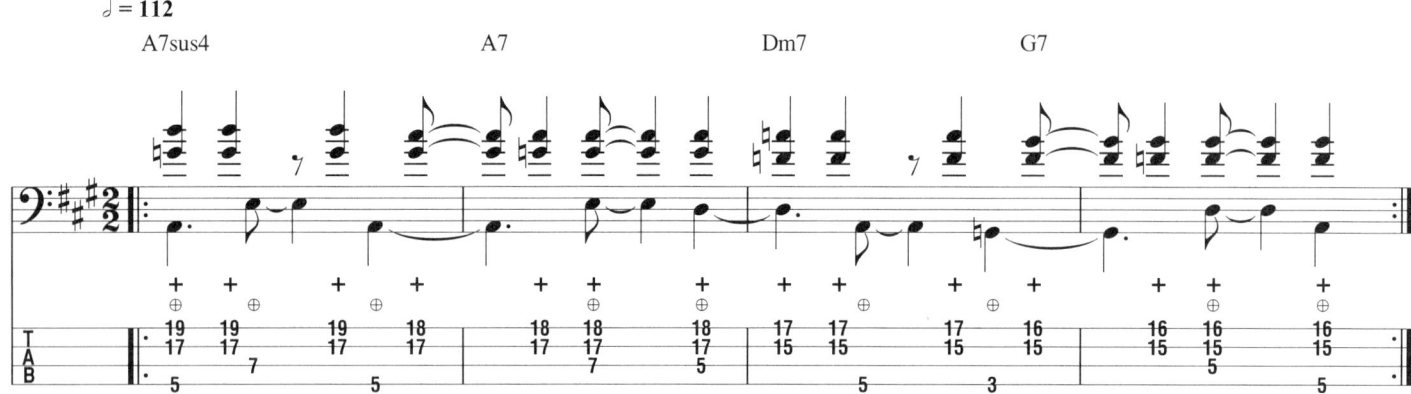

489. It's Montuno Boy 2

490. Montuno Line Cliché with Pedal Tone

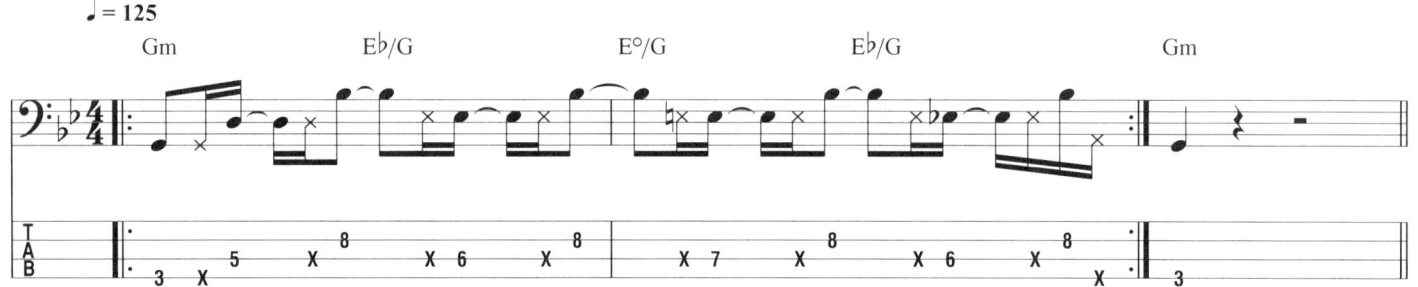

491. One-Man Two-Handed Latin Ensemble 1

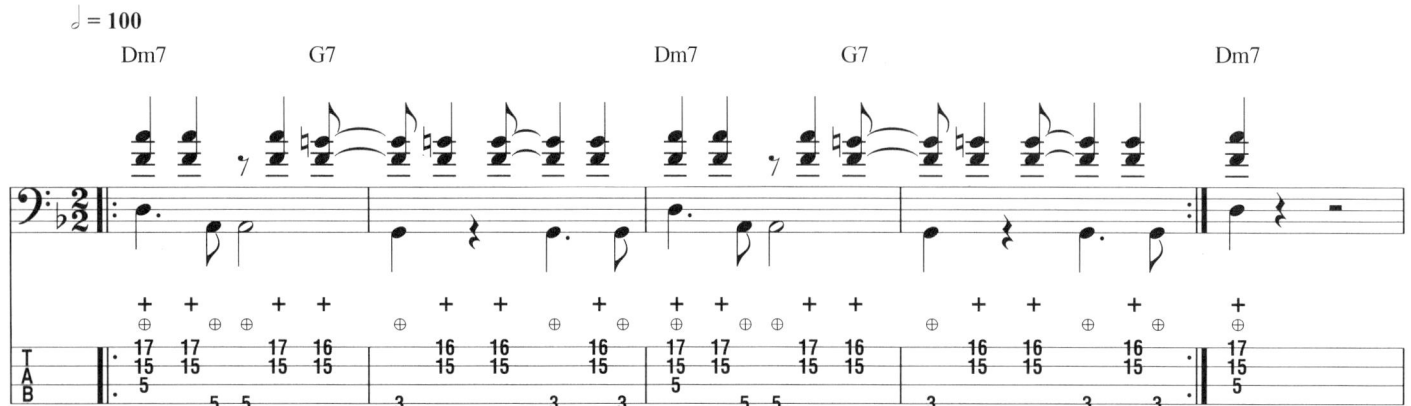

492. One-Man Two-Handed Latin Ensemble 2

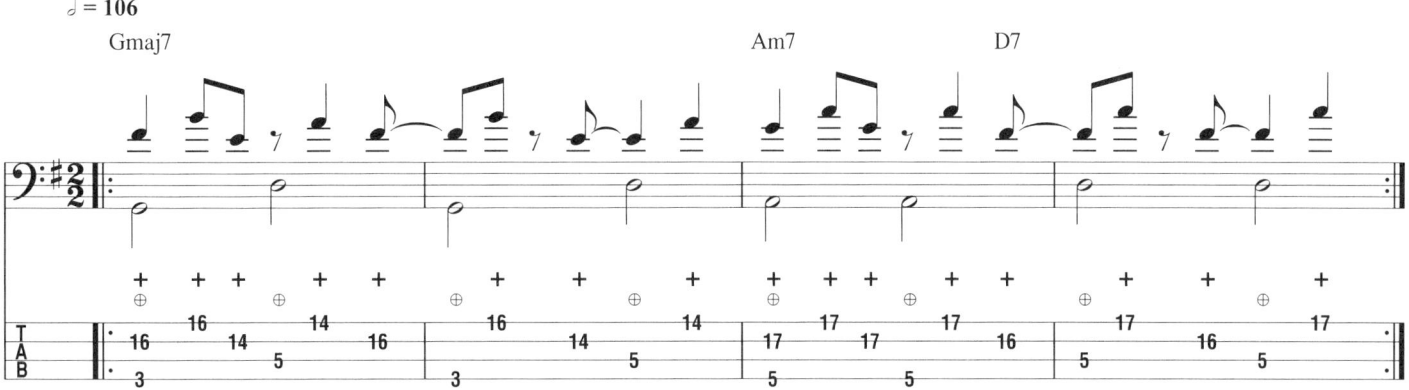

493. Latin Fusion

494. Cumbia 1

495. Cumbia 2

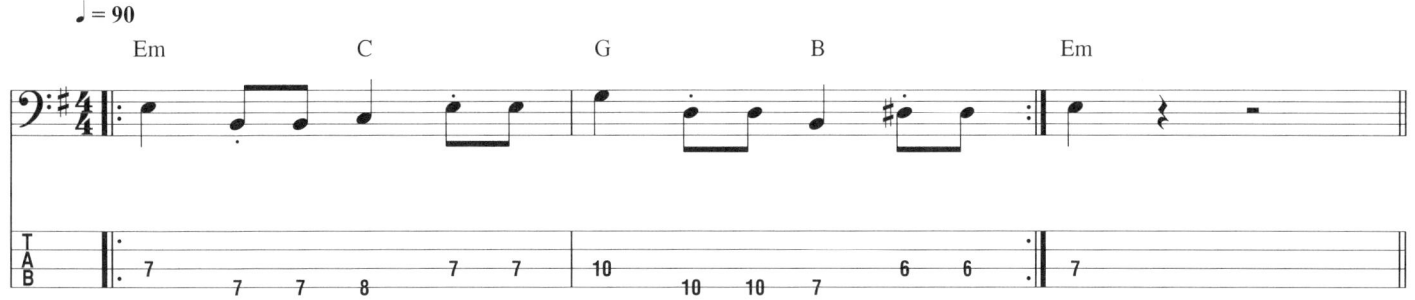

496. Cumbia 3

497. Cumbia 4

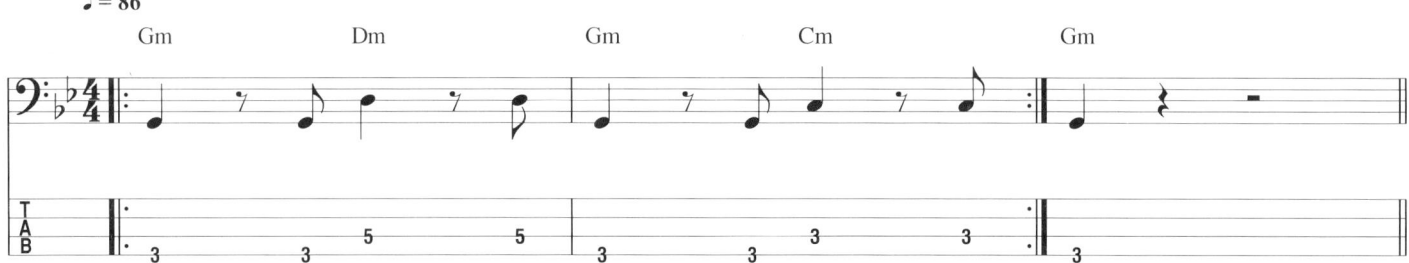

498. Dark Worldbeat

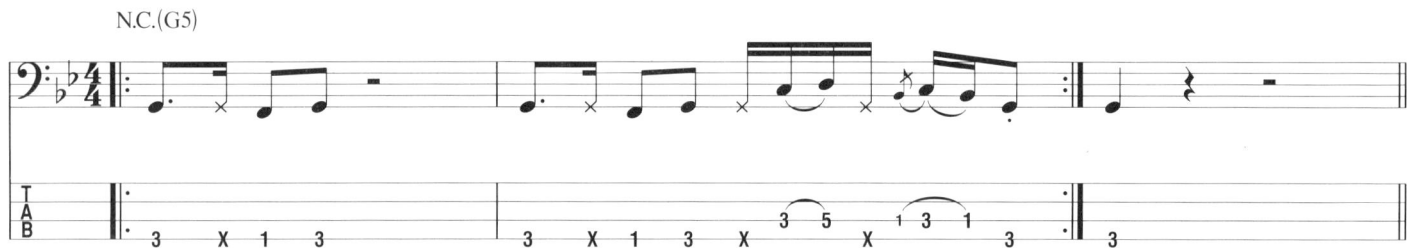

499. Odd-Time Desert Blues

500. Afrobeat

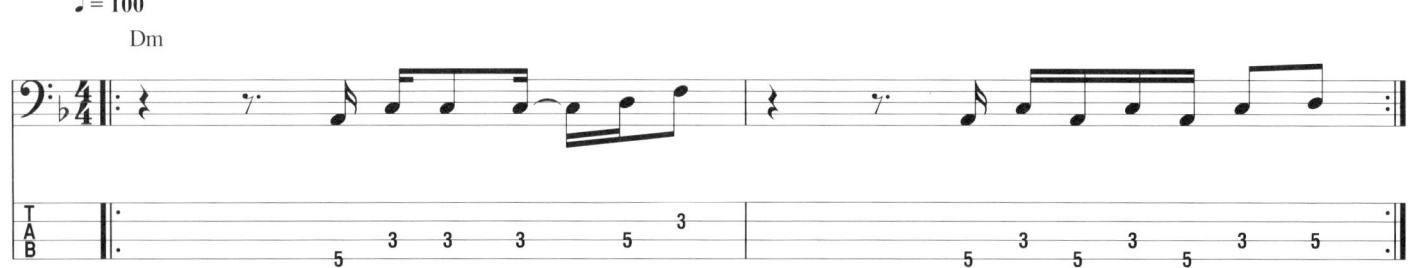